Resonant Space

Religion, Theatre, and the Chinese Martial Arts

Daniel Mroz

*with prefaces by Gey Pin Ang and Peter Lorge,
a chapter by Colin Lalonde, and a postface by Guy Cools*

Cardiff | Gwasg
University | Prifysgol
Press | Caerdydd

Published by
Cardiff University Press
Cardiff University
Trevithick Library
Trevithick Building, The Parade
Newport Road
Cardiff CF24 3AA

https://cardiffuniversitypress.org

Text © Daniel Mroz 2025

First published 2025

Cover design by Hugh Griffiths
Cover image: Landscape with Talisman
Cover image credit: Brandi Beckett

Series name: Physical Cultural Studies

Print and digital versions typeset by Siliconchips Services Ltd.

ISBN (Paperback): 978-1-911653-56-1
ISBN (Hardback): 978-1-911653-57-8
ISBN (PDF): 978-1-911653-52-3
ISBN (EPUB): 978-1-911653-54-7
ISBN (Mobi): 978-1-911653-55-4

DOI: https://doi.org/10.18573/book11

The full text of this book has been peer-reviewed to ensure high academic
standards. For full review policies, see https://www.cardiffuniversitypress.org
/site/research-integrity/

Suggested citation: Mroz, D. 2025. *Resonant Space: Religion, Theatre, and
the Chinese Martial Arts*. Cardiff: Cardiff University Press. DOI: https://doi
.org/10.18573/book11. Licence: CC-BY-NC-ND

To read the free, open access version of this book
online, visit https://doi.org/10.18573/book11 or
scan this QR code with your mobile device:

To Laura Astwood, Richard Fowler, and Sui Meing Wong

In loving memory of Ker Wells and Lisa Wolford-Wylam

Contents

Acknowledgements

Deep thanks to Gey Pin Ang, Guy Cools, Colin Lalonde, and Peter Lorge for their thoughtful writing; to Brandi Beckett, Martin Borth, Rick Cousins, Jim Davies, Jack Rusher and Maya Yoncali for their artwork; to Rex Lee and Aisling Murphy for research and editorial assistance; to Kel Pero for copyediting; to Matthew MacLellan for creating the index; to Paul Bowman and Ben Judkins for creating Martial Arts Studies and for supporting this book in so very many ways; to Scott Park Phillips for inspiration and conversation; to Simon Cox for direction and support; and to Mike Sutherland for presence and assistance.

Thanks to the mentors, colleagues and friends who read and commented on drafts: Marco Adda, Fatema Albastaki, Ellis Amdur, Paul Allain, Laura Astwood, Art Babayants, Aaron Balivet, Graham Barlow, Olivier Bernard, Eric Burkhart, José Carmona, Chen Gong, Ian Cipperly, Erwan Cloarec, Gordon Cooper, Erick Desjardins, Sean Dixon, D.S. Farrer, Steve Geisz, Angela He, Ai-Cheng Ho, Henry McCann, Justin McGrail, Martin Minarik, Jared Miracle, Meaghan Morris, David Palmer, Maurice Passman, John Pence, Rachael Powles, Mat Ravignat, Jo Riley, Michael Rook, Geoffrey Samuel, Debbie Shayne, Ben Spatz, Tim Stanley, Trần Khải Hoài, Evan Webber, Sixt Wetzler, and Grzegorz Ziółkowski.

Thanks to my teachers, colleagues, collaborators, friends, and students for every kind of help:

Jean Abreu, Montana Adams, Gonzalo Alarcon, Daniel Amos, Paul Auclair, Michael Babin, Ian Baker, Peter Batakliev, Christopher Bates, Eugenio Barba,

Artem Barry, Joël Beddows, Diana Belshaw, Lorne Bernard, Emily Bertrand, Mario Biagini, Adriaan Blaauw, Alex Boyd, David Benedict Brown, Jeannine Cameron, Frank Camilleri, Tim Cartmell, Chang Wu Na, Chen Zhonghua, Gene Ching, Zaakira Chubb, Jamie Coates, Margaret Coderre-Williams, Ken Cohen, Yvonne Coutts, Miriam Cusson, Blake Dalton, David Daniel, John Dahms, Stephie Theodora Demas, Elizabeth de Roza, Sylvie Desrosiers, Jean-François Dubé, Koryna Dylewska, Bobbe Edmonds, Elias Edström, Chad Eisner, John Evans, Xing Fan, Adam Frank, Louise Frappier, Kurtis Fujita, Mike Geither, Fanny Gilbert-Collet, Jim Good, Randall Goodwin, Sean Green, Tracey Guptill, Brandon Groves, Marie-Louise Gariépy, Tina Goralski, Angela Haché, Hugo Hanriot, Jill Heath, Asa Hershoff, Emma Hickey, Ismet Himmet, Damon Honeycutt, Kee Hong, Mary Catherine Jack, Badger Jones, Vera Kérchy, Gitanjali Kolanad, Alex Kozma, Mark Klyman, Gabrielle Lalonde, Adriana La Selva, William Lau, Eric Ling, Jon Lockhart, Mei-hui Lu, Lü Suosen, Emmanuelle Lussier Martinez, Ma Yue, Andrea Maciel, Chris Manuel, Stefan Marcec, Sam Masich, Jasmine Massé, Justin McGrail, Sophie McIntosh, Yana Meerzon, Lauren Miller, Martin Minarik, Patrick Mok, Lana Morton, Kiara-Lynn Neï, Katherine Ng, Marije Nie, Natascha Nikeprelevic, Daniel Olsberg, Solomon Ostrojic, Anne-Marie Ouellet, Jean-Michel Ouimet, Kevin Orr, Patrick Orr, Céline Paquet, Emmanuelle Pépin, Andrea Pelegri, Robert Allen Pittman, Kathryn Prince, Jean-Philippe Ranger, Robert Reid, Katelin Richards, Tedd Robinson, Katie Rochford, Arkadiusz Rogozinski, Lola Ryan, Kris Salata, Denis Salter, Geoffrey Samuel, Michael Saso, Sylvain Schryburt, Keith Seeley, Ekaterina Shestakova, Antti Silvennoinen, Lauren Steimer, Jarek Szymanski, James Tam, Marc Tellez, Brennan Toh, Philip Tom, Jason Tsou, Jennifer Venning, Petr Vrána, Naishi Wang, Qijun Wang, Sionêd Watkins, Brian Webb, Marnix Wells, Paul Whitrod, Rainer Wiens, and Doug Woolidge.

Images

Preface by Gey Pin Ang, PhD

Daniel is my *Lǎodì*—my younger brother in the Chinese arts. *Lǎo* means old and wise, while *dì* means younger brother. Daniel has always been a knowledgeable researcher whom I consult on all things related to *wǔshù* 武术, the Chinese martial arts. I became acquainted with Daniel in 2011 when he invited me to the University of Ottawa. During my visit to Ottawa, where I conducted a two-week theatre workshop for a group of Daniel's students as part of his project *Les Ateliers du corps*, I also had the opportunity to see videos of some of the productions he had directed. From what I saw on the screen, he was exploring elements related to his deep connection and heuristic practice using instinctive sensing and discovery, *gǎnyìng* 感应 and *fāxiàn* 发现, in wǔshù. He then associated his findings with performer training and theatre making.

Daniel's long-term practice of wǔshù has been the dominant factor in his work as a theatre artist. In his writing, he delves deep into Chinese culture and its roots in religion, language, social ontology, and cosmology, providing readers with a rich feast of knowledge. It was as if he sought to excavate the depth of the ancient source and wisdom, like reaching the sky from the bottom of the well of his heart.

Phenomenologically, physically, and metaphysically, Daniel's writing uncovers the age-old philosophy—external and internal source works—among varied Asian bodily disciplines that manifest through theatrical presentations. His first-hand accounts, field research, and reflections make his ventures among diverse fields of research even more valuable and insightful.

From his examination of historical and religious sources, Daniel discovered that the practice of *tàolù* 套路, choreographed movements in martial arts, has the ability to develop awareness of the negative space within the practitioner. This perception of space can be used to cultivate a metaphysical layer within the practice, highlighting its potential to facilitate the creative process and enabling the practitioner to play seamlessly with co-performers in a theatrical performance.

It is this strong connection between martial arts and theatre that Daniel clearly envisions and explores. The interrelatedness of these two distinct fields can only exist in the "unspoken" aspect of the practice. These aspects are represented by the Chinese characters *xū* 虚 (subtle), *wú* 无 (empty), and *xīn* 心 (heart), which are essential to any practitioner/performer. This *xīnlǐngshénhuì* 心领神会 (heart realizes and spirit knows) is a fundamental aspect of Daniel's approach, and forms a bridge from his scholarly research to the essence of *wújí shēng tàijí* 无极生太极 (nothingness gives birth to the ultimate), as described in Daoism.

Writing about practice-based research can be quite challenging. It is like moving from a peaceful lake to a stormy ocean or transitioning from silence to the waves and currents. The question is, how can this extensive piece of writing be understood?

This book can be perceived as a window to the concealed world of wǔshù, its multiple layers, and intriguing traces across Asia and globally, as well as its connection to the theatre world, as revealed in this volume. The book's scope uncovers a treasure trove of enriching and valuable resources for academics, students, and practice researchers.

Phenomenologically speaking, not every human experience can be expressed in words. Meanings emerge from practice, whether it is in theatre or martial arts. Practice is the act of being present in the moment and constantly responding to it, deepening one's understanding within a structured environment. Although time and practice are required to master structured and choreographed moves, one must let go of the learned and memorized and instead simply flow with the details of each moment. As Daniel explicitly states, it is by practice that one's perception can be enhanced, the spatial experience of the practitioner altered. As a result, the practitioner can be transported and transformed through the subtlest shift in one's inner landscape.

Any practice that involves the body speaks for itself in a unique and visceral way that is deeply connected to our humanity. The experience of the practice and the research process that goes into it allow the practitioner to encounter the nuances and subtle, intangible aspects of the practice. This experience is not initiated or rooted in the human mind, but rather in the body itself. The understanding that arises from this experience belongs to the bodymind of the practitioner and can only be transformed during the *silent* act of practice.

I am grateful to have read *Resonant Space*, which is filled with treasures about wǔshù, theatre, and much more. It has prompted me to engage in further reflexive inquiries, reflecting on my own practice and questioning of what I know (*zhī* 知), while expanding my awareness of what I don't know (*bùzhī* 不知). As Daniel wisely acknowledged, it is impossible to fully articulate all there is to say about Chinese martial arts. One can be likened to a frog at the bottom of a well, unable to see the whole sky. Thank you, Lǎodì, for providing a space for reflection.

Gey Pin Ang, PhD 洪藝冰, 博士 *is an actor, theatre director, and acting teacher. She is Senior Lecturer in the School of Theatre of the Nanyang Academy of Fine Arts at the University of the Arts in Singapore. Gey Pin co-founded Lǎoniú Jùchǎng* 老牛剧场*—Theatre OX in Singapore in the 1990s, and was a part of the Workcenter of Jerzy Grotowski and Thomas Richards in Pontedera, Italy in the 2000s. She has led Sourcing Within, or Nèi Sù* 內溯*, an international network of theatre makers since 2006. In 2017 she completed her PhD in Drama by Practice as Research at the University of Kent in the U.K. An accomplished international theatre artist, Gey Pin is also a highly adept and lifelong student of the Chinese martial arts, particularly Chén Shì Tàijí Quán* 陳氏太极拳 *under the late Yáng Zhìqún* 杨志群 *of Singapore.*

Preface by Peter Lorge, PhD

Zhuangzi and Huizi were wandering on a bridge over the Hao River. Zhuangzi said: "Look at those mottled fish out wandering at ease. That's what fish like!"

Huizi said, "You are not a fish. How do you know what fish like?"

Zhuangzi said, "You are not me. How do you know I don't know what fish like?"

Huizi said, "I'm not you, so I certainly don't know what you know. And since you're not a fish, you don't know what fish like. There, perfect!"

Zhuangzi said, "Let's go back to the beginning. When you asked how I knew what fish like, you had to know I knew already in order to ask. I know it by the Hao River – that's how."[1]

This passage from Zhuangzi came to mind as I was reading this book and trying to understand Daniel Mroz's unique point of view on the martial arts. I'm not sure whether I see myself as the Daoist Master or his interlocutor, but it is clear to me that Daniel's position with respect to mine is both disruptive and enlightening. Where he seeks to understand the meaning of the martial

---

[1] Paul Kjellberg (trans.), (2001), "Zhuangzi," in Philip J. Ivanhoe and Bryan W. Van Norden (Eds.), *Readings in Classical Chinese Philosophy* (pp. 207–254, p. 247), 2nd edition. Hackett Publishing Company.

arts in theatre, religion, and culture, I have merely focused on the historical representation of the martial arts. My historical and Sinological training taught me to keep the subject of study at academic arm's length, and to concentrate on the linguistic and textual problems of understanding the past. This is because the physical embodiment of any practice is so far from graspable through text that historians either give up or invoke all manner of theories in order to hyper-intellectualize that physicality. From my methodological starting point one can only go so far in examining the martial arts.

Daniel presents an entirely different *route* (and, yes, I am invoking the Dao here) to try to understand that physical practice. The martial arts are per-formed, not just "practiced," and their meaning is often fulfilled through that performance. Fighting in wartime, in self-defense, or in dueling is not the only end or even means to an end for the martial arts. And as much as I should know that performances are real even as they represent something, the inher-ent bias of my socialization and training remains difficult to overcome. Daniel's perspective on the martial arts will therefore be profoundly helpful to people outside of the performing arts if their minds are open to it. But as Zhuangzi makes clear, most people's minds are not open to different perspectives, and there is nothing that can be done about it. You can only have a real exchange of perspectives with the right interlocutor. Zhuangzi and Huizi, also known as Hui Shi, never agreed, but they continued to argue until Huizi passed away.

At least from that comparative sense, I am not Daniel's ideal interlocutor because I usually find myself in agreement with his work. In person, my own limitations as a conversationalist are more than made up for by Daniel's skills in that regard, and we have had many wonderful discussions of martial arts that have profoundly broadened my understanding of the subject. Fortunately for me, and for others not fortunate enough to speak to him in person, Daniel has written down his views. I can now cite him properly and those others can experience him at one remove.

Peter Lorge is an associate professor of History at Vanderbilt University. He is a historian of 10th- and 11th-century China, with particular interest in Chinese military, political, and social history. He is author of The Reunification of China: Peace Through War under the Song Dynasty *(Cambridge, 2015),* Chinese Mar-tial Arts from Antiquity to the Twenty-First Century *(Cambridge University Press, 2012),* The Asian Military Revolution: From Gunpowder to the Bomb *(Cambridge University Press, 2008), and* War, Politics and Society in Early Modern China *(Routledge, 2005).*

Lorge is co-editor with Kaushik Roy of Chinese and Indian Warfare: From the Classical Age to 1870 *(Routledge, 2014), and editor of* Debating War in Chinese History *(Brill, 2013),* Five Dynasties and Ten Kingdoms *(The Chinese University Press, 2011), and* Warfare in China to 1600 *(Ashgate, 2005). His book series with Routledge, Asian States and Empires, has published thirteen books.*

Peter Lorge is one of the founders and executive board members of the Chinese Military History Society. He won the Harriet S. Gilliam Award for Excellence in Teaching in 2004 and has appeared on CNN to discuss Chinese military affairs. In 2007, he attended The Johns Hopkins School of Advanced International Studies workshop on teaching national security at Basin Harbor.

Introductions

The only persistent problem for the artist is to express a subject which is always the same and which cannot be changed, by finding a new form of expression each time.

—Francis Bacon 1992: 80

My persistent artistic problem is the meaning of the Chinese martial arts. After over 30 years of practice, I continue to find every scholarly and practical explanation of their nature, my own included, inspiring yet incomplete. In this book I further reckon with my problem, examining the Chinese martial arts through the lenses of cultural history, highlighting their religious and theatrical aspects. From my first-person point of view as an artist and teacher, I describe the role they have played in the creation of contemporary theatre and dance, using examples drawn from my own work and from that of Asian and European artists of the later 20th century.

Beginnings

The chapters that follow are my detailed response to questions raised by an unusual experience. On October 10, 2006 I attended *Kagemi—Beyond the Metaphor of Mirrors*, a performance by the dance company Sankai Juku 山海塾, choreographed by the late Amagatsu Ushio 天児 牛大 (1949–2024), at the National Arts Centre of Canada in Ottawa. I had bought my ticket at the last minute and was disappointed by my seat in the back row of the balcony, two levels above the stage. I usually made a point of sitting very close to the front at every piece of dance and theatre I attended to better see the details of the performers' work.

Seated far above the action, watching the dance in an almost plan view, I experienced the optical illusion that the dancers left trails of light in their

How to cite this book chapter:
Mroz, D. 2025. *Resonant Space: Religion, Theatre, and the Chinese Martial Arts.*
    Pp. 1–9. Cardiff: Cardiff University Press. DOI: https://doi.org/10.18573/book11.a.
    Licence: CC-BY-NC-ND

wakes, tracing lines and shapes on the floor. I was mesmerized by the complex patterns created by the six dancers whose trajectories formed circles, spirals, and stars in my imagination, each shape effortlessly resolving into the next.

At home after the performance, I found myself replaying the dance I'd just seen in my mind's eye. I was surprised by the level of detail I was able to recall. It occurred to me to try to change the angle at which I was watching my visualized stage. I imagined myself on the floor of the theatre and watched the dance straight on, ideally positioned in the centre of the audience. *Kagemi* was the first thing I thought of when I woke up the next morning. I tried to imagine it again and managed to conjure both the plan and frontal views of several parts of the dance. Inspired, I tried to imagine one of the solo martial choreographies I knew, to see if I could watch my imagined self perform in plan and frontal views. This was more difficult. My image kept flipping as my remembered sensations contradicted the mirror-image of myself I was trying to keep stable in front of me, but after a few weeks' regular work it became possible. I soon began to rely on this ability to recall, replay, and reorient movement in my work. Whether directing, teaching directing and acting, teaching martial arts, or reflecting on exactly how I'd been beaten in different kinds of sparring, these clear visualizations were useful everywhere.

My new skill depended on an unusual parameter: To make it happen, I had to soften and diffuse my attention and feel the warmth of my skin all over my body at once, as though preparing to sleep. If I didn't do this, the images would not appear or move reliably.

How had I developed this ability? I didn't think it was an inherent attribute that I'd simply discovered. Prior to beginning the practice of the Chinese martial arts in 1993, my coordination had been poor. I had not been able to perceive complex movement, let alone generate it in my head. I inventoried my martial training to see what practices might have contributed to my new experience. Three elements stood out: solo choreographies of martial movement that mimed fighting using theatrical, ritual movements; martial games that approximated fighting without too much risk of injury from knockdowns or strikes; and meditative visualizations, often combined with movement and practiced with closed eyes.

I felt that the solo choreographies had developed my understanding of my own position and movement. Partner games and sparring had given me a sense of position and movement relative to another moving body. My ability to visualize abstract images while moving my body in correlated yet distinct patterns—moving in one way while imagining something else—had given me the ability to imagine my body from various external visual perspectives.

How had these practices combined to work on my ability to perceive, recall and imagine movement? How had they come to be a part of the Chinese martial arts? What was their history? What kind of performances could I make using the skills they had imparted to me? Could I share these experiences with willing movers and thinkers who had not undergone the same martial training as I? The ideas in this book evolved out of the investigations, conversations, and reflections provoked by these questions.

To begin to address them I returned to the practices I'd been taught. I met, studied under, and in some cases exchanged with many martial arts experts, explaining that I already had principal teachers and practices, but that I was also very interested in experiencing their perspectives, even in the short term. I further sought out contemporary sources in religious studies, anthropology, and history, which in turn led me to primary texts in Chinese. Friends and colleagues who shared my interest became important inspirations, and I developed an informal network of collaborators around the world whom I would visit on occasion and with whom I'd speak or correspond regularly.

Looking at both martial movement and scholarly writing, I developed an interpretive strategy in which I chose to suspend the Euro-American presupposition that "martial arts," "religion," and "theatre" were siloed disciplinary categories. I adopted what I think of as a more culturally Chinese presupposition that the qualities of *wǔ*, or martial and primal, and *wén* 文, or civil and cultured, might appear and have decisive roles across the firm distinctions assumed by Western-style thinking. I applied the insights of my practice and research to the creation of original theatre, to the teaching of acting and directing, to initiating dancers into new ways of moving, to advising choreographers in the process of making their own work, and to writing about all these activities. In 2016 I was invited to give a keynote address at the Second Martial Arts Studies conference in Cardiff, UK, and I began to think of my writing as a contribution to this new interdisciplinary research area.[2]

Zhuāng Zhōu's Frog in a Well

The ideas that build up over the course of this book are certainly linked, yet each chapter shares a slightly different view. This constellated presentation is the result of my work as a theatre director and creator. As an artist in training in the 1990s, I hoped to share the worlds and stories I imagined with audiences directly. I quickly discovered that when people watched the theatre I had made, they didn't see exactly what I had imagined, but rather conjured worlds of their own inspired by what I had offered them. My experience that performances evoked different things in the imaginations of different audience members resonates with a story from the *Zhuāngzǐ* 莊子, which I have used as a model for this book. I feel it is an appropriate philosophical perspective on the subjects I have written about and matches my experiences as an artist and teacher.

---

[2] Anticipated by Farrer and Whalen-Bridge's 2011 edited collection *Martial Arts as Embodied Knowledge*, British cultural studies scholar Paul Bowman and American political scientist Ben Judkins created Martial Arts Studies in collaboration with researchers from around the world, founding a journal and holding an annual conference beginning in 2015.

The *Zhuāngzǐ* is a collection of stories and anecdotes from the late Warring States period of Chinese history (476–221 BCE.) Attributed to one Zhuāng Zhōu 莊周 it has had an enormous influence on Chinese culture as a whole, in particular on the ideas of the later institutionalized, esoteric religions of *Dàojiào* 道教, or Daoism (Paper 2019: 21). The *Zhuāngzǐ* presents funny and irreverent fables, allegories, and parables, which teasingly subvert any possibility of certain perception and judgement. In one of these tales, a frog who lived in a dilapidated well celebrated his dominion over his tiny home and invited a tortoise from the eastern ocean in for a visit:

> The surrounding crabs and tadpoles are certainly no match for me! For to have such mastery over one whole puddle of water like this, possessing all the joy of this sunken well—that is perfection! Why don't you come in and have a look sometime? (trans. Ziporyn 2022: 140).

The sea tortoise was too large to fit itself into the well, and from outside told the frog about its own vasty ocean home, which was so hard for the little frog to conceive of, that his "mind scattered in all directions in astonishment, beside himself in his puniness" (2022: 140).

Through the story of the frog in the well, the *jǐndǐ zhī wā* 井底之蛙, also called *zuò jǐng guān tiān* 坐井觀天, or sitting in a well, looking at the sky, the *Zhuāngzǐ* suggests that our perceptions are determined and limited by our environments. A creature living in a small well cannot hope to share the view of one living in a vasty ocean. Our *zhì* 智, or intellect, is as unsuited to thinking beyond our given contexts as a mosquito is to carrying a mountain on its back (2022: 140). The story of the frog in the well gently points out the limits our human embodiment places on our knowledge.

The frog's perspective is echoed in a later poem, the *Tí Xīlín Bì* 題西林壁, a short Song dynasty poem attributed to poet, calligrapher, and statesman Sū Shì 蘇軾 (1037–1101): "Horizontal ridges and vertical peaks, all different distances with different heights. / As I live in Lu Moutain, I don't know its real face."[3]

The poem eulogized the *Xīlín*, or West Forest Buddhist temple, on Mount Lu in Jiujang, Jiangxi. Founded in 366 CE, the temple has been renovated, destroyed, and rebuilt many times in its long history. Evoking it, Sū Shì suggests that while we know our immediate environment intimately, from our position within it we struggle to conceive of its larger shape and nature.

I do not experience the limits implied by Zhuāng Zhōu's story or Sū Shì's poem pessimistically. While the instructions behind the Daoist meditations I have learned and practiced do not posit a final, enlightened perspective, they do suggest that we can perhaps change wells, and hold new perspectives, if only

---

[3] The original text of the 題西林壁:

横看成嶺側成峰，遠近高低各不同。
不識廬山真面目，只緣身在此山中。

Figure 1: Untitled work from Jack Rusher's *Astronaut Series* (2021).

in a watery and dreamlike way. Jack Rusher's image, inspired by a shot from the 1946 British film *A Matter of Life and Death*, can serve as a metaphor here. While we cannot occupy the place of Jack's little astronaut, we can perhaps look up through more than one well.

Depending on which one we peer out of, the sky of the Chinese martial arts can look very different. While I don't think we can capture a definitive picture of them, I do believe that the subjects I discuss in this book—from martial movement, through different kinds of religiously inspired contemplations, to the creation of contemporary theatre and dance—conjure distinct worlds, new wells out of which we can look up.

Resonant Space

The late Edward de Bono (1933–2021) described creativity as a lateral linking of asymmetrical sets that uses crosscutting between categories to connect seemingly unrelated domains in novel ways (1993: 16). American theatre director Robert Wilson (b. 1941) offered an evocative, accessible example of this: "If you place a baroque candelabra on a baroque table, both get lost. If you place the candelabra on a rock in the ocean, you begin to see what it is" (1996: 53).

I don't know if René Magritte (1898–1967) was thinking of icebergs when he painted *Le Château des Pyrénées* (1959), but my fictional representation of this process offers a visual analogy of creative crosscutting:

The conceptual space between such ideas as a candelabra and a rock in the ocean, or a castle and an iceberg, allows an artist to relate them creatively. This

Figures 2, 3 & 4: Castle, iceberg, & *Le Château de Pyrénées*, sketches by Martin Borth.

kind of space is what I cut across in my interdisciplinary thinking about the Chinese martial arts, religion, and theatre, enabling gǎnyìng 感應, or correlative resonance, among different activities, people, ideas, geographies, and time periods. Gǎnyìng, a Chinese cultural and cosmological term used to elaborate mechanisms of causality, was first suggested in early works such as the *Zhuāngzǐ* and in manuals of rulership such as the c. 139 BCE *Huáinánzǐ* 淮南子, and significantly developed in later religious conceptions both Daoist and Buddhist.

Gǎnyìng is made up of the characters for *feeling* and *answer* and embraces both the phenomenological experiences generated by artistic practice and the written ideas resulting from scholarly contemplation. Academic disciplines such as religious studies, anthropology, and theatre studies, for example, offer sets between which I make lateral links. My perception of this resonant space and my creative crosscutting within it have been cultivated by the practice and teaching of the Chinese martial arts and of contemporary theatre and dance.

Contemplating these crosscuts, I wrote a poem about the gǎnyìng explored in this book:

武術即巫術
武道即舞蹈
勢即時
若亡若存

巫術即武術
舞蹈即武道
時即勢
若存若亡

wǔshù jí wūshù
wǔdào jí wǔdǎo

shì jí shí
ruò wáng ruò cún

wǔshù jí wǔshù
wǔdǎo jí wǔdào
shí jí shì
ruò cún ruò wáng

martial arts are sorcery
martial arts are dance
space is time
real yet unreal

sorcery is a martial art
dance is a martial path
time is space
unreal yet real

While pronounced with different tones, in Mandarin Chinese the word for martial, *wǔ*, is homonymic with the word *wū* or sorcery and *wǔ* or dance. The characters *shì* and *shí*, which can mean posture in space and time, are likewise similar. The final lines suggest the concurrence of opposites, of existence and non-existence. This poem represents my approach to the possible meanings of *religion, theatre*, and *martial arts*. Rather than operating from a single overarching definition, each chapter proposes a different view of the Chinese martial arts, while developing specific understandings of religions and of the art-forms of theatre and dance. A pun-filled poem in a language I started learning as an adult is perhaps the most judicious and good-humoured way to begin this volume, and I have used its lines to title some of my chapters.

Overview

Chapters 1 and 2 introduce the overall themes of this book: "Mastering Space" presents more conceptual views of wǔshù, and "Spatial Projection" develops these ideas with practical examples drawn from martial, theatrical, and ritual practices. Chapters 3, 4, and 5 constellate different elements of the cultural history of the Chinese martial arts, providing more focussed examples of the general ideas developed in the first two chapters. Chapters 6 and 7 provide detailed practical examples of my own application of wǔshù in the creation of contemporary theatre and dance.

   Chapter 1, "Mastering Space," articulates how the practice of choreographed Chinese martial movement, or *tàolù* 套路, can develop exponents' spatial perception. This chapter was originally published in 2021 as "*Tàolù*—The Mastery of Space" in the open-access journal *Martial Arts Studies*. I have made changes and added material to better integrate it with the chapters that follow.

Chapter 2, "Spatial Projection," describes a specific process of skill development and its application both in different phases of Chinese martial arts training and in the creation of a contemporary theatrical performance. It can be seen as the practical application of the more conceptual exposition of chapter 1. "Spatial Projection" originally appeared in the journal *Theatre, Dance and Performance Training* in the fall of 2022 as an open-access publication. I have made minor changes to better integrate it into the rest of this book.

Chapter 3, "Martial arts are sorcery. Sorcery is a martial art," examines the martial arts of Chinese religious specialists, highlighting the parameters of Chinese orthopraxy and how conceptions of religion that differ from Euro-American assumptions about belief and orthodoxy can be useful in understanding the many social roles played by the Chinese martial arts and their exponents.

Chapter 4, "Martial arts are dance. Dance is a martial path," presents the work of Chinese director Móu Sēn 牟森 and Indonesian director W. S. Rendra, two very different examples of the influence of wǔshù on the work of late 20th-century Asian theatre artists.

Chapter 5, "Real yet unreal. Unreal yet real," investigates *energy*, a Euro-American esoteric term that has become significant in the practice of both the Chinese martial arts and cosmopolitan theatre, through a discussion of 20th-century martial arts and theatrical projects that combined older ideas in novel ways. The intracultural combination of Daoist cosmology and martial training created by Sūn Lùtáng 孫祿堂 and the intercultural theatre practice of Jerzy Grotowski are examined.

In chapter 6, my collaborator Colin Lalonde describes his experience of our process as we created an original performance together. *And Treat the Distant Peoples with Kindness*, in which Colin participated as assistant director, was the third piece of theatre my collaborators and I created over the course of *Les Ateliers du corps*, a three-year artistic research project. Participants learned and practiced Chinese martial arts with a view to applying them to the creation of original contemporary theatre. Colin's account explores how our working methods facilitated the creativity of the performers and further examines how the aesthetic qualities of our work actively involved our audiences in the creation of the performance's meanings.

Chapter 7, "Space is Time. Time is Space," discusses the ways in which space and time have been conceptualized in Chinese martial arts and how these ideas manifested in my work as a facilitator and dramaturg working in contemporary dance. I present work done with students and recent graduates of the contemporary dance program at Fontys University of the Arts in Tilburg, the Netherlands; facilitation for choreographer-dancers Naishi Wang and Jean Abreu at the National Arts Centre of Canada in Ottawa; and my work as dramaturg for choreographer-dancer Katherine Ng as she created a solo for the CanAsian Dance Festival.

This book examines the historical and conceptual, and the artistic and applied, from the perspective of the personal and experiential. I hope that the resonances among these elements will offer readers new ways of considering their work, be it artistic or scholarly or both.

Notes on the Text

Romanization

Chinese characters, or *hànzì* 漢字 logographs, are provided when a name or term is first introduced. Traditional characters are used throughout, except where proper names or citations use simplified Chinese characters. Attempts to reform written Chinese to increase literacy began in the early 20th century, with simplified writing becoming standard in the People's Republic in the mid-1960s. I have used traditional characters here, as they are the basis for research into ancient writings and the older aspects of Chinese culture.

Mandarin, or Pǔtōng Huà, 普通话 is Romanized using *Hànyǔ Pīnyīn* 漢語 拼音, which means "the spelled sounds of the Hàn language." Cantonese, or Gwóngdūng Wá, 廣東話 is Romanized using the Yale system. I have included the diacritical marks that indicate the tonal pronunciation in both cases. I have kept the original Romanization in citations where the authors have used older or idiosyncratic styles, or Pīnyīn without diacritical marks, as well as in instances where individuals spell or spelled their proper names in English without using any standard system. The Romanized spelling of Chinese place names reflects international usage and does not include diacritical marks. Sanskrit Romanization uses the ISO-15919 format, including diacritical marks. Japanese Romanization uses the Hepburn system, which also includes diacritical marks. Terms in other languages maintain the Romanization used in the sources cited.

Citations and Sources

Citations that refer to specific information include page numbers. References to ideas developed over entire books and articles do not. Online references are indicated in the body of the text, with the internet address and date of consultation provided at the end of the book. Chinese language references and online sources are listed separately, as are personal communications, also at the end of the book.

How to cite this book chapter:
Mroz, D. 2025. *Resonant Space: Religion, Theatre, and the Chinese Martial Arts.* Pp. 11–12. Cardiff: Cardiff University Press. DOI: https://doi.org/10.18573/book11.b. Licence: CC-BY-NC-ND

Videos

Links to videos illustrating ideas discussed in the text are provided as they arise. These links, as well as full videos of the performances from which my examples are excerpted, are provided in Appendix D.

CHAPTER I

Mastering Space

Introduction

Tàolù, the choreographed movement practices found in the martial arts of China, are tools for mastering space. They train us to project our imaginations into the negative space around our bodies, and to manipulate that empty space intentionally as though it were a positive object or substance.

Tàolù can be seen as proto-combative behaviour, a level of practical coordination that can be put at the service of combat. The martial movement they express existed prior to the context that will eventually give it meaning as warfare, hunting, duelling, self-consecration, meditation, sporting competition, aesthetic performance, or a host of other possibilities. Tàolù are the human performance *of* combat and include, but also go beyond, human performance *in* combat. The martial movement of tàolù predates our present name for them. It is found not only in Chinese martial arts, but also in Chinese theatres and religious practices, current and historical (Mroz 2011: 22). Tàolù are acts of self-consecration that express martial religiosity using theatrical means. In this chapter I will explore their conjoined combative, religious, and theatrical expression.

Cunning and Surprise

Tàolù teach us how to create surprise.[4] In fighting, surprise enables victory, or the transformation of disadvantage into dominance. In theatre, surprise is used to lead the attention of the audience. In religion, surprise creates insight when we consider the meaning of the two experiences we often prefer not to think about: death and, more critically, life.

---

[4] I owe this important insight to my mentor Ken Cohen, whose dropped pearl "surprise is the only technique," completely transformed my view of the martial arts.

How to cite this book chapter:
Mroz, D. 2025. *Resonant Space: Religion, Theatre, and the Chinese Martial Arts.*
    Pp. 13–31. Cardiff: Cardiff University Press. DOI: https://doi.org/10.18573/book11.c.
    Licence: CC-BY-NC-ND

It may seem paradoxical to associate the repetitive and formal tàolù with surprise. However, the set structures of tàolù create the possibility of mental space. In following their behavioural prescription, we accept external standards of movement. In doing so we can transform, suppress, or at least negotiate with our movement habits and preferences. Having externalized our decision-making process by following the rules of tàolù, we may notice that some of our constant mental chatter and our physical tics are silenced. In this silence, lateral thoughts and unusual movement impulses can arise, and novel avenues of perception and action become available to us. We can see beyond our usual horizons and can act in new ways. As Brian Eno advises in his *Oblique Strategies* for artists, repetition *is* change, as reexperiencing patterns to saturation alters our perceptions (2005). While the pattern of the tàolù won't change in practice, each inspiration that arises offers a new variation when we move without the constraints of routine practice. It may not be obvious in contemporary curricula, but tàolù should serve to facilitate creative, free movement that can be improvised alone, in free play with a partner, in performance, in sporting competition, or in combat.

Describing the Chinese martial arts, Kāng Gēwǔ 康戈武 writes that they are characterized by *qiǎo* 巧, which his translator renders as "ingenuity" (1995: 1).[5] I suggest that "cunning" is a better word for combative training that lets us reliably engineer surprise. Nevertheless, the modernist lens through which we view the Chinese martial arts can make it hard for us to think in terms of cunning.

Our contemporary experience leads us to imagine these systems in two ways: as symmetrical sporting contests, or as responses to asymmetrical self-defence situations. We cannot ignore the powerful and positive effect that the first of these assumptions has had on the practical skill levels seen in combat sports today. From boxing and wrestling, through *Jūdō, Sǎndǎ* 散打, Muay Thai, and BJJ, to the worldwide proliferation of MMA, aggressive competition and training guided by sports science have created consistently improving competence in unarmed fighting.

Since the rise of MMA in the 1990s, tàolù and their related partner training practices have fallen into some disrepute. Learning elaborate choreographies and playing flowing, collaborative martial games do not appear to be of immediate use in a fight. Most of the extraordinary players in contemporary combat sports do not train this way.[6]

To employ qiǎo, however, we must not think like contemporary combat athletes. Rather, we should emulate Odysseus, the archaic trickster archetype.

---

[5] As does Andrea Falk in her English dictionary of Chinese martial arts terms (2019: 70).

[6] Current research suggests that "blocked practice," the rote movement training that characterizes liàn tàolù, is less useful in the acquisition of agonistic, interactive movement skills than "random practice," characterized by variability, improvisation, and high rates of failure (Schmidt 2008: 257).

Certainly, there was close, hand-to-hand fighting after the Greeks emerged from the Trojan Horse, but as soon as that horse was behind Troy's walls, the war was effectively won. In the Chinese martial arts and in military strategy more generally, excellence in fighting is secondary to trickery and wisdom. As far back as the *Liù Tāo* 六韜, a military manual from the Zhou dynasty, deception and surprise hold pride of place, as "the superior fighter does not engage in battle" (Sawyer 1993: 34, 69).

Ideally, qiǎo dictates the fundamental elements of an opponent's experience before physical conflict can manifest. Contemporary Taiwanese *Bāguà Quán* 八卦拳 teacher Hé Jìnghán 何靜寒 explains this, describing the attitude he believes his grand-teacher Yǐn Fú 尹福 to have held:

> We modern people have the wrong idea about the old masters, somehow thinking that they were always fighting. No! People such as Yin Fu, who was a bodyguard for the Empress [Dowager], would maybe have had three fights in their entire life and only then when there was a very good reason and when they were sure they would win. If Yin Fu had to fight, already he had failed. His job was to keep the Imperial family safe, not to get caught up in violence. He would have been expert at all kinds of terrain, geography, weather patterns, local customs, and much more, all kinds of strategy and ways of travelling, to ensure he never had to fight. (Hé, in Kozma 2011: 158–159)

We might also add the mastery of social interactions and cultural forms to this formidable list of necessary survival skills. As Sixt Wetzler proposes, these things we messily call "martial arts" are our attempts to tame the chaos of violence, transforming it into patterns that allow us to perceive it more clearly (Wetzler 2018: 131–132).

Chinese Religions and War Magics

For millennia, and up until 1912, China explicitly understood itself as a religious state. The patterning Wetzler evokes developed over thousands of years within the larger design of Chinese religious practice. John Lagerwey describes this world view in terms of two major spiritual forces: the environment experienced as deities and spirits, and humans honoured as ancestors (Lagerwey 2010: 7–13). In such a system, conflict was managed and understood using two kinds of rituals of propitiation. The Daoist and popular religious approaches were exorcistic, martial, and earthy, associated with place and with space. The Confucian and Buddhist approaches were preoccupied with human genealogies, hierarchies, and texts, and associated with ancestors and with time. Every aspect of Chinese history, society, and cosmology can be understood in terms of a martial/civil binary (Boretz 2011: 40–57). The complement to the martial wǔ is the civil wén, and as much as the official, written, and static elements of Chinese culture reflect wén, so do the violent, chaotic, and performative aspects reflect wǔ.

Rulers preferred the stability of Buddhist and Confucian texts that reinforced the social order. The people preferred the informality and idiosyncrasy of Daoist and popular embodied rites that exorcized troublesome spirits and directly appealed to the humble earth gods for protection and good harvests. The Daoist and popular religious rituals were more influential and widely practiced, but were not given much attention by imperial historians, appearing mostly in local archives (Lagerwey 2010: 7–13). Even seemingly agnostic events or individuals could not escape the consequences of this binary, as these understandings were deeply embedded within both local and elite cultures.

Further describing these fundamental cultural patterns, Lagerwey contrasts *dìyuán* 地緣, a Daoist China of space and cosmos, with *xuèyuán* 血緣, a Confucian China of human lineages (2010: 19). Dìyuán plays a vital role in the constitution of Chinese martial arts and the practice of tàolù. Dìyuán is home to natural forces understood as spirits and coincides totally with the actual physical environment in which conflict occurs. In this worldview, physical, tactical fighting and rituals exorcising and blessing space are in fact the same subject. In other words, martial arts are war magic, containing both physical and metaphysical techniques (Farrer 2016: 1). The distinction between the two is a modern one that reflects Western assumptions and a fundamentally secular worldview that would have been alien to most residents of imperial China.

Concretely, war magic could have included defenders stockpiling weapons, making a large offering to a local deity for protection, and prominently wearing the talismans produced during that rite while patrolling their territory. The enemy encountered on such patrols was likely from nearby and would share the same ritual culture. The defenders' gambit was that their potential raiders would be cowed by the talismans and the good morale produced by such magical protection. An aggressor would not do something as pointless as attacking an enemy rendered invulnerable by a talisman. Should violence nevertheless erupt, the defenders could pragmatically fall back on their physical, tactical training. However, they acted magically first because it projected their power farther out into space, into the territory that they wanted to secure.

This kind of war magic is usually identified with 19th-century rural peasant groups such as the Hóng Qiāng Huì 紅槍會 (Red Spear Society) or the Dàdāo Huì 大刀會 (Big Sword Society). Elizabeth Perry describes the spread of the Red Spears' rituals in the 1800s as the popularization of previously marginalized practices (1980: 256), but the magic performed by these radical groups is far from peripheral to the history of Chinese martial arts. Meir Shahar recounts how imperial troops seeking supernatural protection had petitioned their tutelary deities Guān Yǔ 關羽 and Mǎ Shén 馬神 the Horse King in the 1500s, three hundred years earlier. War magic is a perennial aspect of Chinese martial cultures, from the conventional centre to the idiosyncratic margins (see chapter 5) (2019: 378).[7]

The success of Chinese war magic depends on its antagonists' mutual participation in the shared world of the dìyuán, and on its being deployed with qiǎo. Perhaps the most famous failure of war magic was experienced by the Yìhéquán 義和拳 fighters of the Boxer Rebellion of 1899, who discovered they were not impervious to the bullets of Western colonial powers. The occupying forces didn't participate in the dìyuán of the rebel—and worse, the Boxers did not deploy their magic with qiǎo. Instead of tricking the colonial forces into believing that shooting at them would be useless, they foolishly exposed themselves to enemy gunfire. Unlike Odysseus and Yǐn Fú, the Boxers had not won before they fought. This created a *false connection* between martial ritual and actual combat (Farrer 2018: 37). Despite such false connections, we cannot simply dismiss the dìyuán as a mere world of make-believe that is of no consequence to "reality."

These ideas may be counterintuitive to our usual ways of thinking about the Chinese martial arts. While most of the systems that are practiced today were secularized and largely reinvented between the 1910s and the 1950s, they preserved deeper cultural practices that were created in accordance with a millennial, religious worldview that is now largely forgotten. We cannot grasp the social meanings and skilled fruition of even the most "modern" practices without first dealing with this neglected inheritance. In imperial China, the martial arts had the following general characteristics that are now unfamiliar to us:

- Chinese martial arts idealized cunning and taught the use of trickery before tactics and spiritual combat before physical combat;
- Chinese martial arts took place in a real, material space that was also simultaneously a religious space governed by shared cultural values, including belief in the supernatural;
- Tàolù expressed this shared vision of China as a religious space, by theatrically creating physical narratives that were experienced by their players and received by audiences.

I am not diminishing the tactical brilliance of the Chinese martial arts overall or the fighting skill of the many capable exponents with whom I've had the good fortune to study. Rather, I point to the history and sources that can explain the nature of tàolù and the attributes that their practice cultivates.

---

[7] David Palmer's account of martial rituals performed today in Huangha, in northern Guangdong province, is instructive (2021: 126–130). His online presentation at the 2020 Martial arts studies conference at Université Aix-Marseille included footage of contemporary *wǔ* rites: https://www.youtube.com/watch?v=RAkjt2I9mlI (archived here: https://vimeo.com /891091968?share=copy).

To make an analogy, we could elect to discuss the works of J. S. Bach (1685–1750) strictly in terms of their formal musical structures, with no reference to religion. Bach, however, was a practicing Christian who worked in a church. In his lifetime, his music was received as religious expression. Furthermore, the standardized tuning named A440, which is used to play his music today, was only adopted in the 19th century. If we don't know these things, we will still be able to enjoy contemporary performances of Bach, but we will remain ignorant of the factors that shape our experience of his music. If we attempt to speak with authority on the nature and origins of his music, we will simply be wrong.

Martial movement

Please watch the video example: https://vimeo.com/901925713?share=copy [8]

Let us observe the movement that makes up these ritual, martial, and theatrical activities. In the video on the left, two recreational martial artists who are students of a present-day international Chói Lěih Fáht Kyùhn 蔡李佛拳 lineage, perform a choreographed fight using double sabres and spear.[9] Simultaneously, on the right are two professional teachers of Jīngjù 京劇, or "Peking Opera," from the National Academy of Chinese Theatre Arts in Beijing, demonstrating basic phrases of fight choreography with the same weapons.

There is a slight difference in the tempo-rhythms of the two choreographies, as one is a real performance by amateurs and the other is instructional material presented by professionals. The Jīngjù weapons are made of light and resilient wood reinforced with twine or fibreglass. The Chói Lěih Fáht weapons, while still light and maneuverable, are made of heavier wood and metal, and the spear is about one-third longer. Yet these two presentations are virtually interchangeable. The contexts may be different, but the physical culture and martial movement displayed are the same. Why might this be so?

Theatre, Religiosity, and Chói Lěih Fáht Kyùhn

The Hùhng Sing 鴻勝 Chói Lěih Fáht Kyùhn School was perhaps the first martial arts studio that a contemporary person would have recognized as such. It

---

[8] The Chói Lěih Fáht Kyùhn video was created by the Plum Blossom International Federation and uploaded to the *YouTube* social media platform, https://www.youtube.com/watch?v=5tXl6xv8Sks. It was retrieved on June 24, 2020 at 17:22 EST. The *Jīngjù* video comes from VCDs I acquired in Beijing in the spring of 2013.

[9] I practiced Chói Lěih Fáht Kyùhn intensively from 1993–2005. It accounts for at least 10,000 of the 20,000 or more hours of instruction I've received in Chinese martial arts. I've written in detail about this transmission and about my teacher, Sui Meing Wong 黃小名 (Yale: Wòhng Síu Méng), in my book *The Dancing Word* [Mroz 2011: 66–68]. Sui Meing Wong is heir to Lèuhng Kái 梁啟 (1918–1992), himself a student of Fùhng Yuhk Syū 馮育樞, who studied with Chàhn Gūn Baak 陳官伯, the son of Chói Lěih Fáht's founder. Since 1997 Sui Meing has also studied the Bāk Sing 北勝 variant of Chói Lěih Fáht (Jyutping: *bak1 sing3*, Pīnyīn: *Běi Shèng*) with Chiu Kwok Cheung 趙國忠 (Yale: Jiuh Gwok Jūng).

is thus an interesting test for understanding the worldview of even relatively modern Chinese martial arts. Chói Lěih Fáht Kyùhn was founded by Guangdong native Chàhn Héung 陳享 (1805–1875), in 1836. He presented his style as a synthesis of three earlier practices. In 1848, Chan's representatives opened branch studios in various locations, including Guanxi Province and the Guangdong city of Foshan. In his early career Chan was sought after as a teacher of martial arts and militia drill for smaller communities in the Pearl River Delta region. However, his creation of a chain of studios teaching a standardized curriculum, which individuals could join by paying or bartering, was a new development in the region. The Foshan Chói Lěih Fáht Kyùhn schools were closed when the Red Turban Revolt (or Opera Rebellion) of 1854 was put down in 1856, and when the style resurfaced in the city in 1867 it was as the main activity offered by the newly reformed Hùhng Sing Association (Judkins & Nielson 2015: 97).

The Hùhng Sing Association was a fraternal organization that catered to the working classes of Foshan, who sought social respectability through participation in an increasingly influential group. In addition to martial arts instruction, membership offered individuals a network of social connections and negotiating power in their dealings with landlords, employers, gangster-run protection rackets, and the state. At its height in 1920, the Hùhng Sing Association had some 3,000 members in Foshan, a town of about 300,000 people. Judkins and Neilson estimate that four percent of the adult male population under the age of 40 were members and consequently had some experience of Chói Lěih Fáht Kyùhn (Judkins & Nielson 2015: 97).

Although Hùhng Sing membership required the practice of Chói Lěih Fáht Kyùhn, the association also offered other group physical activities, including military drill. In situations of violence, such as the Hùhng Sing Association's involvement in the militarized aspects of the 1925 Hong Kong general strike, members armed with rifles were deployed to the picket-lines. They grabbed their guns and left Chói Lěih Fáht's powerful punches and its vast arsenal of archaic edged weapons behind in the studio. While violence and hand-to-hand combat were certainly a feature in the lives of the people practicing Chói Lěih Fáht Kyùhn, when push came to shove, they used firearms and group action to defend their persons and their socioeconomic interests. As Ben Judkins clearly affirms, "China's modern schools of hand combat were all created in the era of firearms" (Judkins & Nielson 2015: 40). Like the vast majority of Chinese martial arts extant today, Chói Lěih Fáht Kyùhn was never used on a battlefield, nor did it descend from practices that were. While its exponents may have used it for skirmishing, its principal relationship to violence was in the civilian context of duelling, and in self-defence against the kinds of limited social conflicts that Patrick McCarthy has called Habitual Acts of Physical Violence (2005: 2).

While the Chói Lěih Fáht Kyùhn practiced by the members of the Hùhng Sing Association undoubtedly helped them to negotiate individual social positions through fisticuffs, it also intersected visibly with religious behaviour. Chói Lěih Fáht exponents playing tàolù enacted a magical, religious role in and for their community. The play of tàolù and Lion Dancing in a seasonal calendar of popular festivals demonstrated the adepts' martial prowess while earning spiritual merit for the entire community. By practicing and demonstrating the arduous and humbling physical training Chói Lěih Fáht requires, these performers consecrated and re-consecrated themselves to what Daniel Amos refers to as a "religion of the body" (1997: 31–61). This self-consecration made them spiritually inviolable and venerable in the eyes of their community. Their demonstration of skill acquired through perseverance, or gōngfū 功夫, was a meritorious act performed on behalf of the collective. This was one of the ways that the Hùhng Sing Association's plebian students could achieve status within their broader social system.

This self-consecration was also tacitly expressed in theatre. Theatre permeated public and private life in 19th-century China. While professional actors belonged to a marginalized underclass, people loved the entertainment they provided, and hired them not just to perform, but also to teach and coach amateurs. For professional, amateur, and private groups, the learning, rehearsing, and presentation of theatre was beloved, constant, and intense. While non-actors would never play professionally, virtually everyone was involved in performing at some level. Given its spectacular nature and emphasis on dramatic fights, it comes as no surprise that Chinese theatre, or xìqǔ 戲曲, employs many training methods that are virtually identical to those used in martial arts. While it would be possible to provide multiple examples, Jo Riley relates a particularly interesting case:

> In 1991 I filmed a wǔshù club training in the village temple in Zhong Suo village in Guizhou under their master Lu Huamei, who was also the head of the village theatre company. Lu teaches tang quan style, which is in the middle level range of skills, and over three hundred villagers train regularly with him (nowadays girls included). Six small boys also take part in the training, the youngest of whom is ten years old, and the skills they learn from Lu are also observed from standing on the stage with the village theatre company when they perform. As in many villages, the village temple, martial arts training and performance indivisibly form the cradle of acting in and spectating theatre.[10] (Riley 1997: 17)

Whether amateur or professional, actors portraying deities and ancestors on stage would achieve an exponential self-consecration: the actors performed martial movement, and in doing so, self-consecrated. Their performances presented the stage figures of ancestors and deities, a further act of self-consecration.

---

[10] Riley's interview with Lu was conducted through an interpreter who spoke the local language, rather than in Mandarin. She did not learn the character for tang, nor did her informant Lu elaborate on what he meant by a "middle range of skills" (Riley, personal communication). I speculate that Lu might have been referring to a regional style named Táng Quán 唐拳.

These stage figures in turn performed martial movement within the fiction of the dramatic narrative, self-consecrating for a third time.

The Red Turban Revolt of 1854 gives some sense of the theatre's public value in 19th-century China: in an altercation over taxation with the faltering and distant imperial Qing government, a theatre troupe leader named Lǐ Wénmào 李文茂 joined forces with a secret society gangster named Chén Kāi 陳開 and other malcontents, eventually capturing the city of Foshan. Lǐ's revolutionary actors turned their rebellion into a theatrical performance, fighting and then governing in costume. Dressed as the folk-heroes, deities, and ancestors they would normally play onstage, they brought the archetypal, outsized, and chaotic world of myth and fiction into everyday politics in the most direct way imaginable (Lei 2006: 160–161). When the rebellion was quelled in 1856, those actors who didn't flee or hide their identities were massacred. Local theatre was banned for a period of 10 years.[11]

The Hùhng Sing Association reopened its Chói Lěih Fáht Kyùhn studio in 1867, eleven years after the Opera Rebellion and one year after the theatre ban was lifted. Given the sheer density of theatre being practiced in Chinese culture in the 19th century, it is easy to imagine all of that commitment and effort being transferred from theatre to martial arts, bringing with it a wealth of martial choreographies.[12] Regardless of the details of how this came about, the Chói Lěih Fáht tàolù are theatrical artefacts, and demonstrate a discreet yet robust site of resistance to imperial power: "No officer, of course it's not theatre—it's Kung Fu!"

Structure and Phenomenology of Martial Movement

More recent concepts used in the teaching of Chinese physical culture may help us to further understand the theoretical and historical propositions outlined above. What makes us move? Tàolù always imply the presence of another body, even if the practitioner is training or performing alone. The impetus for

---

[11] The ban was not only meant to punish the actors who had risen above their station. The secret societies resisting the Qing government conducted their ideological teaching and initiations through elaborately produced amateur theatre productions, further stoking the imperial ire against local theatre artists (see chapter 4.)

[12] In 2013, a day after arriving in China, I visited the class of my friend and colleague Prof. Lǔ Suǒsēn 吕锁森 at the National Academy of Chinese Theatre Arts in Beijing. He introduced me to his 30-odd Jīngjù students as a visiting theatre artist and immediately had me learn a partner stage-fighting choreography for the qiāng or spear, which his Finnish student, Antti Silvennoinen, taught me on the spot. Because of my previous training I learned the short, paired set very quickly. He called all the students over to watch while giving them a most thorough scolding, pointing out that they had failed to memorize the series in question after three weeks of work, whereas I, a foreigner who had arrived in Beijing the day before and who spoke Mandarin poorly, could already perform it! I'd never played with any Jīngjù weapons before, but I had of course trained in Chói Lěih Fáht Kyùhn and its spear-play forms. I explained this to Lǔ, but he didn't choose to enlighten his stunned students any further.

movement in Chinese martial arts comes from outside of the exponent's body. They may begin the process of movement because of an imagined natural force, an ancestor, deity, teacher, or opponent. They may even have a real teacher or an actual audience to salute, but from there on in they are moving in response to the prompts and demands of an attacker, present or implied (Mroz 2017: 48).

This extroversion is fundamental to all the developmental agendas we might attribute to Chinese martial movement. To respond competently to violence, I must reject my instinctual or preferred reactions in favour of responses that help me neutralize my aggressor by using my environment. To perform capably in a martial competition or demonstration, I must externalize my decision-making process to respond to my partner's actions and timing. To self-consecrate through training, I must abandon my self-involvement and conform my body to preexisting ritualized shapes and sequences. This rejection of habit and preference is accomplished using a durational training that, over time, changes how I perceive my body.

The externalization created through this training process is practical. When called upon to respond to an outside stimulus, such as dodging a ball, I will move faster than if I am merely asked to move as quickly as I can without the stimulus of the ball.[13] In the absence of an actual ball, the solo-movement training process of the Chinese martial arts teaches me how to construct movement tasks for myself that allow me to use my imagination to access abilities normally recruited by real stimuli. I achieve this by learning to project my imagination outwards into the space around my body.

Both the Chinese martial and theatrical arts describe externalization using the five-character formula *shǒu yǎn shēn fǎ bù* 手 眼 身法 步, "the method of integrating the hand, the eye, the steps and the body."[14] In the theatrical version, the character for body is replaced with *zhǐ* 指, or finger (Riley 1997: 88). Some martial arts formulations add the character for loosen, or *sōng* 松 (Childs 2020: 84). The formula denotes the elements that need to be differentiated and individually emptied of habitual reactions, and then reintegrated to produce an expert level of performance.

A practical example: we use our hands to eat. As we prepare to take a bite, we lean forward and drop our head while we move our hands toward our face. As a result, when we begin to learn martial movement, any action of our arms unconsciously pulls our heads forward, sabotaging our balance and disturbing our peripheral vision. In swordplay this tendency allows our training partners

---

[13] I owe this clear example to my friend and collaborator Scott Park Phillips.

[14] Yung Sai-Shing notes that in Chinese theatre

The five Chinese characters of the *wufa* denote: "hand" (*shou*), "eye" (*yan*), "torso" (*shen*), "method" (*fa*), and "step" (*bu*). Since the other items without exception refer to parts of the human body, the fourth, *fa*, seems not to belong in the same category. Thus, another version of the *wufa* postulates that the written character for the term *fa*, rather than being the character to denote "method", should be the character that means "hair" [髮 *fà*] which specifies the skill of spinning "hair". The confusion is a result of the same pronunciation of the two different characters (in Morris, Li & Chan eds., 2005: 28).

to tap us on our fencing-masks every time we move our sword, as our heads come forward automatically, presenting themselves as easy targets. Consciously separating the actions of the head from those of the hands is essential in learning martial movement.

Mid-20th-century martial practitioner Tāng Rǔ Kūn 湯汝昆 describes how mastering the five characters actually feels.[15] Tāng was a teacher of the 20th-century Chinese martial art named Yì Quán 意拳, founded by Wáng Xiāngzhāi 王薌齋 (1885–1963.) Tāng writes that martial training produces qì gǎn 氣感 or "the sensations of the life force," which are heat, weight, vibration, and expansiveness (Tāng in Cohen 1997: 270).

Qì is a term with many meanings, and its use in the discussion of Chinese martial arts is contested. It's been described by Chinese experts as everything from the *sine qua non* to nothing but "bogus talk" (He 2006: xxvii). For our purposes, qì is a phenomenological correlate to the circulation of blood. My blood is a material substance with an obvious location and flows along predictable paths. When I practice the basic exercises of Chinese martial arts that realign and strengthen the tonic, supportive muscles of the body, both my circulation and the depth of my felt sensations of heat, weight, and vibration will improve dramatically. To use Tāng's terms, as my body empties of compulsion, it can fill with qì.

The last term on Tāng's list is expansiveness, a euphoric "subjective feeling of blending into the environment" (Cohen 1997: 271). As our experience deepens, rather than being hypnotized by ever-smaller physical sensations, we reverse our inward focus and project ourselves out into the space that surrounds us. This reversal should emerge tacitly from training and then be supported directly with visualization.

Like the externalizations mentioned above, expansiveness is practical. Our ability to orient ourselves has been developed through the practice of stances, postures, and stepping. We can predict the shape of our space and our position in it using our felt sense of the position of our feet, the distribution of our mass, and the orientation of our bodies. We have also learned to measure the space around us using the body of another, through partner training and collaborative martial games. Using the body of another to measure space is called extended physiological proprioception, or EPP, and we experience a version of it every time we write with a pen and feel the surface of the paper through the stylus we are holding (Simpson 1974: 146–150). In expansiveness we combine the potential of all these capabilities to create an imaginal rendering of the space we are moving in.[16] We experience our body inside our mind, which is co-equal with space.

---

[15] Tāng was the Yì Quán teacher of Ken Cohen, who is in turn my teacher. He also gave Ken a copy of his book Yì Quán Qiǎn Shì 意拳淺釋.

[16] The word *imaginal* is a neologism coined by scholar Henri Corbin to describe the visualized and visionary experiences of Islamic mysticism that exist between sensory experience and discursive thought (Corbin 1977: viii–ix).

Spatial Perception

How much space can we embrace with our minds? I was introduced to three magnitudes of space in my training in the swordplay of the *Wǔdāng Dàojiào Xuán Wǔ Pài* 武当道教玄武派.[17] The first distance was the range at which I can, with a leap, strike my opponent with my sword, but where I hope they cannot reach me. The second distance allows me to touch my opponent with one hand while also striking them with my sword, while at the third distance, I can strike them with both my elbow and my sword.

These three concentric spaces are named after features and phases of Chinese cosmology. The first range is named after the *bāguà* 八卦, the second is referred to as the range of *tàijí* 太極 or *yīnyáng* 陰陽, and the third is called *wújí* 無極. These cosmological designations are surprisingly tactically concrete.[18] At the bāguà range, there are many possible striking actions available. At the yīnyáng tàijí range, those possibilities have been curtailed to a few binary options—and at the wújí range, I cannot differentiate clear striking lines, as my limbs are entangled with those of my opponent.

Visualization is used in solo and then in partner practice to map the space of play. As part of my training in Wǔdāng swordplay, I memorized the octagon of the bāguà and practiced projecting it outwards in front of me to encircle my training partner. I also learned to project it downwards towards the ground to encircle myself with the eight principal directions of movement. Lastly, I was asked to visualize the vertical circle in mirror image, to be able to see how my training partner was seeing me.

These projections were preceded by a series of meditations done holding the *jiàn*, or straight-sword, in lying, seated, and standing positions. In these *shēn jiàn* 身劍 or "body and sword" meditations, the student practices merging the felt sense of different parts of their body with the felt sense of the sword they hold. Initially the student imagines breathing in to their lower abdomen, and breathing out along the blade of the sword, which is imagined to extend infinitely.[19] Gradually, increasingly complex feelings and intentions are asked

---

[17] I studied this approach privately with Ismet Himmet in Berlin, in the fall of 2018, for 30 hours. Ismet learned from Yóu Xuán Dé 游玄德, the head of the *Wǔdāng Xuánwǔ Pài* in China. My recent studies with Ismet supplemented my earlier work with Chinese sword-play teachers Jason Tsou (Zōu Jiāxiāng) 鄒家驤 (2013), Chang Wu Na (Zhāng Wùnà) 張悟納, and Lu Mei-hui (Lǔ Měihuì, PhD) 呂美惠, 博士 (2013 and 2015), and regular fencing practice with my mentor Michael Babin (2012–2018).

[18] While readers will recognize these cosmological elements as a part of Chinese religion, we must recall that the ostensibly Daoist students of this swordplay system would be effortlessly familiar with such references and find them easy to recall and project.

[19] Having practiced these methods almost daily since the fall of 2018, I have noticed a marked improvement in my ability to manipulate the jiàn in solo tàolù, in practicing cuts and thrusts on a swinging, suspended brass pendulum and in free swordplay using limited targets and light protective equipment. Heavier gauntlets seriously inhibit EPP, and I do not yet notice much improvement in "all-in" swordplay from this particular practice. I don't spend much more than

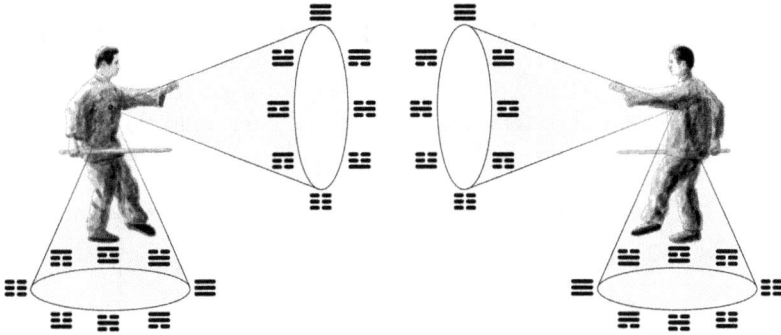

Figure 5: Bāguà projection in Wǔdāng swordplay.

of the student. During training retreats, for example, students are expected to sleep beside their swords, holding a particular body shape corresponding to the handle, guard, and blade of the jiàn.

The three ranges of *Xuán Wǔ Pài* swordplay correlate well with the general categories of spatial perception posited by neuropsychology. Extrapersonal space, corresponding to the bāguà range, is the space that occurs outside of our reach. Peripersonal space, corresponding to the yīnyáng or tàijí range, occurs within the reach of our limbs. Percutaneous space, corresponding to the wújí range, occurs at and just above the surface of our skin, where even if there is no contact, we will sense heat and motion (Elias & Saucier 2006: chapter 10.1). A contemporary, if reductive, interpretation of Tāng's evocative term "expansiveness" casts it as the ability to transfer the immediate sensitivity we have at close tactile and visual range to spaces farther and farther from ourselves.

First-Person Experience

In my fifth year of martial training, I began to experience an expanded sense of the space around me. I began automatically to project a grid onto the floor of any space I worked in, divided along the diagonal and cardinal lines. The area of the grid was defined by its geometric centre and its peripheral boundaries, either lines on the floor for sporting play or actual boundaries such as walls or level changes in the ground:

Asymmetrical, curved, or random shapes were adjusted in my perception to angled two-dimensional figures such as squares, rectangles, and triangles. My training partner defined a second, mobile, and dynamic centre to this area.

---

20 minutes a day doing these meditations, and I am surprised at their effect, given they are static and do not model swordplay movement or fighting in a direct manner at all.

I also began to sense the position of the ground and objects in the environment through the play of tensions in my training partner's body during controlled, collaborative free-play partner drills such as *tuī shǒu* 推手. I used my partners' bodies to develop extended physiological proprioception to parse the space around us in into three-dimensional cubic cells, through which I perceived their movements:

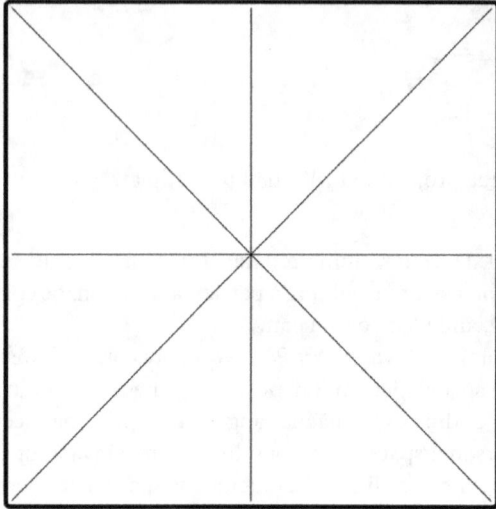

Figure 6: Centre, Periphery, Cardinal, and Diagonal Lines.

Figure 7: Three Dimensional Cubic Cells.

Over years this awareness developed to the point where I perceived the empty, or negative, space around people and objects as a positive object. It felt as though the space was full of a thick, viscous fluid that flowed around me and my training partner, forming a vast, abstract Henry Moore sculpture made of liquid metal. Swordplay further clarified this experience as I used the positive, solid shape of the sword to craft the shape of this negative space "sculpture," determining the pathways of movement of my training partner.

In my professional work as a theatre director, choreographer, and teacher of stage movement, I discovered that I was developing performances from beginning to end by making sequential changes to the overall shape of the negative space on stage. My mental picture of the stage space, the initial positions of the performers, the viewpoints of the audience, the height of the ceiling, and the objects I had planned to use as the set were enough to set the "sculpture" in motion. The change of emphasis from the positive objects I engaged with in the early years of my training to the negative space that currently preoccupies me seems characteristic of training in Chinese martial arts.

Reversals in Training, Reversals as Training

When we begin to learn Chinese martial movement, we are extroverted. We hope to be able to defend ourselves from others, to demonstrate martial skill in competition or performance, and perhaps in doing so to self-consecrate in ways our community will find meritorious. Once initiated into practice, we experience a first reversal. We are asked to differentiate our bodily movement, to breathe with the abdomen in mind, to focus on the personal and internal world of sensation. When we come to express the results of this withdrawal into our soma, we encounter yet another reversal. The self-sensing that we have refined through inward focus becomes an outward projection of perception and action.

Such reversals, or *fǎn* 反, are fundamental to the Chinese religious practice of *jīndān zhī dào* 金丹之道, or the cultivation of the golden elixir, which dates from the around the third century and has contributed importantly to the lore and training methods of Chinese martial arts as both metaphor and practice (Pregadio 2019: 2). Also known as *nèidān* 內膽, or inner elixir, it is found in Daoist and other branches of Chinese normative religion.[20] It is composed of physical exercises and visualization, or *cún xiǎng* 存想. It is undertaken with the view that engaging with our mortality can lead to us toward agency and meaning, rather than to banal social and material careerism. While not literally

---

[20] For example, the practice of jīndān and the worship of Zhāng Sān Fēng were essential elements of the heterodox *Sānyī Jiào* 三一教 sect created by Lin Zhao'en (1517–1598) whose most distinguished follower was Qī Jìguāng 戚繼光, 1528–1588, the Ming general today celebrated as a possible source of the martial art that became *Tàijí Quán*. Scott Park Phillips made this discovery correlating the religious studies archive with the more commonly trawled military history one (Phillips 2019: 48–64; see also Dean 1998, for a history of the *Sānyī Jiào*).

concerned with the transmutation of metals, jīndān takes its name and its metaphors from alchemy, comparing the reversal of the normal process of human
maturation and decay with the transformation of dross into gold.[21] The preparatory phases of jīndān found in formal religious practices have been diffused
into common knowledge informing the practice of Chinese martial arts.

The reversals of jīndān are expressed in the narratives of folktales and popular theatre through the trope of divine madness. Consider Zhāng Sān Fēng
張三丰, the Daoist immortal and jīndān master who some late 19th- and early
20th-century oral traditions credit with the invention of the supposedly peaceful and enlightening martial art of *Tàijí Quán* 太极拳. Despite the fact that he
is a spiritual being and thus an example to be imitated, he tests the tolerance
and openness of all who encounter him by appearing as a filthy, contrarian
drunkard who likes nothing more than a good brawl (Phillips 2019a: 42–48).
While this perspective resembles a conventional, literary trope such as
Bakhtin's carnivalesque, it is important to keep in mind that jīndān existed
as a widely distributed and varied technical and embodied process, not just as
a funny story. Its reversals are specific procedures that produce particular
psycho-physiological effects. For instance, the *Wǔdāng Xuán Wǔ Pài*, an oral
transmission attributed to Zhāng Sān Fēng, offers advice on adapting training
to various climatic conditions:

1. Waxing Moon   – practicing sword enhances *qì*,
2. Waning Moon   – practicing slow, even open-hand movement develops
   force or *lì* (力),
3. Windy Night   – hike and climb uphill to train the endurance of the
   lungs,
4. Rainy Night   – read Daoist texts and contemplate them
5. Midnight   – meditate to become aware of our "human qualities,"
   chief among these, our mortality and our tendency to
   deny it.[22]

While still quite general, the specification that training should take place at
night reverses the social norm of being active by day and sleeping after dark,
setting the would-be student of martial arts on the path toward jīndān.

This reversal, using internalization followed by spatialization, is also found in
the preparatory phases of formal jīndān practices I have learned. In the *Dàojiào
Qī Pán Dà Zuò* 道教七盤大坐 of the *Wǔdāng Xuánwǔ Pài*,[23] one passes through
seven levels of consciousness by visualizing and inhabiting their representative
bodies. In the *Huāshān* 花山 tradition one moves from dynamic movement,

---

[21] I discuss nèidān, the core formal practice of jīndān, in chapter 5, differentiating it from the
preparatory process described here.

[22] I received these instructions from Ismet Himmet, October 2018, Berlin.

[23] From Yóu Xuán Dé via Ismet Himmet, since 2018.

sound, and breath-holding called *Qì Fā Gōng* 氣發功 to the circulation of qì in the *Xiǎo Zhōu Tiān* 小周天, or the small celestial circuit meditation; to the raising and lowering of qì in the *Jīn Guān* 金光, or golden light meditation; to the concentration of qì in the *Jīn Zhū* 金珠, or golden pearl meditation. All of this results in the creation of the *Yǐng Xíng* 影形, the projected self which further assists in cultivation.[24] Finally, in a reversal worthy of jīndān, *Zhìnéng Qìgōng* 智慧氣功 begins with a visualization where the body expands to the "top and bottom of the universe," starting, rather than closing, with spatial projection.[25]

While all these methods are relatively quiescent preparations for the actual practice of jīndān, they nevertheless assume the martial movement found in tàolù as a prerequisite. When meditation or *qìgōng* students lacked this training, all the teachers I've studied with would introduce them to some kind of fundamental martial movements, to allow them to make the process of externalization and its reversals clearer for themselves.

Correlation with Tibetan Yoga

"As is now well-known after forty years of unprecedented study of religion in Chinese society and history, we Westerners have a congenital incapacity to see the religious dimension in China" (Lagerwey 2010: 1).

The same is not so of Tibet and India, where the Western imagination has not just noticed the religious dimension but magnified and exoticized it. Looking to the Himalayas and to South Asia, we see that jīndān, wherever we may find it in the religions of China, is comparable to a yogic path. It is a series of "disciplined and systematic techniques for the training and control of the human mind-body complex, which are also understood as techniques for reshaping human consciousness towards some kind of higher goal" (Samuel 2008: 2).

Textual references to a wide variety of practices all named "yoga" abound in Indian and Tibetan history. Much like the Chinese martial arts, however, almost all of what is practiced as *yoga* today dates from the 1800s (see chapter 5.) The Tibetan *Six Yogas of Naropa* is one of the few extant pre-19th-century traditions of yoga. It follows a comparable series of reversals to the ones found in jīndān preliminaries. The practice begins with intense physical training, called *trulkhor*, that includes extensive martial and theatrical movement (Phillips & Mroz 2016: 148). The heat, weight, and vibration experienced in trulkhor is turned within using visualization and breath retention to produce heat in the body, called *tummo*. The resulting expansiveness is used to project the imagination out of the body, into a variety of spaces. The adept visualizes and projects multiple bodies for themselves. They project themselves into the liminal space

---

[24] From Ken Cohen, since 1998.
[25] From Liú Yuán Míng 刘垣明 via Sui Meing Wong, since 1993.

between life and death, and subjectively experience the ejection of their consciousness into pure space (Baker 2019: 200–210).

The correlation of this process with jīndān is unmistakable. Historically, Vajrayana Buddhism has identified with Indian sources to discourage Chinese territorial claims. Culturally however, Tibetan yoga was influenced by Chinese *Chán* 禪, Buddhist and Daoist methods developed on Mt. Wutai in Shanxi province (Baker 2012b: 222). Further, the imaginal body system of centres and channels, or *cakras* and *nāḍīs*, now considered characteristic of yoga and tantra writ large, also appears to have entered the Indian tradition from China, appearing in the eighth century (Samuel 2008: 278–282, and see chapter 5).

Perhaps our easy acceptance of the religiosity of India and Tibet, and the documented exchanges between Chinese religions and these cultures, can allow us to explore further the Chinese martial arts as religious expressions.

Conclusion

Tàolù are ingenious acts of martial preparation, religious self-consecration, and theatrical performance. The practice of tàolù can train us to project our imaginations into the negative space around our bodies. This perception may allow us to manipulate that empty space intentionally as though it were positive object or substance. To develop this skill, we transfer the immediate sensitivity we have at close tactile and visual range to spaces farther and farther from ourselves. Extended physiological proprioception, cultivated in both the open-handed and armed collaborative partner games of the Chinese martial arts, seems to play a major role in this process. As our sensitivity expands, we experience our mind occupying all the space that it can encompass, perceiving and moving our bodies as though from outside. This phenomenological experience has its roots in the Chinese religious conception of dìyuán, the Daoist China of space and cosmos, and was originally actualized with cunning, or qiǎo, in the physical and metaphysical practice of martial arts as war magic.

Tradition does not provide a single term or definition for this unusual skill or attribute. Daoist traditions speak of the projected self, or Yǐng Xíng. The Tàijí Quán Lùn 太極拳論, one of the martial essays that compose the cannonical *Tàijí Jīng* 太極經, describes knowing how to move intuitively and effortlessly as the state of *shén míng* 神明, literally a "radiant spirit" (Doherty 2009: 64; Masich 2020: 1; Zhang 2016: 68–70). Turning to contemporary authors, D. S. Farrer describes the feats of spatial memory performed by the "Coffee Shop Gods," the master martial artists of Singapore (Farrer 2011: 203–237). Scott Park Phillips proposes the "tangible imagination" as the field in which this perception and action takes place (2019a: 221). Writing about the correlate ability of perceiving trajectories in space as tangible geometric shapes, Soviet sports psychologist Grigori Raiport describes the "objective imagination" (1998: 50–51). All these terms are compelling, but there is still much research to be done; for now, we must be content to know that tàolù cultivate a very special spatial sense, about which we can always learn more.

Tàolù call upon us to examine the unseen. The implied but absent elements suggested by these choreographies are signs of their combative, theatrical, and religious nature, but also of the presence of qiǎo in their design. The fighting usage of the movements must be filled in by the individual player or their audience. If the shape the player takes is a character from Chinese theatre, it is the viewer who recognizes that figure and places it into a story or a fragment of a story. Visualizing the fictional assailant trapped between our limbs makes us aware of the empty and the full, the xū 虚 and shí 實, or the imaginary and real elements found in our peripersonal space. This implies a larger realization of the complementary relationship between form and emptiness and the fundamentally composite nature of our reality. A well-presented tàolù might convince us that its player has fighting ability they in fact lack, or that they are in possession of special skills or war magic when in fact there is none. From the perspective of the performer or the witness, we can experience violence transformed, exorcism, trickery, entertainment, ritual and increased depth, all because of the evoked unseen.

Tàolù play a ubiquitous, symbolic role in Chinese culture, not unlike the lóng 龍, or dragon. The lóng is a composite creature with the head of a tiger, the horns of a ram, the body of a snake, the claws of an eagle, and the scales of a fish. It represents the original fusion of the nomadic hunting tribes who merged to practice agriculture along the banks of the Yellow River, becoming the Han people (Tu 1997: 4). In the calendrical cycle of totemic animals, each creature has its own pattern of behaviour, characterized by a quality, or qì. The lóng is described as moving up, out and down, over and over, in an undulating sine wave that mirrors the progressive reversals of jīndān preliminaries. The cultivation of the spatial sense is one of the many coils revealed by this endless dragon. In combative training, theatrical performance and religious expression, the practice of tàolù actualizes this unusual and powerful experience.

CHAPTER 2

Spatial Projection

Introduction

The practice of *Zhōng Guó Wǔ Shù* 中國武術, the Chinese martial arts, can train us to project our imaginations and felt senses into the empty space around our bodies. Developing this skill, we transfer the immediate sensitivity we have at close tactile and visual range to spaces farther and farther from ourselves. As our sensitivity expands, our awareness can embrace an increasing volume of space. I call this experience spatial projection. While martial artists find it useful in unarmed and armed sparring games, it has also been decisive in my work as a theatre director. Metaphorically, I feel the empty parts of the performance space as a giant sculpture made of liquid metal. I create the mise-en-scène by intuiting the movement possibilities suggested by the initial shape of this sculpture, moulding it into a form that I hope will suggest meanings to audiences. Spatial projection involves both an extension and a reversal of perception: I viscerally experience empty space as though it were full, a material object, the shape of which I can influence with my imagination. The more the performers with whom I work are able to experience spatial projection themselves, the more effortless and holistic our creative process becomes. Here, I share the practices and perspectives that develop this mode of perception for the benefit of creators, performers, teachers and scholars.

Terms and Sources

Making "theatre" and practising "Chinese martial arts" can mean many things. The theatre that I create and refer to here is devised and choreographed. Its elements are determined through careful selection and composition. Its aesthetic is contemporary and metaphorical. Its texts are created in partnership

How to cite this book chapter:
Mroz, D. 2025. *Resonant Space: Religion, Theatre, and the Chinese Martial Arts.*
    Pp. 33–49. Cardiff: Cardiff University Press. DOI: https://doi.org/10.18573/book11.d.
    Licence: CC-BY-NC-ND

with living authors. Since 1996, my various collaborators and I have presented our works in festivals and spaces dedicated to both original theatre and contemporary dance. These crafted performances aim to set audiences' imaginations in motion, while affording those who act in them a means of deepening their skill and their self-awareness through the conscious repetition of precise physical and vocal actions (Lalonde 2012: 36–37, 73). The artistic procedures I learned as an apprentice came from Canadian theatre artist Richard Fowler, who was a student and then a collaborator of directors André Gregory, Jerzy Grotowski, and Eugenio Barba (Brask 1992: 150–177). In this chapter, I draw on examples from the rehearsals and performances of *Ismene*, an original theatrical production I directed with my students in 2017.[26]

By "Chinese martial arts," I refer to cultural practices that began to assume their present forms from the mid 19th to the early 20th centuries, at the end of the Imperial and the beginning of the Republican periods of Chinese history. These arts develop credible fighting abilities through exacting physical conditioning, through partnered, combative drills and games, and through the practice of prearranged movement patterns called tàolù (Mroz 2020: 9–22; 2017: 38–49). Prior to the end of the Imperial period in 1912, China explicitly understood itself as a religious state (Lagerwey 2010: 1–17). Communities across China not only used their martial arts to defend themselves, they also performed them as theatrical acts of religious self-consecration, communal blessing, and entertainment in an annual calendar of sacred festivals (Ward 1979: 18–39; Sutton, 2003; Amos, 2021). Modernization and secularization at the end of the Imperial period removed the original context of these practices. The Chinese martial arts were transformed over the course of the 20th century by their worldwide spread and by their ideological appropriation by the Chinese Republic of 1912 and the People's Republic of China that succeeded it in 1949 (Morris 2004: 185–229; Kennedy and Guo 2010: 1–17). Their religious heritage now forgotten in many social and cultural contexts within greater China and internationally, the arts we practise today combine a legacy of pragmatic combat skill, religious enaction, participatory recreation, competitive athleticism, and performed entertainment.

I have practised the art of Chói Lěih Fáht Kyùhn 蔡李佛拳 since 1993, Dūng Pìhng Taai Gihk Kyùhn 東屏太極拳 and Zhìnéng Qìgōng 智能氣功 since 1995, and *Chén Tàijí Quán* since 2005. I have written about these apprenticeships and my teachers Sui Meing Wong 黃小名, Ken Cohen, and Chén Zhōnghuá 陈中华 in *The Dancing Word* (2011: 45–91). Swordplay has further clarified the experience of spatial projection: from 2012 to 2018 I learned *Tàijí Jiàn Shù* 太極劍術, or *Tàijí*, fencing methods in regular private lessons with Michael

---

[26] *Ismene*: text by Michael Geither, directed by Daniel Mroz, produced by the Department of Theatre, University of Ottawa, November 2017, six performances, 500 spectators. Performed by Montana Adams, Emily Bertrand, Zaakirah Chubb, Emma Hickey, Sophie McIntosh, Jasmine Massé, Kiara-Lynn Neï, and Stephanie Velichkin. Set and lights by Paul Auclair, costumes by Margaret Coderre-Williams, stage managed by Katie Rochford.

Babin in Ottawa, Canada. I learned three different approaches to Wǔdāng 武当 style swordplay in short-term, private study with experts Zhāng Wùnà 張悟納 and Lǚ Měihuì, PhD 呂美惠, 博士 (Seattle, 2013 and 2015), Ismet Himmet (Berlin, 2018) and Simon Cox (Ottawa, 2022).[27] Due to the great variety of training methods found in the Chinese martial arts, the following path to spatial projection is surely only one of many possible routes.

1. Foundation Training

Jīběngōng 基本功 is a contemporary term for the foundation training that shapes beginners' bodies. Students learn how to assume key positions and how to move among them. The practice of positions and transitions builds the fundamental attributes of strength, flexibility, and endurance, with attention to alignment, coordination, and concentration. During this training, they learn the essential skill of power generation, the rapid display of strength needed to kick, strike, throw, and grapple with consequence. Individual arts each have their own specific jīběngong. This example is from the southern Chinese martial art of Chói Lěih Fáht Kyùhn. The exercise is named *Ńgh Lèuhn Máh* 五輪馬, the "Five Wheel Horse-Stance." The Five Wheels are the physical abilities needed to move in five basic directions: forward, backwards, left, right, and remaining in place. The series contains eight movements, which are first trained individually, then as three movements, and then as a single flow.[28] Students repeat each version ten times per side. In Video 1 the cast of *Ismene* demonstrate *Ńgh Lèuhn Máh* after forty hours of practice spread over six weeks.

Video 1: https://vimeo.com/935113528?share=copy

Ńgh Lèuhn Máh teaches orientation through proprioception: we learn to orient ourselves based on the local positions the parts of our bodies occupy relative to one another as we progress along a linear trajectory. The visible parts of the practice are the clear shapes and alignments required. The invisible aspect is the selective tension and release within the body created by the transitions from shape to shape. The sequence produces *guhk bouh lihk* 局部力 or "sectional power." We push off the ground with the rear leg, braking our momentum with the front leg, while turning the waist to channel the force created up from the ground to the torso. *Ńgh Lèuhn Máh* restricts the hands and arms, which usually dominate our attention, keeping them at the waist throughout. The vocalization made while kicking develops resonance and ensures that we exhale completely at the end of a complex phrase of movement, the resulting vacuum creating an automatic and rapid subsequent inhalation (Mroz 2011: 127).

---

[27] I also learned all too briefly from expert Jason Tsou in 2013 and 2014.

[28] See also Mroz, 2011: 174–179.

The movements of *Ńgh Lèuhn Máh* are an important first step for spatial projection, taught in terms of the geometrical figures they carve out in the space around the practitioner's body. We draw lines, arcs, and curved planes on the ground and in the air with our heels and toes, our knees and hips, and our elbows and shoulders, surrounding ourselves with the contours of our own imagined abstract art.

2. Tàolù

If jībĕngōng are the equivalent of musical scales and études, then tàolù are essential pieces of repertoire, the notes of which are mimed fighting movements. From cinema through online streaming videos to public parks, these choreographies are the most readily identifiable element of the Chinese martial arts seen today. They link *jībĕngōng* into more complex sets, adding repetitions, variations, and virtuosic elements such as rolling and leaping. The emphasis practitioners continue to place on tàolù reveals the strong roots of Chinese martial arts in the theatrical rituals of war magic (Farrer 2016: 1). Should you ask boxers, wrestlers, or fencers—or Muai Thai or Jūdō competitors—for a demonstration, you will likely be shown two people engaged in agonistic competition. Should you ask Chinese martial artists for a demonstration, they will almost certainly show you a solo tàolù. Evocative performance rather than literal demonstration remains the standard for displays of martial prowess, even if the use of such abstracted movements in fighting and the quality of their execution cannot easily be understood by an uninitiated audience (Mroz 2017: 42–45).

Tàolù can be trained in solo, partner, and occasionally three-person formats. Performed as duets, they are called *duìdǎ* 對打, "set sparring," or *duìliàn tàolù* 對練套路, "partner choreography." The acrobatics of the rarer, three-person combinations seem especially indebted to xìqǔ 戲曲, or Chinese theatre. Clearly theatrical and religious group choreographies also exist: the Taiwanese *Sòngjiāng Zhèn* 宋江陣, "battle arrays," for example, are performed by groups ranging from 36 to 107 people to honour local deities, and the heroes of the epic *Shuǐhǔ Zhuàn* 水滸傳, the "Outlaws of the Marsh," after whose leader, Sòng Jiāng 宋江, they are named (Sutton 2003; Chin, Chen & Tsai 2010: 120–132). As Avron Boretz observes:

> The techniques of martial performance troupes are unambiguously derived from the martial arts. The lion dance and the Song Jiang Battalion can be considered modes of martial arts training in themselves. A powerful lion dance or well-coordinated Song Jiang Battalion drill is, to untrained and expert eyes alike, a convincing, sometimes awe-inspiring demonstration of the performers' potential to do real damage. (2011: 55)

Tàolù can be trained extensively or intensively, emphasizing either the memorization of multiple, increasingly difficult sequences or the transformation of an individual choreography. Chói Lěih Fáht Kyùhn, the first style I practised, has a long and increasingly complex curriculum of unarmed and armed forms. I learned twelve elaborate Chói Lěih Fáht choreographies from Sui Meing Wong, each one more demanding than the last. However, the Dūng Pìhng Taai Gihk Kyùhn, which I also learned from Master Wong, has but one open-handed sequence. Once students have learned the 108 movements of this set, they then learn to restrict its stepping patterns to fit it into four square meters of space. After this, students solve the puzzle of how to perform the sequence in mirror image. Students practising this way learn how movements can be rearranged and reversed, and their sense of the possible transitions and relationships among positions develops significantly.

In contrast to these approaches, my teacher, Chén Zhōnghuá, suggests students practise the principal tàolù of Chén Tàijí Quán 10,000 times, a process that takes years. He attributes his prescription to tradition, explaining that the routine is so well composed that steady practice is sufficient for development. Video 2 shares my performance of this routine at a martial arts competition organized by Master Chén at his training centre in rural Shandong, China, in 2011.

Video 2: https://vimeo.com/935118737?share=copy

Unlike the *guhk bouh lihk* of Chói Lěih Fáht Kyùhn, the power trained by *Tàijíquán* movement can be described as 整合力 *zhěng hé lì*, or "whole body force." While both Chói Lěih Fáht Kyùhn and Tàijíquán contain both strikes and grappling manoeuvres, Chói Lěih Fáht Kyùhn stresses punching, while Tàijíquán emphasizes wrestling. Its terminology reflects this preference, evoking

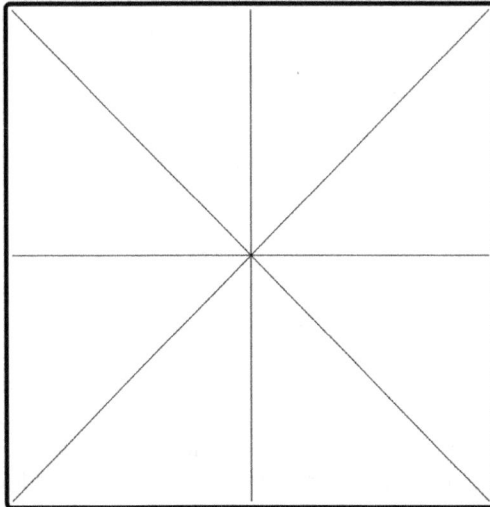

Figure 8: Centre, Periphery, Cardinal, and Diagonal Lines.

the pressure exerted by the entire mass of the practitioner against an antagonist engaged at very close range.

While jīběngōng developed my sense of the lines traced in space by individual movements, training tàolù gave parameters to space itself. After about five years of regular practice, I began to feel an imaginary, idealized grid defining the space in which I moved. On the ground, it was defined by its geometric centre, its peripheral boundaries such as walls or level changes in the floor, and its cardinal and diagonal lines:

These lines arose spontaneously in my felt perception of space, invisible boundaries that I had to respect. It was only upon reflection that I conceptualized my experience in terms of a drawn grid that I could share with collaborators and students.

3. *Tuī Shǒu* 推手

The martial partner game of tuī shǒu, or "pushing hands," a form of wrestling that emphasizes off-balancing and deception, further refined my sense of spatial projection. While tuī shǒu is a very important part of Tàijí Quán, Chinese martial arts as distinct as southern Chói Lěih Fáht Kyùhn or northern *Bāguà Zhǎng* 八卦掌 all have some version of this training game. Introductory tuī shǒu emphasizes position, gravity, and consequent momentum, while limiting the momentum of impellent force. We can get knocked down and fall at the speed of gravity because our partner has compromised our position, but neither of us should suddenly accelerate to initiate an attack. Training usually begins with a tuī shǒu tàolù, a set pattern of attack and response, performed with constant contact between two players. As they become more experienced and comfortable, this pattern gives way to improvised, free movement in which different attacks and defences are attempted. Since the 1970s, Tàijí Quán tuī shǒu has also been interpreted as a combat sport, and today different intensities of this standing grappling event are found in the People's Republic of China, Taiwan, and around the world.

In Tàijí Quán tuī shǒu training, we use touch to perceive the position and orientation of our training partners' bodies as well as the distribution of their mass across their structures. Then we try to compromise their balance and knock them down without allowing them to do the same to us. Over time our ability to interpret our partners' positions also gives us an impression of the space surrounding them. Reading the selective tensions in their bodies, we sense how they adjust their alignment based on what they feel of us through touch, and what they can see of the space behind us, which we ourselves cannot see. Constant touch means that this reading is mutual: we also provide them with our felt interpretation of what we see of the space behind them. In the oral traditions of Tàijí Quán, such "sensing with the skin" is referred to as *pífū gǎnjué* 皮膚感覺.

The ability both partners gain from using each other's bodies to sense space is a kind of "extended physiological proprioception," or EPP (Simpson 1974: 146–150). We experience EPP in daily life when we write with a pen and feel the surface of the paper through the stylus we are holding, as though our fingers formed a tip that touched the paper directly. While there are many different styles of Tàijí Quán, they all seem to build their fighting strategy around the idea of *zhān nián jìn* 粘黏勁, the ability to stick and adhere to one's opponent in order to proactively read their movement, neutralize their advantages, and knock them to the ground. Regular, sustained Tàijí Quán tuī shǒu helps us learn to process the changing physical sensations provided by our *duì fāng* 對方, or training partner. In Video 3 Jean-Philippe Ranger and Brennan Toh demonstrate Chén Tàijí Quán tuī shǒu.[29]

Video 3: https://vimeo.com/935146975?share=copy

Like tàolù, tuī shǒu changes our perception of space. Using touch, we determine the position of our partner's limbs, torso, and head, but also the shape of the empty or negative space around them into which we could step or insert our own limbs in order to compromise their position. We further became aware of our opponent's points of imbalance, found on a line orthogonal to the mid-point between their feet. For example, if I stand with my feet parallel at shoulder width and my partner pushes on my chest, I will fall backward. If they push on my back between my shoulder blades, I will fall forward (Figure 9). The two points of my training partner's feet and their points of imbalance fore and aft generate the triangular tiles shown in Figure 10:

Long-term practice of tuī shǒu refined my experience of two of the three general categories of spatial perception posited by neuropsychology. It sharpened my perception of *percutaneous* space, which occurs at and just above the surface of our skin, and of *peripersonal* space, which occurs within the reach of our limbs. The last category is *extrapersonal* space, the space outside of our reach, which leads us to swordplay (Elias & Saucier 2006: 323–332).

4. *Nián Jiàn* 黏劍

The game of *nián jiàn*, or "sticking sword," further develops the elements of spatial projection cultivated in tuī shǒu. Players target their opponents' hands and wrists, gradually progressing to the legs, torso, and head, while keeping their practice swords in constant contact as they cut and thrust at one another. Players begin using wooden swords, switching to metal ones, and adding protective gear as the game becomes more dynamic. Versions of nián jiàn are principally

---

[29] Jean-Philippe Ranger, PhD and Brennan Toh are Canadian instructors of Chén Tàijí Quán under Chén Zhōnghuá.

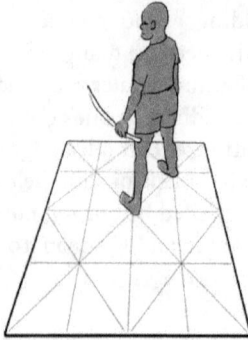

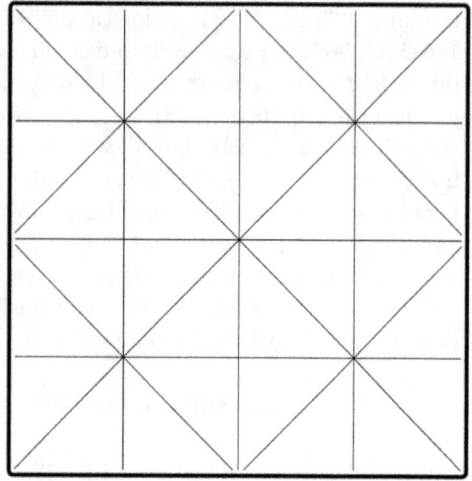

Figure 9: Points of Imbalance.   **Figure 10:** Triangular Tiling.

found in the sword-centred martial arts of the Wǔdāng mountains and in various transmissions of *Yáng* style Tàijí Quán 楊太極拳. Nián jiàn is likely a 20th-century development extrapolated from drills focussing on wrist cuts and inspired by the relatively safe learning game of Tàijí Quán tuī shǒu.[30]

As with tuī shǒu, training begins with set patterns of attack and response, which serve as a basis for free play. *Jiǎo* 攪, a movement in the horizontal plane which translates as "stirring," is fundamental to nián jiàn. Students learn partnered, sticking jiǎo first because this movement both attacks and protects the wrist. Unlike tuī shǒu, there is no combat sport directly derived from nián jiàn. There is, however, a style of competitive fencing with short, padded weapons using both sword and sabre or *dāo* 刀 techniques named *Duǎn Bīng* 短兵, which was developed in the Republican period and carried over by Communist China (Mǎ 2003).

Nián jiàn extends the range of our spatial projection by interposing tools between us and our duì fāng. Reading the vibrations we receive from our partner's sword through our own weapon, we feel the shape of the space surrounding us both, an imagined shape that we co-create through our conjoined perception and action. During play, we attempt to mould this shape to our own advantage. In Video 4, Badger Jones and I demonstrate the game of nián jiàn.[31]

---

[30] *Kūn Wú Jiàn* 昆吾劍, as taught by the late Taiwanese expert Liú Yúnqiáo 劉雲樵 (1909–1992), contains partner training that emphasizes sticking and that might be another important source of this practice, given Liú's prominence in Taiwan and his many students and grand-students who teach worldwide.

[31] Badger Jones is the head instructor of the contemporary Filipino martial art Siling Labuyo Arnis, and a full member of the international Dog Brothers real-contact weapons-fighting fellowship.

Video 4: https://vimeo.com/935149191?share=copy

Playing nián jiàn, I feel that I am in the central courtyard of a building. There are eight "rooms" surrounding me, one at each of the cardinal and diagonal points (Figure 11). I try to be in a separate room from my duì fāng, to give myself the largest range of options, while using my sword to threaten them as though sculpting the space to limit their movement. The building I imagine can be represented as a nine-cell grid, in which the central square is the courtyard. My awareness of the eight directions, bā xiàng yìjí 八向意極, hopefully allows me to display eight-directional control of the space, bā xiàng kòngzhì 八向控制.

While the courtyard house is my own felt metaphor, the nine-cell grid is an important structure in Chinese martial arts, religion, and theatre. Called the Luò Shū 洛書, or Luo River Map, it is a key element of Chinese architecture, determining the shape of cities, temples, and stage spaces (Schinz 1996; Swetz 2008; Lü 2009). Dating from the seventh century BCE, the Luò Shū presents the numbers one to nine, as the magic square of order three, in which the sum of any three cells in any direction is always fifteen (Figure 12).

In the principal annual rite of Orthodox Daoism or Zhèng Yī Dào 正一道, officiants dance the numbers of this grid to empty themselves ritually of their self-involvement, enter the presence of the transcendent Dào 道, and return with blessings to nourish their communities (Saso 1990). The originally exorcistic Nuó Xì 儺戲 theatre found in rural Guizhou, Anhui, Jiangxi, Hubei, and Hunan provinces serves a similar purpose and organizes its performers within an axonometric projection of the Luò Shū (Riley 1997: 255):

Understanding of the Luò Shū has been equated with advanced knowledge in such northern Chinese martial arts as Bāguà Zhǎng, and Tàijí Quán (Tyrey & Brinkman 1996; Carmona 1997: 47–49). Today, students of the Chinese martial

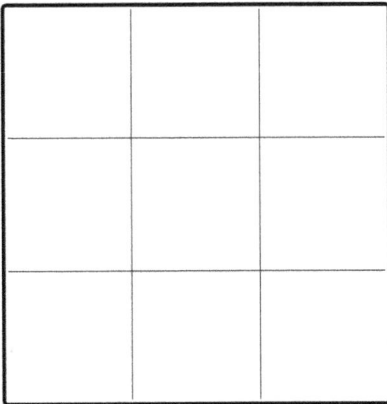

Figure 11: Nine-Cell Grid (left).

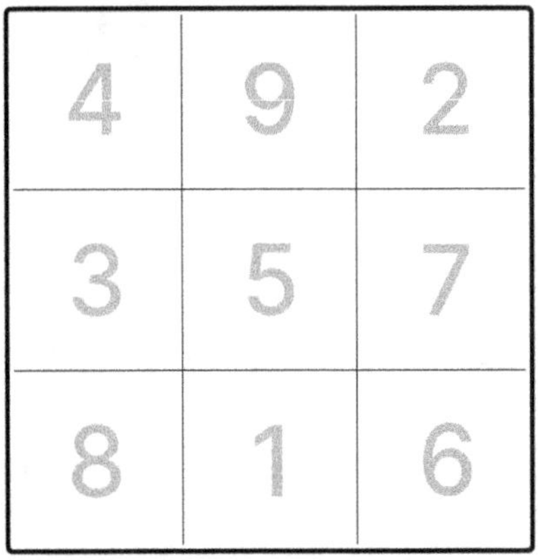

Figure 12: Magic Square of Order Three (right).

Figure 13: The Martial Artist's Peripersonal Space.

Figure 14: The Martial Artists' Interpersonal Spaces.

arts learn to sense this cube by parsing their physical structure into three sets of three. The *sān jié* 三節, or three sections of the arm, hand, forearm and upper arm, describe depth. The *sān pán* 三槃, or three basins of the hips, thorax, and cranium, describe the vertical. The *sān mén* 三門, or three gates of left, right, and centre, describe the horizontal.

The spaces of the players intersect in an encounter. Figure 14 shows the percutaneous and peripersonal spaces meeting within conjoined cubes within the extrapersonal space beyond it. Through regular play we aim to control the empty space, or *kòngzhì kōngjiān* 控制空間. Moving from the foundation training of jī běn gōng through the elaborations of tàolù to the partner games of tuī shǒu and nián jiàn, we extend our senses into our environment.

Rehearsing *Ismene* for Spatial Projection

Ismene is a contemporary retelling of Sophocles' *Antigone*, written at my request by playwright Michael Geither. The text combines dialogues between Ismene and Creon with scenes between Antigone and Ismene.

Ismene was staged for an audience of 80, seated on either side of a rectangular playing space. A cast of eight actors collectively portrayed the sisters Ismene and Antigone, and their uncle Creon. The space was empty except for eight plywood boxes, which the performers reconfigured to create the architecture of each scene. The boxes were inspired by the ones Anthony Gormley created for Sidi Larbi Cherkaoui's choreography *Sutra* (2008), to which our designer Paul Auclair added transparent surfaces and LED light ropes.

In addition to practising *Ńgh Lèuhn Máh*, the cast of *Ismene* composed their performances and developed spatial projection by playing a martial game I invented. This game of avoidance and entanglement approximates striking and grappling, the two principal actions found in hand-to-hand combat, while minimizing the impact of punches and throws. It lacks the depth and finesse of tuī shǒu, but it can be learned and played far more quickly.

In Videos 5, 6, 7, and 8, my collaborator Damon Honeycutt and I demonstrate the elements of the avoidance and entanglement game during our 2017 artistic research and teaching residency at the School of Dance in Ottawa, Canada.[32]

In avoidance, partner A points to a spot on B's body, making sure the line indicated is clear. In response, B must move off the line while establishing a point in return. Players can work very close to one another to develop trickery and stepping, or focus on precision by moving far apart.

Video 5: https://vimeo.com/935155592?share=copy

Once some flow has been achieved in these exchanges, we change the pointing action into a touch. Partner A puts a hand on B's limbs or torso. B slips away from the contact point, while placing one of their own, and so on.

Video 6: https://vimeo.com/935158724?share=copy

---

[32] Damon Honeycutt, MA, MFA, is a composer, dancer, and martial artist specializing in *Dà Shèng Pī Guà Mén* 大聖劈掛門, the "Monkey King" style of Chinese martial arts.

The next level is entanglement: partner A puts two hands on partner B and steps deeply into B's peripersonal space to set up a possible trip. Partner A then twists partner B toward a direction of imbalance, stopping short before B falls. In the short pause at the end of the twist, B steps, taking grips and a position on A.

Video 7: https://vimeo.com/935166015?share=copy

The complete game moves from avoiding projected lines through avoiding contact points to recovering from imbalance. When it is played by beginners, it uses an even rhythm in which partner B only responds once partner A has completed a movement. With experience, pre-emptive and proactive timing can make this simple structure much more demanding and exciting.

Video 8: https://vimeo.com/935172945?share=copy

During the first week of the rehearsals for *Ismene*, we played this game daily for an hour. Once the performers were familiar with it, we used it to compose physical scores, the pre-arranged movement patterns created by individual actors which the director combines in an eventual performance (Mroz 2011: 21). Physical scores resemble tàolù, as their mimed movements evoke interactions with unseen elements. Using the avoidance and entanglement game in composition, I hoped to preserve the credibility of response that the performers had when being touched and manipulated by their partners in situations where they were not physically in contact with one another. Our first step was to create a set duet, using the parameters of the avoidance and entanglement game. In Video 9, Emma Hickey and Stephanie Velichkin demonstrate the duet they created:

Video 9: https://vimeo.com/935176102?share=copy

The actors then transformed their duets into pairs of solos, by performing their actions alone as though still being touched by their partners. Videos 10 and 11 show Emma Hickey's solo along with one composed by fellow performer Jasmine Massé:

Video 10: https://vimeo.com/935186049?share=copy
Video 11: https://vimeo.com/935194326?share=copy

Creating these solos, we composed our own short, very modest tàolù. Each one was informed by the individual idiosyncrasies of the performers, but they all shared a common movement vocabulary, created by the parameters of the avoidance and entanglement game.

Solo scores are palimpsestic, evoking unseen elements that inform the visible causality created when two solos are integrated into a duet. The actors simultaneously preserve the felt senses of their original solos, while also accommodating the context created by their new stage partners. This layering ideally creates a live version of magic realism, in which the invisible world of dreams and the imagination is always present at the edges of the action. With this in mind, I recombined the cast's solos into duets that created causality through timing, rather than touch.

Video 12: https://vimeo.com/935197527?share=copy

Video 13 presents the scene in which the recombined duet created by Emma Hickey and Jasmine Massé appears. The role of Ismene is shared among seven of the performers, while the role of Creon is played by Zaakirah Chubb. In this fragment, which begins in the middle of the last scene in the play, Ismene tells Creon stories about Antigone's eccentric behaviour–in particular, that she often built cairns!

Video 13: https://vimeo.com/935202723?share=copy

Ismene's final words evoke Tiresias, the blind prophet of Thebes. To suggest his presence, members of the ensemble don blindfolds to perform their final movements, then sit on their heels, sphinx-like, in the semi-darkness. The cast's ability to perform blindfolded with relative confidence in this fragment suggests that they were able to actualize a degree of spatial projection during our short rehearsal process.

The text of this fragment is found in Appendix A, below.

Levels of Perception

Progress in wǔshù can be expressed in terms of the Three Treasures or *Sān Bǎo* 三寶, used to conceptualize embodiment in the Chinese tradition (Cohen 1997: 36–41).[33] At the *jīng* 精, or physical level, of training we are concerned with the position of our bodies, and we focus on precise alignments:

Figure 15: *Jīng* Level Perception.

---

[33] Thanks to Scott Park Phillips for the idea of using the *Sān Bǎo* as a kind of perceptual grid.

As we progress to the qì 氣 level, the learned shapes of the jīng level become second nature. Our attention can turn to our somatic experience. The sensations of weight, heat, and vibration within and around our bodies are called *qì gǎn* 氣感, or "qì sensations":

Figure 16: Qì Level Perception.

Figure 17 illustrates the reversal of perception, or fǎn, involved in spatial projection, where the normally empty space that surrounds us is perceived as a positive object.

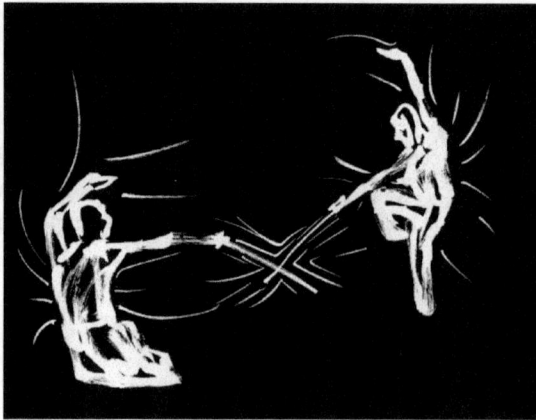

Figure 17: Reversed Perception of Space.

This is a glimpse of the spiritual *shén* 神 level of experience. Shén refers to the transpersonal and visionary aspects of our lives, and is also the word for deity. This level can be experienced in swordplay when players' sensitivities fill the field around them, and they feel the space occupied by their bodies as empty. We dis-identify with our bodies, and paradoxically identify with space. Our bodies are empty, or *xū* 虛, and the space around us becomes full of *shì* 勢, or potential.

This reversal of perception and its resulting spatial projection grant us insight. We sense the possibility of unusual movements, images, and associations that can be transformed into artistically meaningful elements:

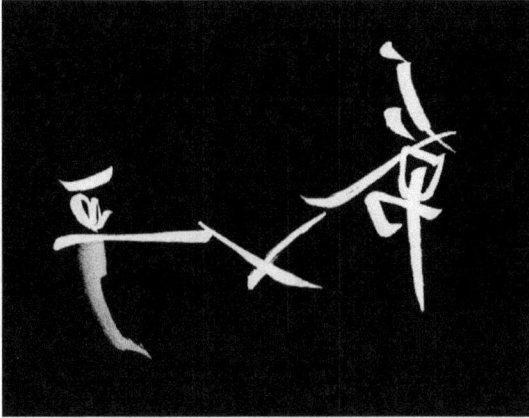

Figure 18: Creative Insight.

The result of this process is expressed to an audience that experiences it in positive space. In our metaphor, the figures above resolve into a calligraphy of the characters for dance and language, *wǔ* 舞 and *yǔ* 語:

Figure 19: *Wǔ Yǔ*, calligraphy by Joseph Lo, 1997, from the author's collection.

While the suite of images above is an original idea, there is a long relation-ship between swordplay and calligraphy. The *Bǐ Zhèn Tú* 筆陣圖, a Jin dynasty manual by Wèi Fūrén 衛夫人 (272–349 CE), or Lady Wei, itemizes the basic training methods of calligraphy. Its title translates as *The Battle Plan of the Brush*.[34] It describes seven essential brush strokes, the *qī shì* 七勢, as the "seven powers," using terms that evoke sword strokes (Pegg 2015: n.p.). The intentionally empty space or *liúbái* 留白 which surrounds calligraphic strokes allows the viewer to engage with both what is present and what is absent, inviting the imagination.[35] In the Chinese tradition, art is a visceral response to the world, one that can use a pragmatic activity like swordplay, experienced at the level of shén, to set our imaginations in motion:

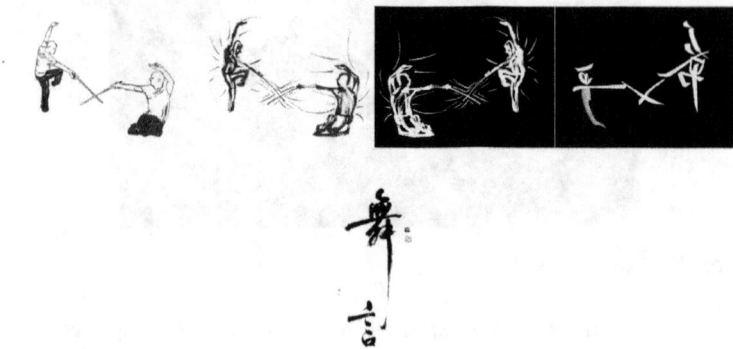

Figure 20: Body, Energy, and Imagination.

From Space to Language

Like the metaphorical example above, our relationship to character and language in *Ismene* was also the result of spatial projection. Watching the performers shape the space around them while practising Ńgh Lèuhn Máh in unison, I imagined them as a single body that spoke with many voices. We transformed the usual one-to-one correspondence between actor and character into a distributed, improvised, and transpersonal expression. In the scenes between the sisters Ismene and Antigone, we divided the actors into two teams. While all the dialogue had to be delivered, there was no rule regarding when each individual actor would speak. Sometimes each of the sisters would be voiced by four people, sometimes only one or two would speak the lines. In the scenes between Ismene and Creon, one performer would play Ismene, while all the others would speak Creon's lines in unison. Over the course of the play, performers switched from playing Creon to playing Ismene, their additional voices

---

[34] The 1627 CE edition can be consulted online: https://curiosity.lib.harvard.edu/chinese-rare-books/catalog/49-990079015200203941.

[35] Thanks to Hé Yīng 何櫻 for her thoughts on this concept.

underscoring her disillusionment and growing determination. The performers evoked the piece's characters collectively as musical, poetic constructions.[36]

Conclusion

While wǔshù employs precise terminology and sophisticated conceptual structures, it is principally transmitted by example through unspoken teaching, or *bù yán zhī jiào* 不言之教. The Chinese martial arts are experienced phenomenologically, and their depths are sounded through practice. Writing about the unusual skill of spatial projection and its role in the creation of original theatre is a departure from this quiet tradition. I hope that readers will find this account of use in their own work. In the next chapter, I shall examine some of the possible religious sources that have informed the practice of Chinese martial arts.

---

[36] Video recordings of two complete performances of *Ismene* are found in Appendix C, below.

CHAPTER 3

Martial arts are sorcery. Sorcery is a martial art

武術即巫術 。 巫術即武術

Wǔshù jí wūshù. Wūshù jí wǔshù

Introduction

In this chapter I shall expand on the relationship between what we now call Chinese martial arts and Chinese religious practices. My objective is to introduce new and fruitful ways of considering this subject, but in doing so I must critically address a series of common views:

That the historical Chinese martial arts can be considered secular by our contemporary standards; that ritual specialists were not involved in their creation as a part of their specializations; that the widely diffused martial arts practiced by civilian populations had their origin in the workaday training of soldiers.

These are hasty suppositions.

Separating the Chinese martial arts from religious expression is an anachronistic projection; Chinese ritual specialists created and taught martial arts; the Chinese martial arts are not simply derived from military drill. Rather than declining from the dignity of functional minimalism to the shame of a fanciful display, the cultural role of the Chinese martial arts has remained remarkably consistent over a very long history. Examining the religious elements of their genesis and natures allows us to appreciate them, and the cultures that produced them, in all their rich and complex detail.

Tàolù and Dìyuán

The Wǔdāng Sān Fēng Pai is a contemporary Daoist order that expresses its unusual version of *Quánzhēn* Daoism 全眞道 through the practice of martial

How to cite this book chapter:
Mroz, D. 2025. *Resonant Space: Religion, Theatre, and the Chinese Martial Arts.*
Pp. 51–68. Cardiff: Cardiff University Press. DOI: https://doi.org/10.18573/book11.e.
Licence: CC-BY-NC-ND

arts and meditation. It is named after the legendary Daoist immortal Zhāng Sān Fēng. This sect's oral tradition considers Qiū Xuán Qīng 邱玄清 (1327–1393) to be the *sānfēng pài dì yī dài zhǎng mén dà dìzǐ* 三丰派第一代掌門大弟子, the first-generation head of its lineage (钟 Zhōng 2014: 22). Qiū is also credited as the creator of a *tàolù* called the *Yìbǎi Líng Bā Shì* 一百零八式, the One Hundred and Eight Actions. Qiū is said to have composed this tàolù to expand an earlier sequence named the *Shísān Shì* 十三式, or the Thirteen Actions, in order to "make it more martial" (Cox online 1).

The creation of the Thirteen Actions is attributed to Zhāng Sān Fēng (1279–1368), a near-legendary figure remembered as Qiū's teacher. Unlike in the Western tradition, Chinese historiographies have little difficulty incorporating such heavily mythologized characters, recognizing their significance due to the subsequent social importance their stories are accorded, rather than because of their simple historicity. Figures named Zhang San Feng appear in the Six Dynasties period (220–589), the Song dynasty (960–1126) and the Yuan dynasty (1279–1368), with slight variations in the characters used in their names. Qiū mercifully appears in the archive of but one period. According to his biographies, he served as the abbot of Five Dragons temple, or *Wǔ Lóng Gōng* 五龍宮, on Mount Wǔdāng. He was promoted to the role of imperial inspector, or *yù shǐ* 御史, and later to the position of *Tài Cháng Qīng* 太常卿, or minister of state sacrifices (Efurd 2012: 189). Late in life, he returned to Wǔ Lóng Gōng. He was buried in 1393 along the banks of the *Hēi Hǔ Jiāng* 黑虎江, or Black Tiger River. All told, Qiū was a high-ranking ritual specialist charged by the first Ming Emperor *Hóngwǔ* 洪武 (r. 1368–1399) to lead rites on behalf of the entire empire.

One of his biographies describes him as "meeting Zhāng Sān Fēng," and "performing rites of sacrifice to *tiān* 天" (Efurd 2012: 191). Tiān, which is usually rendered as "Heaven," is more helpfully translated here as "Sky," a part of the complementary cosmological force of Sky-and-Earth, or *tiān dì* 天地, which Chinese emperors and empresses were believed to embody (Paper 1992: 8). Rites to tiān can be described as "weather magic," rituals to help ensure the precarious fertility of the arid soil of northern China. These also included the dramatic and martial *Léi Fǎ* 雷法, or Thunder Rites, which were practiced within the Daoist traditions.

Initiates describe the Léi Fǎ as giving them the ability to "control the power of thunder to cure illness or expel evil," (Saso 2012: 243). Commentaries accompanying Léi Fǎ texts explain that they are used to "pray for rain, offer sacrifices to clear the skies, examine bewitching and evil forces, decapitate and extinguish animal spirits around mountains, rocks, earth and woods and the illicit ghosts and spirits" (from the *Shàngqīng Léi Tíng Huǒ Chē Wǔ Léi Dàfǎ* 上清雷霆火車五雷大法, in Reiter 2002: 171). Describing the practice of the Thunder Rites in the Ming dynasty, Mark Meulenbeld explains,

> Thunder Rituals are used to capture the unruly and uncanonical spirits
> that enthrall local communities and to transform them into bona fide

sacred beings aligned with cultural institutions that transcend any single locality or region. (2015: 2)

The Léi Fǎ are operated by embodied actions that recall the tàolù of the Chinese martial arts:

> The formulas for thunder magic found in manuals such as the twelfth-century *Wang Wenqing Leishuo* (The Thunder Discourse by Wang Wenqing) are all performance-based. As with all Daoist rituals, this involves dancing esoteric choreographies to music and incantations: the performer controls his breath in a specific manner and uses magical hand and finger gestures. The efficacy of thunder magic is clearly martial. (Chan 2016: 39)

As Meulenbeld elucidates,

> individual gods are associated with specific martial "methods" (*fa*) that can be executed as ritual by trained religious experts in wars against demons but that can also be enforced as divine laws for communal organization during times of actual war. At those moments, ritual masters, who summon the "demon warriors" (*guibing*) of martial gods, join forces with martial institutions like local militias (*yibing*, "Righteous Troops"). Akin to the procedures of ritual masters (who sometimes act as commanders), local militias also defend their communities against threats by assuming the role of demon warriors. Men and gods thus fight shoulder to shoulder in a liturgical network of divine protection. (2015: 3)

According to oral tradition, Qiū, a Daoist who performed Léi Fǎ on behalf of the entire empire, composed a lengthy tàolù. If we recall the relationship between tàolù and dìyuán from chapter 1, an expression of martial movement is both apotropaic and exorcistic with respect to a given territory and the community that lives there. Qiū's expansion of a short set might well have added new close-quarters combat methods to a modest syllabus of fighting movements, but his act of making the Thirteen Actions "more martial" was accomplished on an entirely different plane.

Simon Cox suggests that the 108 movements could have been created by rotating the nine cells of the Luò Shū square (see chapters 1 and 2) through the twelve houses of the *Rì Shù* 日數, or Chinese solar zodiac, aligning it with the Chinese calendrical periods and the annual cycle of festivals and offerings (Cox online 1). Placing the Thirteen Actions on the Luò Shū grid creates a new series, one that moves through all nine points of the chart in the correct order. If we then rotate the entire composition 12 times, changing the orientation by 30 degrees each time to match the movement of the Big Dipper constellation across the sky, we will have completed a full circle, representing all the positions of the stars over a year, and we will have generated 108 move-ments. As it creates both a fundamental movement vocabulary and developed variations, this kind of choreographic technique can be used to generate a lot of movement without having to start from scratch with each new phrase of a composition. Changing the angle of a particular martial movement transforms both how it can be used, and how it appears to viewers.

In the oral tradition of the *Sānfēng Pài*, the Thirteen Actions served as a pre-paratory exercise for meditation, to ensure that the adept's body was strong and supple enough to sit comfortably for extended periods. The scale of the dìyuán involved was modest and apotropaic, not to mention pragmatic, suitable for a single or small number of adepts. In the early years of the Ming dynasty, how-ever, the imperial dìyuán needed more than just the local good fortune brought about by the performance of a short tàolù by a mountain recluse.

The Ming had just overthrown the Mongol dynasty that had conquered China, invading from the north. Their victories, which led to the establish-ment of the Yuan dynasty in 1271 CE, were believed to have been assisted by war magic. Dampa, a Tibetan Buddhist Lama in the service of Qubilai Khan, summoned Mahakala, a wrathful deity adopted by the Mongol State:

> The Mongols adopted the Tangut practice of employing Tibetans as their preceptors, and the wrathful deity Mahakala became the state protector and focus of the imperial cult. Mahakala ("The Great Black One") was credited with intervening in several key battles. For instance, early in the Mongolian campaign to push south in China, Qubilai Khan's ritual spe-cialist at court, the aforementioned Dampa, summoned Mahakala, who was seen going house to house on the battlefield. When the Chinese petitioned their god of war Zhenwu to deliver them, the Chinese god left a note on his altar saying that he had to yield to the Black God leading the Mongol army. (Debreczeny online & 2019: 31)[37]

The Perfected Warrior Zhēnwǔ first appeared in the early Northern Song dynasty (960–1126 CE) as the personification of the spiritual forces associated with the north in the Chinese dìyuán. Despite his surrrender to Mahakala, his worship continued during the Yuan dynasty, and he was believed to have played a key role in the creation of the Ming dynasty, during which his influ-ence peaked. In the tumultuous early years of the Ming, the Yǒnglè 永樂 Emperor claimed that he had received Zhēnwǔ's assistance in overthrowing his nephew in the *Jìngnàn Zhǐyì* 靖難之役 campaign (1399–1402 CE). Zhēnwǔ's apotheosis was popularized in the *Běi Yóují* 北遊記, or *Journey to the North*, a folk novel written in 1602 by Yú Xiàngdòu 余象斗. As recently as the 1970s, Zhēnwǔ was found to be one of the ten most popular deities to whom sacrifices were offered in contemporary Taiwan (Chao 2011: 4).

---

[37] Thanks to Scott Park Phillips for recommending Debreczeny's writings.

Zhēnwǔ was a key figure in Thunder Magic. In the mid-fourteenth-century *Model Rites for Submission, Dispatch, Fusing, and Refinement*, the *Zòu Chuán Hùn Liàn Fàshì* 奏傳混煉法式 found in the *Retrieved Pearls from the Sea of Rituals* or *Fǎ Hǎi Yí Zhū* 法海遺珠, adepts employ the technique of cún xiǎng, or visualization, to transform themselves into Zhēnwǔ in order to call their spiritual armies to order:

存丹田內　一嬰兒漸大，披發跣足，皂袍金甲，如真武相，足下有蒼龜吐炁，掐子，龜頭動。 與腎炁合， 有赤蛇吐炁，與心炁合。 掐午，蛇頭動。

Next visualize an infant growing larger in your cinnabar field. See him with loose hair and barefoot, clad in a black robe and golden armor, looking like the Perfected Warrior. Beneath his feet, there is a dark green turtle exhaling qi which merges with that of the kidneys. Form the "zi" mudra and visualize the head of the turtle moving; there is also a red snake exhaling qi that merges with the qi of the heart. Form the "wu" mudra and visualize the head of the snake moving. (Cox 2022a, unpublished translation)

The Yǒnglè Emperor commissioned the construction of temples on Wǔdāng in honour of Zhēnwǔ to thank the deity for his assistance in winning the throne, in tandem with the construction of the Forbidden City in Beijing. He referred to the unified project as "constructing the Forbidden City in the North, affixing Wǔdāng in the South," or *běi jiàn gùgōng nán xiū wǔdāng* 北建故宮南修武當 (Cox 2019: 194). The Wǔdāng temple complex was one of the more ambitious construction projects in Chinese history, creating splendour in a mountainous, inaccessible region, far from running water. Considering the precarity of the early Ming empire and the fall of the Song to the Mongols, the project makes sense from the perspective of war magic. Simon Cox suggests that these shrines created a massive architectural talisman in Zhēnwǔ's name. The performance of Qiū's 108 Actions activated this talisman, assisting the god of the north to seal the dìyuán of the empire against spiritual aggression (Cox, personal communication). Qiū's tàolù can thus be understood as a part of a larger state effort to ritually protect the Ming's northern border.

Yīnyáng and Wū in *Yuè*

Complementary expressions of the Chinese martial arts in which both military pragmatics and magical figures are employed in the defence of the state are documented as far back as the *Yuè Jué Shū* 越絕書, a compilation of histories dating from the early Eastern Han dynasty (25–220 CE). A biographical account of Yuèwáng Gōujiàn 越王句踐, or King Goujian of Yue (496–465

BCE), describes his selection of experts in the use of the sword and the cross-bow as trainers for his troops.

The sword expert, called the Daughter of Yue, is a nameless young woman from the countryside. Her approach to fencing is completely personal, and she has refined it with assistance from a strange old man who, after a duel in which he shared his sword methods with her, transformed himself into an ape and vanished up a tree! She describes her swordplay in terms which evoke the yīnyáng 陰陽 cosmology, and her story is strange: she has lived in the remote forests training alone, yet she describes her approach in terms of two-person duelling. Her claim is fantastical: "With a method like this, one man can match a hundred; a hundred men can match ten thousand" (trans-lated in Selby 2000: 157).

In contrast, the crossbow expert is both concrete and expansive. He is named Chén Yīn 陳音, and his presentation to the king begins with a lengthy discussion of historical precedents, followed by a thorough discourse on the many parameters of marksmanship (2000: 157–161). As Steven Selby[38] observes, "By contrasting the tale of the 'Daughter of Yue' and the account of Chen Yin, we can observe two aspects of martial arts. The swordswoman's way is an art, full of spiritual allusions and grace. Chen Yin's approach is pure science" (2000: 161).

A nameless, solitary, forest-dwelling woman who intuits her fencing, duels with magical creatures, and can teach one man to defeat one hundred with a sidearm is a figure who recalls the 巫 wū, the female shaman or magician of China's distant past. While such sorcerous figures have been present in the myth, folklore, and popular culture of China for millennia, the contribution to the Chinese martial arts of the ritual specialists that the Daughter of Yue might represent has been marginalized. The waves of Westernization and modernization that swept China from the late 19th through the 20th cen-turies have made it next to impossible to recognize the martial role played by such specialists. Since the reforms of the turn of the century, the Chinese martial arts have been categorized in many ways, the broadest of which are determined using the social role of the participants. These include 军事武术 jūnshì wǔshù, or military practice; 民間 武术 mínjiān wǔshù, or vernacu-lar, popular martial arts; and 競賽武术 jìngsài wǔshù, or competitive wǔshù. Today however there is no category of 巫師武术 wūshī wǔshù, which might designate the martial arts descended from the practices performed and taught by the ritual specialists of the Chinese religions throughout history. The biographies and oral history of Qiū allow us to see how such specialists would have expressed themselves martially and artistically, in the service of the state, while cultivating the Dào.

---

[38]   Thanks for Ben Judkins for recommending Selby's commentary.

The Chinese Martial Arts Encounter Modernity

Modernity transformed such complementary binaries as the Daughter of Yue and the Marksman Chén Yīn into contesting ones. Douglas Wile summarizes close to a century of debate over the origin of the martial art of Tàijí Quán, dividing the contenders into two distinct camps: those who see the art as founded by the Daoist immortal Zhāng Sān Fēng in the 1300s, and those who believe it was developed by retired soldier Chén Wángtíng 陳王庭 in the mid-1600s, based on his experience of military exercises:

> [T]he old myth versus history binary [has] to overcome three gaps in the record: 1) how to bridge the gap from the Internal School of the Wudang mountains in Hubei to taijiquan in Chen Village in Henan, 2) how to trace the transition from hard Chen style to soft Yang style, and 3) how to account for the paucity of written theory in the Chen family and its richness in Wu and Yang. (Wile 2016: 23)

The elements under consideration include the tàolù and practices of the various styles, and a set of writings named the *Tàijí Jīng*, which lay out the theory of the art and are now deemed canonical.

A case has been made for a kind of evolutionary development, suggesting that the Wú tàolù comes from the Yáng, and the Yáng from the Chén. These claims are initially satisfying as far as the tàolù are concerned: the structures of the first Chén tàolù and the Yáng and Wú tàolù are strikingly similar, even if the names of the individual actions listed in their form scores or *quán pǔ* 拳谱 differ somewhat. However, the *Tàijí Jīng* do not follow a similarly effortless path, appearing relatively late in the story and in the wrong family: "The old official origins orthodoxy was: the lineage is Chen to Yang; the writings are Wu to Yang; the art is Yang to Wu. This has made for a very untidy picture" (Wile 2016: 26).

Wile's description of the situation emphasizes what he feels is a specifically Chinese contemporary political struggle between traditionalists and modernizers, one that Western scholars should be cautious about entering (2016: 32). Yet since the 1980s, Western authors have endorsed Wile's "modernizing" faction, importing the political position of early 20th-century Chinese reformers to the Anglo-American archive without explaining the ideological context in which such claims were first made. For example, in Green and Svinth's *Martial Arts of the World, An Encyclopedia*, we find:

> The connection between the Chinese martial arts and religion is an artificial construction. Individuals from all walks of life and religions practiced martial arts for their own reasons. Some were religious; some were not. The martial arts themselves were essentially secular activities. Attribution of a religious mystique to the Chinese martial arts is, for the most

part, a comparatively recent phenomenon based on misunderstandings of the past. (Henning, in Green & Svinth 2010: 344)

The author of this entry is American soldier and Sinophile Stanley Henning (b. 1952). Henning's popular articles introduced Anglo-American readers to the ideas of the first representative of Wile's modernizing faction, Communist reformer Táng Háo 唐豪 (1897–1959). Praising him as a "serious scholarly researcher" for attacking "myths," Henning sympathetically, if mysteriously, described Táng's influential efforts as an unheeded "cry in the dark" (1981: 177). It is unusual to see the outlook of a Chinese Communist ideologue enthusiastically endorsed by an American soldier during the Cold War, but their perspectives meet in their desire for an instrumental, secular, and military expression of wǔshù, one whose history is distanced from Chinese cultural practices and the religions from which these inevitably derive.[39]

Táng Háo himself was a lawyer and amateur historian who sought to demonstrate that the origins of the Chinese martial arts lay in military field exercises. A Communist apologist, his many pamphlets attempted to debunk the idea that martial arts had been transmitted by such culture-heroes as Zhāng Sānfēng, the Daoist immortal associated with Wǔdāng mountain, or Dámó 達摩, the 28th Patriarch of Chan Buddhism associated with the Shàolín Sì 少林寺, the famous monastery on Sōng 嵩 mountain (1930/1968 and 1964/2004).

Táng wanted to convince his readers that the Chinese martial arts were originally secular and pragmatic. They had been misappropriated by religious sects and corrupted by superstition, but could be redeemed, modernized, and placed at the service of the state. In 1955 he was appointed to an advisory position with the China State Sports Committee, and his overall view has become normative, its developmental narratives espoused by subsequent authors in the People's Republic (Judkins 2014: online).[40]

Through Henning, Táng has influenced later Anglo-American scholarship.[41] In his definitive survey of martial arts in the military history of the Sinosphere, *Chinese Martial Arts: From Antiquity to the Twenty-First Century*, Peter Lorge

---

[39] Táng's writings focussed on those Chinese martial arts that could be studied without serious personal risk, using rudimentary methods of archival research and fieldwork among living exponents. He did not study groups involved in shén dǎ 神, or spirit boxing like the Yìhéquán and the Hóng Qiāng Huì—the Boxers and the Red Spears—whose initiates entered a trance state to attack the perceived impurities and hegemonies of the status quo. While the Boxers were no more, The Red Spears posed a serious threat to national stability well into the 1940s. While his writings were ideologically inflected, we should remember that Táng's secularizing outlook was also born of the very real dangers posed by large groups of entranced marauders who identified themselves as martial artists.

[40] In English see, for example, Fuhua Huang & Fan Hong 2018, and Zhouxiang Lu, 2018 and 2019, from Routledge press. In Chinese, see Yú Shuǐqīng, 2006.

[41] Peter Lorge begins this book with a thoughtful appreciation of Henning's essay *Academia Encounters the Chinese Martial Arts* (2012: ix).

provides much-needed nuance to a strictly functionalist, secularizing view. He defines the Chinese martial arts as:

> the various skills or practices that originated as methods of combat. This definition therefore includes many performance, religious, or health-promoting activities that no longer have any direct combat applications but clearly originated in combat, while possibly excluding references to these techniques in dance, for example. (Lorge 2012: 3)

While this is a more inclusive and, to my mind, accurate characterization, I nevertheless worry that the suggestion that all Chinese martial movement has evolved from or devolved away from literal fisticuffs makes it harder to apprehend those culturally religious practices of China which for millennia have not involved close quarters combat but have been considered martial by the people who developed and practiced them.

Accepting and generalizing the position of China's modernizing faction, as Henning does Táng's, oversimplifies the nature of martial practice in pre-20th-century Chinese cultures. Attempts to find clean lines of transmission—either by modernizers seeking a Marxist-inspired evolutionary development or by traditionalists hoping for a Neo-Confucian genealogy—stand in the way of our further understanding of the cultural meanings and social functions of the practices that gave rise to such arts as today's Tàijí Quán. In restricting ourselves to the options presented by the contemporary Chinese political debate as Wile outlines it, especially if our views are also informed by a bias written into recent Anglo-American scholarship, we perpetuate a limiting, Western binary between secular and sacred, and the single point of origination it necessitates.

Simon Cox lays bare the problem created by the search for a simple, single origin for Tàijí Quán:

> It seems like Tai Chi was really a Republican era (1912–1949) category that became a sort of umbrella term for various Chinese martial arts that are practiced slowly, containing such multitudes as the ancient martial arts of Chen village, the later arts of the Yang family, and the weird things people were doing at Wudang, in Zhaobao village, and even the government-created variations on these styles. From this view, asking which style started it all is rather meaningless. The historical connections simply aren't there. From the densest of historical positions, there is no evidence anyone practiced anything called Tai Chi Fist before the 20th century. It arises as a high prestige category in the context of post-Qing Chinese nationalism. Every slowish martial art in China seems to have been automatically re-branded as a form of Tai Chi. (Cox online 2)

Cox's speculation about a 20th-century origin is even more likely if we consider the taboo against using the names of emperors, a prohibition ended by the fall of the Qing dynasty in 1912 (Wile 2016: 25). The Jurchen Khan who became the founding emperor of the Qing dynasty, Qīng Tàizōng 清太宗 (r. 1636–1643), adopted the title of Huáng Tàijí 皇太極 or "Tàijí Emperor." This made it a heretical act for imperial subjects to use the term *tàijí* in writing or in speech to refer to anything other than the emperor Tàizōng himself and the cosmological principle from which he took his name.

The oral histories of the various schools also demonstrate just how recent the use of the term Tàijí Quán is. Prior to the 20th century, the Chén clan practiced *Chén Shì Quán Xiè* 陳式拳械, or "the boxing and weapons of the Chén family." *Chén Shì Tàijíquán Huìzong*,[42] a book by Chén Xīn 陳鑫 (1849–1929) published in Nanjing in 1935, after his death, was the first instance of the family's practices being referred to as Tàijí Quán (Carmona 2007: 177). In the oral tradition of the Yáng family, founding figure Yáng Lù Chán 杨露禅 (1799–1872) variously called his practice Cotton Fist, or *mián quán* 綿拳, and Transforming Fist, or *huà quán* 化拳 (Carmona 2007: 154). An apocryphal account published in the 1930s claims that the scholar Wēng Tóng Hé 翁同龢 (1830–1904) observed Yáng performing a tàolù and named the art he witnessed Tàijí Quán in a subsequent poem.[43] Qiū Xuán Qīng's 108 Actions was re-branded as the *Wǔdāng Sānfēng 108 Tàijíquán* sometime in the 1980s (Cox, personal communication). As Marnix Wells has suggested, the Chinese martial arts have been spread by the diffusion, and the recombination and accretion, of practices, rather than through linear transmission (Wells, personal communication).

The naming of all of these previously distinct martial practices took place in the 20th century. The flurry of martial arts activity and publication that began at the end of the Qing dynasty can be ascribed to the lifting of a stricture imposed in the 18th century. In 1727, the Manchu Qing Emperor Yōngzhèng 雍正 (r.1723–1735) issued an edict to suppress ethnic Chinese martial arts and boxing, hoping to limit the growth of subversive, anti-Qing religious sects. The 禁止拳會諭旨 *Jìnzhǐ Quán Huì Yùzhǐ* or Edict Forbidding Martial Arts Societies seems not to have been uniformly applied by court officials, as there are manuals that claim a mid-Qing origin such as the 1781 Cháng Shì Wǔjì Shū 萇氏武技書 by Cháng Nǎi Zhōu 萇乃周.[44] Nevertheless, gaps appear in the

---

[42] Interestingly, this manual begins its genealogy of practitioners with one Chén Pū 陳仆 (alternately Chén Pǔ陳卜) a generation before Chén Wángtíng, the founder identified by Táng Háo (Carmona 2007: 110).

[43] In a further example, a text named the *Tàijí Fǎ Shuō* 太極法說, attributed to Yáng Bānhóu 楊班侯(1837–1890) and claimed to be from about 1885, was first published only in the late 20th century, with allegedly previously withheld manuscripts appearing only in 1985 for the Wú family version, and 1993 for the Yáng family version (for translations and images of these sources, see Brennan 2013: online). Fragments of these works might have been published under other names in the early 20th century, but do not appear before 1912. This seems to be the case with all references to the martial art of Tàijí Quán occurring between 1636 and the end of the Qing dynasty.

[44] Thanks to Petr Vrána for pointing out various possibly post-1727 manuals to me.

archive between the flourishing of martial publications in the 16th and 17th centuries and their reappearance in the early 20th century (Wells 2005: 2).

The oral histories of the 19th-century martial arts now referred to as Tàijí Quán all posit a trajectory of development from the margins to the centre, with rural masters emerging from the unknowns of the 18th century to bring the seeds of authentic practice from the countryside to the cities (Wells 2005: 2). Who were these seed-bearers, and why would oral history accord them such authority?

Authenticity and the Peking Field Force

Expert martial artist and author José Carmona breaks with the long timelines posited by both traditionalist and modernizing Chinese nationalists by situating the synthesis of what we now call Tàijí Quán in the Qing dynasty culture of late 19th-century Beijing. Where Táng's ideological construction had degenerated from ancient, rural, peasant, ethnically Chinese, yet ultimately military sources, the synthesis that Carmona proposes appears to be recent, urban, upper-class, and multi-ethnic, refined by soldiers who drew on materials with ethnic Chinese religious roots.[45]

In the latter half of the 19th century, a group who were members of the Shénjīyíng 神機營, or "Peking Field Force," a Qing battalion of fusiliers who were being taught rifle drill by the British, informally hired a young man from the countryside named Yáng Bānhóu 楊班侯 (1837–1892) to tutor them in martial movement in their off-duty hours. This private salle d'armes included such figures as Wànchūn 萬春, Língshān 凌山, Quányòu 全佑 (1832–1902), and Cháng Yuǎn Tíng 常遠亭 (d. 1918) (Carmona 2007: 156). Quányòu was notably the father of Aishen, better known by his Chinese name, Wú Jiànquán 吳鑑泉 (1870–1942), the founder of the Wú style of Tàijí Quán (2007: 157).

History remembers these Qing bannermen as Manchu, but the Shénjīyíng was composed of 50 percent Manchu, 25 percent Mongol, and 25 percent Chinese soldiers (Crossley 1990: 145). The Manchu banners were hereditary armies that were as much social configurations as imperial institutions (Horowitz 2012: 266). In the political and economic chaos of 19th-century China, such soldiers lived very modestly, despite their seemingly prestigious affiliation. In 1864, no longer able to properly support or arm them, the government allowed the members of these garrisons to enter the skilled trades. By 1911 only one in 20 bannermen managed to live on their commissions, and the least fortunate eked out a living as street performers, noodle-sellers, and prostitutes (Crossley

---

[45] Carmona is not alone. Other practitioners who have investigated the theatrical and ritual character of the Chén Tàijí Quán first routine have speculated on its origins. Scott Park Phillips locates it in a performance of the stories of the god Zhēnwǔ and Daoist Zhāng Sān Fēng (2019). David Roth-Lindberg speculates that it derives from a Buddhist rite to the silkworm god, Mǎmíng 馬鳴 (online).

1990: 148). Those bannermen who were active as soldiers were idiosyncratic in attire and formation: they wore their own clothes and fought individualistically within Qing armies, adopting Western-style uniforms and close order drill only in 1896 (Horowitz 2022: 155). The élan that created the Shénjīyíng, a rapidly modernized force allegedly composed of 6,000 men with a rotation of 2,000 specialist teachers, was provided by Wénxiáng 文祥 (1818–1876), a Manchu statesman and member of the *Jūnjī Chù* 軍機處, or military, privy Grand Council of the Qing (Carmona 2007: 168). The Shénjīyíng project was abandoned on his death in 1876, and the unit slowly dissolved into the civilian life of early 20th-century Beijing (Horowitz 2002: 160).

Yáng Bānhóu was not alone among the Chinese teachers hired by the Peking Field Force. Martial artists Liú Dékuān 劉德寬 (1826–1911)[46] and Sòng Màilún 宋迈倫 (1809–1893)[47] are also remembered as having taught other members of the Shénjīyíng (Carmona 2007:156). As far back as the late 1700s we find references to rural masters such as Wang Lincang being invited to Beijing to teach Chinese martial arts to upper-class Qing (Wile 2017: 28).[48]

Considering that these bannermen hired ethnic Chinese civilians as teachers, modernizing claims that Chinese martial arts had a strictly functional purpose and a military origin seem very strange. Members of the Shénjīyíng were professional soldiers. No simple, instrumental purpose could be served by the hiring of an amateur like Yáng Bānhóu to train them to fight. They were already professional fighters. They were clearly getting something else out of his teaching.

An important Chinese cultural value that can help us understand the attraction rural masters held for the urban elite is the aesthetic category of *púshí wúhuá* 朴实无华, meaning "simple," and "unpretentious." High status and even *shénmì* 神秘, or mystique, were accorded to *fǎshī* 法師, or "masters of methods," often otherwise unsophisticated teachers of martial rituals—such as the Daughter of Yue—who, because of their proximity to the spirits of the dìyuán, were considered to possess great authenticity (Chao 2011: 10).[49] The physically virtuosic, ritualized martial methods they taught were seen as apotropaic acts of self-consecration, linked to the spiritual powers of the land. Manchu participation in these teachings could reflect curiosity about and participation in Chinese ethnic spiritual practices, as well as professional interest in the duelling and skirmishing they included. Carmona characterizes the late 19th-century boxing and weapons synthesized by the Shénjīyíng practice group as having ritual meanings due to the shape, frequency, and spatial orientation of certain movements (2007: 106). The seeming contradiction of the members of a partially modernized military unit perfecting such ritual movement can

---

[46] Skilled in many styles, Liú is principally remembered today as an adept of *bāguà zhǎng*.

[47] Sòng Màilún was an expert player of *sān huáng pào chuí* 三皇炮捶. He founded the *Huìyǒu Biāojú* 會友鏢局, a security service for caravan merchants, based in Beijing.

[48] I have been unable to find the characters for Wang Lincang's name.

[49] Thanks to Gey Pin Ang and Jarek Szymanski for helping me remember the phrase *púshí wúhuá*, to Marnix Wells for suggesting *shénmì*, and to José Carmona who worries that *púshí wúhuá* might not be an aesthetic category appropriate to the performance of martial arts.

be understood in light of the cultural value these practices still held in chaotic late-19th-century China (2007: 157).

The Imperial Military Service Exams were abolished in 1905, and in the last years of the Qing empire, Wàn Chūn, Líng Shān, and Quán Yòu founded one of North China's first commercial martial arts studios in Shuǐmò 水墨 Alley in Beijing, near the recently established Peking University. Out of necessity, they taught their boxing and weapons, along with archery and weightlifting methods, to paying students, a very new configuration for such instruction (Carmona 2007: 29). With the dissolution of the Qing forces, this studio was key to the spread of Tàijí Quán in the early 20th century. Carmona suspects that the important developmental role of these Manchu bannermen has been downplayed due to the nationalism of both traditionalist and modernizing accounts and the discrimination all Manchu faced after the end of the Qing (2007: 16).

Liberal Arts, Elite Athletics, and Serious Leisure

The assumption among scholars and practitioners that today's Chinese martial arts have descended, to their detriment, from military roots is shared by contemporary disciples and historians of the Japanese martial arts. Karl Friday comments that

> ryūha bugei [Japanese martial art] was an abstraction of military science, not merely an application of it. It fostered character traits and tactical acumen that made those who practiced it better warriors, but its goals and ideals were more akin to those of liberal education than vocational training. In other words, bugeisha [Japanese martial artists], even during the Sengoku era [1467–1615 CE], had more in common with Olympic marksmanship competitors—training with specialized weapons to develop esoteric levels of skill under particularized conditions—than with Marine riflemen. They also had as much—perhaps more—in common with Tokugawa-era [1603–1868 CE] and modern martial artists than with the ordinary warriors of their own day. (2005: 15)

Friday's Western, contemporary analogies of the liberal arts and the Olympic Games clearly express both the abstraction and specialization specific to martial arts. Both the performance and the kickboxing events of today's competition wǔshù require "training with specialized weapons to develop esoteric levels of skill under particularized conditions," exactly as Friday describes. It has remained distinct from military training in the contemporary period, as wǔshù athlete, translator, and author Andrea Falk, who was among the first international students to study at Beijing Sports University in the 1980s, relates:

> [D]uring the brief time in the early 1960s that wushu was considered integral to military training, the wushu department and the army

worked together on fighting skills. During the brief period of "militarism training," Zhang Wenguang was tested out by the army and police trainees, who lacked the politeness of wushu students—sessions could get a bit rough. He also taught the security men at the government compound in downtown Zhongnanhai for a few months. But this fun did not last for long. (Falk 2022: Kindle locations 1212–1216)

Zhāng Wénguǎng 張文廣 (1915–2010) was head of the wǔshù program at the Beijing Sports University in the late 1970s and 1980s. A graduate of the Central Guoshu Institute during the Republican period, he had performed his specialty of Chāquán 查拳 as part of the famous wǔshù demonstration at the 1936 Olympics in Berlin as a youth (Falk 2022: vii).

As Mǎ Yuè 马越 (b. 1959), son of Mǎ Xiándá,[50] and himself a graduate of Beijing Sports University and wǔshù tàolù champion, relates, "[T]he development of wǔshù in the PRC was really a conversation [among] the coaches responsible for the three major university martial arts programs: Mǎ Xiándá 马贤达 [1932–2013] in X'ian, Zhāng Wén Guǎng 張文廣 [1915–2010] in Beijing and Cài Lóng Yún 蔡龙云 [1928–2015] in Shanghai" (personal communication, 2019).

Mǎ stressed that in addition to being expert practitioners of martial styles inherited through their families, these three coaches were also trained in the Western combat sports of boxing, wrestling, and fencing (Mǎ 2019). It is significant that these three outstanding practitioners were made responsible for elite athletics, rather than the training of soldiers.[51] The national system they helped to create is unique both for the scale on which the state supports it, and for its university programs, which offer licensure in the practice of wǔshù at the undergraduate, master's, and doctoral levels.

A related helpful contemporary concept in imagining the social role of the Chinese martial arts is the Serious Leisure Perspective in Social Science developed by Robert Stebbins:

---

[50] The Mǎ family are members of China's Muslim Huízú 回族 minority, which appears to influence expressions of their family wǔshù. A preliminary survey of the movement names in their quán pǔ finds that they use literal descriptions and avoid the mention of Chinese cosmology and cultural figures commonly found in wǔshù quán pǔ. When Mǎ's student Chad Eisner went to perform the kētóu 磕頭 prostration that he assumed to be a standard part of a martial discipleship ceremony, Mǎ Yuè stopped him, saying, "our family is Muslim, we don't do that" (Eisner, personal communication). The terms used in the quán pǔ, and the rejection of the kētóu, suggest the association of the Chinese cosmological terms and initiatory practices with Chinese religions.

[51] Mǎ's grandfather, Mǎ Fèngtú 馬鳳圖 (1888–1973) had served under Republic-era leaders Féng Yùxiáng 馮玉祥 (1882–1948) and Zhāng Zījiāng 張之江 (1882–1966). In 1924 they created the báirèn zhànshù jiàochéng 白刃戰術教程, or cold weapons training program for infantry, using a large, single-edged cleaver, or dàdāo 大刀. This approach emphasized rudimentary up-and-down manoeuvres: kē 磕, or knock, to lift an opponent's bayonet away, and kǎn 砍, or cut, to then strike that opponent's neck. Mǎ's personal mastery of wǔshù allowed him to create such simplified practices for soldiers, rather than the other way around.

Serious leisure is the systematic pursuit of an amateur, hobbyist, or volunteer core activity that is highly substantial, interesting, and fulfilling and where, in the typical case, participants find a career in acquiring and expressing a combination of its special skills, knowledge, and experience (Stebbins, 1992, p. 3). The adjective "serious" (a word Stebbins' research respondents often used) embodies such qualities as earnestness, sincerity, importance, and carefulness. This adjective, basically a folk term, signals the importance of these three types of activity in the everyday lives of participants, in that pursuing the three eventually engenders deep self-fulfillment. (Stebbins, online)

Friday's analogies, in combination with the qualities and values Stebbins describes, can help us understand the examples of both the nature of the Shénjīyíng practice group and the backgrounds of the 20th-century experts who developed the modern wǔshù curricula. Their systematic and long-term practice of the Chinese martial arts gave them special skills, cultural knowledge, and access to a unique phenomenological experience. Their martial arts were a devotional, recreational performance *of* combat which included, but also transcended, the need for performance *in* combat demanded by their profession.

Even as we recognize such contemporary analogies and sociological categories, we must not naively apply a modern sacred-versus-secular binary to the culture; as Friday describes it, "the distinction between the physical and the spiritual ... is Western and artificial. Traditional Japanese worldview and pedagogy [don't] separate mind, body and spirit the way that post-Cartesian Western thought does," (Friday, online). While he lived after Descartes, we should recall that Isaac Newton (1642–1726), a thinker we now associate with a secular, materialist worldview, was both a theologian and an alchemist (Hanegraaf 2013: 325–326).

Orthopraxy and Ritualism

We would also do well to keep both Newton's theology and his occult practices in mind when we consider the cultures of the Chinese martial arts before 1912. Fǎshī certainly taught armed and barehanded fighting, but they did so as participants in one or more 教學 *jiàoxué*, or "teachings." The hard distinction we'd make today between the concrete and the metaphysical elements of such teachings would be alien to the residents of imperial China, as would our present-day distinctions between "religion" and "culture."

While Lagerwey describes Chinese religions in terms of the spatiotemporal categories of dìyuán and xuèyuán, the late Jordan Paper (1938–2021) differentiated the many *jiào* of China into *zhèng* 正 and *xié* 邪, or orthodox and heterodox teachings. Orthodoxy honoured the emperor, his empress, his ancestors, and his descendants as embodied manifestations of the natural order established by the interactions of the earth and the sky, *dì* and *tiān* (Paper 1992: 8). The orthodox rites which honoured the imperial genealogy were administered by the *Rújiā* 儒家, the ritual specialists and de facto historians whom Western scholars refer to as Confucian (1995: 8). With the Neo-Confucianist revival that began in the early 1000s CE, the right to worship genealogies was slowly extended to clans other than the imperial family, and gradually became zhèng as well (1995: 3).

Teachings such as Daoism and Buddhism were xié, even if they enjoyed different degrees of proximity to imperial power at different times. Quánzhēn Daoists were closer to imperial power in the early Ming, for example, while Tibetan Buddhists had been favoured by the Mongolian Yuan rulers who preceded them. Daoism and Buddhism are themselves general, low-resolution categories that become less and less precise as we focus on the composition of the teachings found in different parts of China at different times in history. From a high-resolution, local perspective, we see that people sampled from the teachings they were born into or that were available in their environments to best create meaning for their situations, taking part in the sacrificial rites of a variety of deities and sects. The result has never been described satisfactorily in English, with such names as "animism," "folk religion," "popular religion," "normative religion," and even "state religion" being used to attempt to account for the diversity of jiào while giving readers the false impression that they were a homogenous phenomenon of modest importance.[52]

> A standard Chinese response to being queried on "religion" in China is to say that the Chinese do not have one. Few Western scholars are acquainted with the actual Chinese equivalent question: "To whom (or what) do you offer sacrifice?" It is a question that elicits a detailed response on Chinese religious understanding and behavior from many of the same people who state that China has no "religion." (Paper 1992: 3).

The term jiào—"teachings" rather than the more usual "religion"—better articulates the nature of Chinese spiritualities. Generally, religions can be looked at intentionally, in terms of their belief systems, an *orthodoxic* view; they can be looked at as codified behaviour, an *orthopraxic* view; or they can be looked at in terms of their specific rites, a *ritual* view. *Jiào* refers to cultural practices that benefit from being described orthopraxically and ritually. Rather than being linked by professed beliefs or dogmas, jiào create meaning through codified behaviour which ritualism further locates in the precise execution of rites. Belief in the ideas of a jiào is secondary to the individual and collective experiences provided by the enaction of codified behaviour and ritual.

---

[52] Paper proposes the neologism Huárén Jiào 華人教 as a general term for the Chinese religions, a very useful, if not yet widely adopted, name (Paper 2019: 2)

A male subject of imperial China could take part in a capping ceremony, or *guān lǐ* 冠禮, to mark his graduation from the village Rújiā school at age sixteen, attend his village's Daoist-led sacrificial rites as an adult, petition deities associated with his local environment as needed, and be buried in a Rújiā funeral accompanied by either Buddhist or Daoist liturgy (Saso 1990: 133, 152). In contemporary Japan, where such rites were not interrupted by the period of enforced secularism experienced in 20th-century China, it would not be unusual for a citizen to have a Shintō naming ceremony, a Christian wedding, and a Buddhist funeral (Kavanagh, online).[53] Viewed orthodoxically, the dogmas of the traditions involved in both examples seem to conflict, but given the orthopraxic focus of these cultures, it is the correct performance of the rituals that matters to the participants, who combine them without experiencing contradiction.

> Chinese religion is not a universal religion as Buddhism, Christianity, and Islam but is an ethnic religion. In ethnic religions, such as Judaism for a Western example, religion can only be meaningfully separated from culture for the purpose of comparison with universal religions. Within the relevant cultures, the separation is so artificial and dependant on Christian expectations, it has little if any analytical validity. (Paper 1992: 3)

As readers of English, our assumption when we see the word "religion" is to think in terms of orthodoxy. "Faith" and "belief" are synonyms for religion in English, but we must not assume that this equivalence can be simply applied to other cultures. Our orthodoxic assumptions about religion are not helpful in looking at jiào and the martial expressions these have involved.

Conclusion

> The religious dimension of Chinese society and the Chinese state being inseparable from each other, not taking that dimension into account makes it impossible to make sense of anything Chinese: the state, local society, history. (Lagerwey 2010: 1)

---

[53] Expert martial artist and author Ellis Amdur explains the Japanese orthopraxy that he feels underpins the contemporary Japanese martial art of Aikidō and the views of its founder, Morihei Ueshiba:

> Shintō rites are actions offered as pleasing to the Gods or, in Ueshiba's case, actions that harmonize the powers of the cosmos. Unlike Buddhism, mindfulness is not a requirement—merely the proper enactment of the rite … If the rites are correctly performed … the gods and various realms will be harmonized, whether we know what we are doing or not. (in Chierchini 2021: 12)

The Chinese martial arts are a product of Chinese culture, which is synonymous with its jiào. Warfare and violence are downstream consequences of culture, and restricting our study of wǔshù to such lowlands obscures the contexts of its creation. Beginning our examinations upstream we find that the history of the Chinese martial arts includes the shamanistic wū, Daoist ritualists, war magic, and embodied rites to the dìyuán. Even today, "Wushu makes more sense in Chinese than in English. It makes a difference how you think when you are doing it, and, because of how I learned wushu, I think of it in Chinese" (Falk 2022: Kindle location 1712).

We can extend our own "thinking of wǔshù in Chinese" to considering it in terms of the religious cultures that produced it, and in terms of the tacit assumptions we English-speaking researchers and practitioners bring to our own efforts at interpretation. Different approaches to wǔshù were developed variously to display power in the spiritual realms in which war magic takes place, to give people already skilled in fighting a virtuosic pastime, and to keep people in precarious circumstances busy, preventing them from becoming involved in violence in the first place. While wǔshù contains methods of teaching and learning to fight, what instruction in self-defence, paired duelling, and group skirmishing it has offered has been, historically, far from uniform. When considering any Chinese martial art, from the war magic of its tàolù to its tactics in fisticuffs, it seems we should not only ask *How does this activity teach people to fight?* but also *How does this activity prevent violence?* Remembering the complementary, ever-shifting relationship of wǔ 武 and wū 巫 offers us a wider field in which to study, practice, and reflect on the martial arts of China.

As we shall see in the next chapter, wǔshù, jiào and xìqǔ also provide a helpful perspective on the practice of contemporary theatre in Asia.

CHAPTER 4

Martial arts are dance. Dance is a martial path

武道即舞蹈。舞蹈即武道。

Wǔdào jí wǔdǎo. Wǔdǎo jí wǔdào

Introduction

In this chapter I propose examples of the implicit and explicit Chinese martial ideas and practices found in late 20th-century art theatre made in the People's Republic of China and in Indonesia. The two examples I introduce form a yīnyáng pair. Although it was only indirectly influenced by Chinese martial arts, the work of director Móu Sēn 牟森 (b. 1964) can be seen as a wén contemporary theatre project that produced the wǔ qualities of traditional martial rituals. In contrast, Javanese director W. S. Rendra (1935–2009) used the wǔ of Chinese and Indonesian martial arts training to express the wén of European dramatic literature in a new way. I choose these two examples from among so very many possibilities not only because they demonstrate specific facets of a fascinating phenomenon, but because they have had a decisive impact on my own thinking.[54]

---

[54] Contemporary Chinese theatre and dance artists began to take an interest in the Chinese martial arts in the late 20th century. Pioneers among them include Cloud Gate Dance Theatre, U Theatre and Theatre OX.

Cloud Gate Dance Theatre, *Yúnmén Wǔjí* 雲門舞集, was founded by choreographer Lín Huáimín 林懷民 in Taiwan in 1973. Company dancers have been taught by martial arts experts Xióng Wèi 熊衛 and Adam Hsu or Xú Jì 徐紀.

U Theatre, *Yōurén Shéngǔ* 優人神, of Taiwan was founded by director Liú Jìngmǐn 劉靜敏, whose stage name is Liú Ruòyǔ 劉若瑀, in 1988. Her long-term collaborator is expert drummer and martial artist Huáng Zhìwén 黃志文, whose stage name is Huáng Zhìqún 黃誌群.

Theatre OX, *Lǎoniú Jùchǎng* 老牛剧场, was active in Singapore between 1995 and 1997, and internationally until 2000. In 1998 various members of Theatre OX joined the Workcenter

---

Blurred Genres

In his influential essay *Blurred Genres: The Refiguration of Social Thought*, anthropologist Clifford Geertz discussed the enormous amount of genre mixing in late-20th-century Euro-American scholarship. Offering examples, he asked rhetorically whether Michel Foucault was a historian, a philosopher, or political theorist, or whether Thomas Kuhn was a historian, a philosopher, or a sociologist. Noting that Edward Said presented ideological arguments as historiographical inquiries, that Paul Feyerabend's epistemological studies were constructed as political tracts, and that Claude Lévi-Strauss's theoretical treatises took the form of travelogues, Geertz demonstrated how one genre of writing and thinking adopted the aims of another to advantage (1980: 165).

Colin McGuire applies Geertz's idea outside of the Euro-American intellectual tradition to describe the martial arts of China and Indonesia. Writing about the Chinese martial arts, he suggests:

> Traditional kung fu already incorporates aspects of meditation and cultural rites with self-defence, weapons, fitness, performance art, and personal development into what might be considered a "blurred genre," as proposed by anthropologist Clifford Geertz. (McGuire 2010: 3)

In his discussion of Indonesian *pencak silat*, he further specifies that

> interdisciplinarity in *pencak silat* results in a field of practice where it is advisable not to separate the constituent parts, but rather to deal with them as a single whole. Music, dance, drama, costuming, performance, and ritual are not independent from the fighting skills of *pencak silat*— they form an integral part of it. (2016: 105)

In McGuire's adoption, the blurred genre becomes an English-language concept that can help us perceive the interpenetration of the categories of religion, theatre, and martial training that are firmly differentiated and seem incompatible or paradoxical in Euro-American thought. The blurred genre complements the idea that China's traditional theatres can be seen as martial expressions: apotropaic entertainments using martial movement that give pattern and form

of Jerzy Grotowski and Thomas Richards in Pontedera, Italy, eventually becoming the company in residence. Different configurations of personnel remained working in Italy until 2000. The ensemble was co-founded by Ang Gey Pin, Tan Pei Hwee 陈佩卉, Koh Leng Leng 许玲玲, Low Yuen Wei (Beverly Yuen) 卢韵微, Lee Chee Keng 李集庆, Julius Foo Jong Soon 符永春 and Chong Tan Sim 庄丹心. They studied martial arts with the late expert Yáng Zhìqún 杨志群, among others.

Ang Gey Pin continues her work today, accompanied by her younger collaborator, *xiàndài wǔshù tàolù* competitor and theatre artist Ranice Tay (Zhèng Kǎixīn) 郑凯心 (see Ang & Tey 2022). In September 2023 both Ang and Tay appeared in U Theatre's production *Five Colours of Ink 2.0, Mò Jù Wǔsè 2.0*, 墨具五色 2.0, presented in Taipei.

to the chaos of change, transforming space positively for its human inhabitants (see chapter 1). Cultural expressions that blur artistic, religious, and martial practices have also nurtured the examples of 20th-century Asian theatre discussed below, which are remembered for their transformation of physical, social, and spiritual space.

Móu Sēn

Independent Beijing-based director Móu Sēn led the development of a performance entitled *File Zero*. Coproduced by and premiered at the Kunsten Festival des Arts in Brussels in May of 1994, *File Zero* came to the Festival du Théâtre des Amériques in Montréal in the spring of 1995.[55] It was a rare opportunity for Euro-American theatre audiences to see contemporary work from China. *File Zero* was performed over 100 times internationally, making it both one of the most-seen pieces of Chinese theatre in the world, and something of a legend in China itself, where it was never performed.

File Zero took its name from and included the text of *Líng Dǎng'àn* 零档案 a poem published in 1994 to acclaim and controversy by Yú Jiān 于坚 (b. 1954). *Líng Dǎng'àn* is a relentless account of how people's official and private lives were recorded, and consequently determined, by the state filing system.[56] Should an individual's file be lost, it was as though they had never existed.

Like a person without a file, Móu's company Xìjù Chējiān 戲劇車間, the Theatre Workshop, was not recognized by the state. While Móu was socially connected to a whole generation of Chinese artists who have since become influential, officially his theatre did not exist.[57] Móu's company could rent spaces in which to present, but its lack of status meant the artists were not

---

[55] At the time *File Zero* came to Montréal, I was in my third year of training in Chói Lěih Fáht Kyùhn and the first year of my Maîtrise en arts dramatiques (Master's in dramatic arts) at l'Université du Québec à Montréal or UQAM, working on the application of Chinese martial arts to the training of actors under the supervision of actor and playwright Larry Tremblay. I had just met Olivier-Hugues Terreault, an actor who was completing an undergraduate degree in contemporary dance, also at UQAM, with whom I would eventually co-create three performances. Olivier introduced me to filmmaker Sébastien Bage, who later became dramaturge for La Compagnie du Pont-fleurs, the theatre ensemble Olivier, Tamar Tembeck, and I co-founded in the late 1990s. In 1995, Sébastien translated the six Montréal performances of *File Zero* from Chinese to French live, an impressive feat as much of the text was improvised and changed slightly every night. The late Denis Salter (1949–2022), my undergraduate supervisor at McGill University and an early mentor, interviewed Móu and actor Wú Wénguāng while they were in Montréal and described that experience to me as well. It all made a deep impression on me.

[56] An English translation of *Líng Dǎng'àn* begins:

In an architectural construction on the fifth floor / behind locks and more locks / in a secret room / his dossier is held in a document folder / it is evidence of a person / two floors separating it from the person himself / he works on the second floor / the folder / is 50 meters away along a corridor / and 30 steps up on another floor … (Yú trans. van Crevel, in Huang 2016: 492).

[57] In addition to his immediate collaborators, he also mentions rock musician Cuī Jiàn 崔健, and film directors Zhāng Yìmóu 张艺谋 and Chén Kǎigē 陈凯歌, for example (Shank 1996: 10).

allowed to sell tickets to their performances. Their income and production budgets depended on the discreet and very modest contributions of friends and audiences. Móu describes his process and preoccupations:

> [*File Zero*] began with a poem—Ling Dang An by the avant-garde poet Yu Jian, who was one of my classmates at Beijing Educational University. In 1992, he read the unpublished manuscript of the poem to me and I felt it, instinctively, as a driving force for a piece of theatre. Many people disagreed with me, because they have a preconception—based on the presence of story, characters, and so on—of what theatre should be like. I had no clear understanding of how the poem would turn into a theatre piece, but I knew I could trust my impulse. (Salter, Móu & Wú 1996: 223)

File Zero was performed by three people, Wú Wénguāng 吴文光, Jiǎng Yuè 蒋樾, and Wén Huì 文慧. Wú and Jiǎng were documentary filmmakers, and Wén was a choreographer becoming known for her use of daily movement on stage. In 1994 she co-founded Shēnghuó Wǔdǎo Gōngzuò Shì 生活舞蹈工作室, the Living Dance Studio, with Wú, her then-partner, in Beijing.

In *File Zero* Yú Jiān's poem framed two stories, told by Wú and Jiǎng, who addressed the audience directly. Wú extemporized the story of his father, who had been a fighter pilot for the Kuomintang, and whose life under communist rule was thus very difficult, and baffling for his young son, who was proud of his father's achievements. Jiǎng read the sad story of his first love from his journal: as an actor originally trained in Beijing Opera, he didn't want to leave China, where he could practice his art. This alienated the woman he was in love with, who very much wanted to travel. She impulsively married a visiting foreign teacher and left China. Wén Huì, silent, ran much of the stage action, turning the recording of the poem on and off, her entrances and exits punctuating the action. The performance built to a violent conclusion: the actors impaled apples on a thicket of twisted metal rods that Jiǎng had cut and assembled onstage. They hurled fresh fruit into the spinning blades of industrial fans as the voice on the tape recorder intoned Yú Jiān's words.

The actors based their performances on personal accounts and concrete tasks. The director created a composition that juxtaposed the impersonal text of the poem with the emotional memories of the actors, underscored by their evocative activities. The simplicity of their delivery contrasted with the impersonal recording of the poem, the industrial objects onstage, and the intensity of the destruction at the end of the piece. The meaning of the elements created by the performers and assembled by the director was determined by the experience and interpretation of each audience member.

Xìjù Chējiān's work sounds contemporary, and yet this performance was made in isolation from the tendencies of late-20th-century world theatre. Beyond the difficulties imposed by their economic marginalization, it was their aesthetic isolation that Móu listed as first among the many challenges he and his colleagues faced:

> [I]n China we are not able to know or see a lot of what's happening in the world in theatre. We don't have this kind of comparative perspective. We have to set our own criteria to assess ourselves, what we are doing and whether it's successful or not. (Shank 1996: 7)

The Other Shore

While *File Zero* toured to international acclaim, Xìjù Chējiān's first production played to small audiences in a Beijing classroom. Over four months in 1994, Móu worked with students at the Beijing Film Academy on an adaptation of *Bǐ'àn* 彼岸, or *The Other Shore*, by author, painter, political refugee, and later Nobel Laureate Gāo Xíngjiàn 高行健 (b. 1940). *Bǐ'àn* was not an easy choice. It had been deemed critical of the state, and its 1986 premier was cancelled by the authorities before it even opened.

Móu named his project *Bǐ'àn Hé Guānyú Bǐ'àn De Hànyǔ Yǔfǎ Tǎolùn* 彼岸和关于彼岸的汉语语法讨论, which in English could be understood as *The Other Shore, and a Discussion of the Philology of The Other Shore*.[58] The expression *bǐ'àn* is a literary term for the opposite bank of a river, and is also used to translate the Sanskrit *paramita*, the specific virtues to be acquired on the path to Buddhahood. The figures in the fragmentary episodes of Gāo's play already inhabit another shore, but reveal themselves to be just as complex and curious as those of us who have not yet achieved the paramitas. Poet Yú Jiān gutted the script of *The Other Shore* for Móu's class production, transforming its cultured political critique of communist China into a much shorter, playful game of language and performance. Yú's short text undercut the idealism and intellectual abstraction of Gāo's original, emphasizing the contrivances of theatrical presentation, a transformation that was clear to audiences:

> An actor asked: *What is the other shore?*
> All the actors replied: *The Other Shore is a play, and it is what we perform.*
> ...
> *What is the other shore?*
> *The other shore is just one word, one noun, two syllables, sixteen strokes.*
> The actors climbed the ropes hanging over the audience's heads one by one, and they kept shouting:
> *Now*

---

[58] In Chinese the title manages to sound witty, sober, and slightly pedantic all at the same time. In English, the pleasing symmetry of the phrases *Bǐ'àn Hé Guānyú* ("of the other shore") and *Bǐ'àn De Hànyǔ* ("philology of the other shore") is lost.

there is a rope
Instead of a river
Ahead of us
We shall cross this river
To the other side.
But have they really reached the other side? No, they know they've only
reached the other end of the room (Hè, online, my translation).

Móu's project was in every way unusual. In 1993 the Beijing Film Academy,
Běijīng Diànyǐng Xuéyuàn 北京電影學院, offered a special workshop for a
group of 30 or so students who had been cut in the final round of auditions for
their acting program. The refused candidates didn't want to leave Beijing, and
academy officials hoped to alleviate their profound disappointment. Móu was
interested in teaching, and he put together a team of artists to work with the
students. Féng Yuǎnzhēng 冯远征 and Móu taught theatre theory, Ōu Jiànpíng
欧建平 and Wén Huì taught dance, and two teachers with the surname of Kǒng
孔 taught acting, while Móu directed the final project (Lǐ, online). Over half of
the participants dropped out over the course of the program due to the intensity of the work. Móu explains:

> It was performed in a rehearsal studio at the Beijing Film Academy
> because that is where the four-month training course had taken place.
> We had no money, so we did it in a very simple way. We did seven per-
> formances, and it created a very, very strong reaction in the audience,
> among the cultural circles. The audience was mainly people from the
> theatre and other art circles as well as teachers and students, not only
> from the film academy, but from other schools and theatre academies.
>
> The fourteen young actors were not what people would consider
> professional or "real" actors, but the production transmitted a very
> strong impression for the audience. The audience was surprised that
> theatre could be like this, unlike that dramatic, naturalistic theatre at
> all the official companies. This is very physical, movement-based work,
> so the audience discussed whether this is theatre and how theatre could
> be like this. (Shank 1996: 8)

The student actors transformed their classroom space, plastering the walls,
pipes, conduits, and chairs with newspaper. More crumpled papers covered the
floor. They stretched lengths of rope across the room, dividing the space from
multiple angles. The eventual audience of 60 sat on bleachers surrounding the
performance area on all sides. The young, rural student-actors performed with
passionate commitment and rough physicality. Móu's environmental staging
and the transitions he ably created between episodes juxtaposed the obvious
innocence and exuberance of the performers with what I believe to be his more
ambivalent point of view.

The Other Shore played a handful of times for small audiences between June 21 and 27, 1993 (Lǐ, online). Even though very few people saw it, it is remembered as "a transformational work of Chinese contemporary drama," becoming an important node in late 20th-century Chinese theatre culture—Cuī Jiàn, China's first rock star, even wrote a song called "The Other Shore," inspired by what he'd seen (Yáng, online). Both the rehearsals and the performance were captured on film in Jiǎng Yuè's documentary *The Other Bank*, released in Japan in 1995.[59] In it we see the young actors seethe, wrestle, and tangle in the ropes; their collective gyrations and cries juxtaposed with still and intimate moments of dialogue.[60]

Martial Resonances

Two aspects of Chinese martial movement were at work in this production. A modernist interpretation of martial movement was provided by Gāo Xíngjiàn's stage directions, and a more contemporary manifestation appeared due to Móu's collaboration with choreographer Wén Huì.

Gāo had written *Bǐ'àn* in part as an actor-training exercise aimed at creating an evocative theatre inspired by older Chinese aesthetics:

> *The Other Shore* was written with a view towards training actors. The playing with the rope, the observing and looking into the eyes of one another, and the listening intently to music in the play are at the same time physical responses to the other shore of the imagination, and all of these help the actors free themselves from the modes of their daily movements and feelings. (Gāo 2012: 167)

Gāo hoped to create theatre that departed from Russian-inspired realistic acting and didactic Communist orthodoxy. As he writes in his production notes for *Bǐ'àn*, he hoped to "restore it to the multiple performance elements of total theater, including recitation, singing, mime, and movement" (Gāo, trans. Riley, in Cheung and Lai 1998: 153).

Gāo's key idea, the "neutral actor state," was inspired by his observation of Beijing Opera training and performance. He describes the neutral actor state as a requirement for the instant changes he believes an actor must manifest

---

[59] The film was screened in the fall of 1996 at the *Cinéma Parallèle* in Montréal, Canada.

[60] The documentary also captured the aftermath of the project. While Móu received a commission from a new piece from the Belgian arts festival, the funding for the project he planned with the *Bǐ'àn* students fell through, after much of the group had returned to Beijing to resume their rehearsals. The impoverished rural students took jobs as delivery people, night club hostesses and menial workers, and were almost without exception completely disillusioned. The film juxtaposes these tragic outcomes with Jiǎng and Móu's moving trip to rural Hebei to watch their former students Cuī Yàpǔ 崔亚普, Zǔ Er 祖儿 and Tang Zhǎngliàn 唐长炼 perform an original piece of theatre they created for their small, rural community audience entitled *A Blackbird Flying Across the Sky, Yī Zhī Fēiguò Tiānkōng De Hēi Niǎo* 一只飞过天空的黑鸟.

in performance. His conception of the actor is tripartite, a consciousness that moves among the self, the neutral state, and the role (2012: 166). It is a purified and concentrated experience to which the actor returns again and again as their performance progresses:

> On the stage the consciousness of this purified self transforms into a third eye that controls and modulates the performance, and from time to time the actor using his status as neutral actor observes the audience and the role he is acting, going in and going out so that he both experiences and acts. (2012: 165)

He links this skill to the martial arts and related practices:

> It is not difficult to grasp these essentials from qigong and taijiquan that have their origins in Chinese martial arts, but the difference is that the consciousness of self is not extinguished. Instead, the consciousness of self is refined into a third eye or, in other words, is the lucid observation of one's own body. (2012: 166)[61]

Gāo was drawn to these contemplative and individualistic aspects of Chinese martial training. Of a different generation, Móu and his collaborators brought their own preoccupations and artistic procedures to Gāo's pedagogical project. Nevertheless, although Yú eventually transformed Gāo's text, the performance emphasized movement as a primary mode of expression, used ropes to transform both the actors' bodies and the space they played in, and emphasized the collective acting of the group and the close rapport between them that it required—all staging devices that Gāo had proposed as the tools of his actor-training exercise.

Before he began to adapt Gāo's script, Yú Jiān visited the class:

> In June 1993, I watched Móu Sēn's physical training class in the second rehearsal room of the Beijing Film Academy. The actors' movements, which were ugly and rough—hideous when one expects to see polished dancing on stage—had a powerful effect on me. I was deeply impressed. It was the first time in my life that I had seen human bodies manifest so many intense, meaningful, yet unnameable movements. (Yú, online, my translation)

---

[61] While I do not believe that Tàijí Quán or qìgōng players aim to or do extinguish their consciousness of self, Gāo's idea of a state from which instant change is possible does resonate with the reality of these practices. Interestingly, the expression tiānyǎn 天眼, which his translator Mabel Lee renders as "third eye" in both citations, more accurately suggests an eye in the sky that sees all things as though from above. The expression refers to clairvoyance, but does so in a way that suggests a broad, calm, and detached perspective, rather than an anatomical location.

Given her aesthetic interests and her subsequent acclaim in China and abroad, I speculate that the unusual quality of the young actors' movements owed as much to Wén Huì's influence as it did to Móu's.

"As Long as People are Alive, They Are Verbs"

In the early 1990s Wén Huì was developing her own independently conceived version of an approach to dance that earlier Euro-American artists had named "task-based movement." While all human movement requires bodily actions, dance is often made of designed movements, at one remove from daily function and personal idiosyncrasy. Task-based work asks the dancer to accomplish a certain action while also allowing them to choose the way in which they do it. A contemporary choreographer might ask a dancer to move from one point to another by making five jumps. Unlike the ballet or modern choreographer, who would assume the use of a pre-existing stylistic movement vocabulary—a *jeté* or leap from one foot to the other in ballet, for example—a task-based approach allows the dancer to choose what kind of jumps they make. This brings the individual dancer's choices, attributes, and experience to the fore. It can also accommodate improvisation on the part of the dancers, who, as long they fulfill the requirements of the choreographic score by making their five jumps, might choose to jump differently in each performance. Task-based performance, improvisation, and the use of transformed daily movement as a performance vocabulary were already of interest to Wén before her contact with Euro-American contemporary dance. They were also central to the work of the Judson Dance Theatre, a collective working in New York City in the early 1960s, whose influence was decisive for later Euro-American dance artists (Burt 2006: 14).

Right after her work with Móu and the students, Wén visited the New York studio of one the major founding Judson Dance Theatre artists, the Tricia Brown Company Workshop, where her movement interests, unique in China at the time, could be understood and elaborated. On her return to Beijing in 1994 she presented *Yìbǎi Gè Dòngcí*—百个动词, or *100 Verbs*, the piece she'd created while away. The title revealed both her aesthetic preoccupations and the kind of movement she put on stage. As she said, "As long as people are alive, they are verbs"[62] (in Huáng, online).

In each of its four iterations between 1994 and 1995 Wén, alone or with different groups of dancers, performed a structured improvisation using a dance vocabulary developed from daily tasks.[63] While dressing and undressing, walking, kneeling to clean the floor, even taking photographs, she created

---

[62] *Rén zhǐyào huózhe jiùshì yīgè gè dòngcí*, 人只要活着就是一个个动词.

[63] An archival recording of one of the four versions of *100 Verbs* is held in the video library of the VMAC: Videotage Media Arts Collection, Cattle Depot Artist Village, To Kwa Wan, Hong Kong.

arresting images within a montage of ordinary doings. Remaining clothed, she bathed in a large tub full of rice; she inverted and contorted her body on a chair as she removed her sweater with her mouth. Wén used her task-based approach to interpret creatively the simple objectives she had set herself and her fellow performers. Accomplishing such tasks as bathing in a bowl or removing a sweater while sitting on a chair led to involved personal, unusual, and effortful actions, reversing the expectation of routine created by the more daily movements of which her dance was composed.[64]

Expressing actions that accomplish a concrete task as a choreographic presentation is a key element of wǔshù. While tàolù are not imagined as allowing much ambit for improvisation and personal decision-making, they are nevertheless composed of task-based movement vocabularies. In representing fighting, they require adepts to move in a way that would accomplish a concrete task. Strikes, kicks, grappling, and throwing are tasks given to the wǔshù performer by the form they are practicing. Even when performed alone, these movements must change the body of the adept in the same way they would if a training partner or assailant were present, within that performer's reach. While their precision gives them a stylized quality, the movements of the tàolù of wǔshù have a fundamental concrete dimension that always implies the presence of another body that is acted upon.

Transformed by Móu and Wén, Gāo's actor-training proposals yielded a performance composed of task-based, concrete actions. The relationship between Gāo and Wén's contributions reflects a complementarity of wén and wǔ. These two sources, one intentional and the other structural, and the visceral impact felt by the audiences of *Biàn Hé Guānyú Biàn De Hànyǔ Yǔfǎ Tǎolùn* are why I believe it was informed by the martial movement that characterizes Chinese wǔshù, theatre, and ritual.

Where Gāo was explicitly inspired by the physical, martial, and musical virtuosity of traditional Chinese theatre, Móu was critical of such expressions, suggesting that Beijing Opera and related activities offered "nothing more than an artificial and superficial cultural experience" (Salter, Móu & Wú 1996: 220). Artistically and aesthetically, Móu's work with the young rural students seemed distant from the virtuosic performers of Jīngjù, and the ancient stories of its repertoire. It was also distant from Gāo's playwright-driven, European- and Modernist-inspired, experimental spoken drama, or *huàjù* 话剧. Móu's iconoclastic disruption of the literary sources of his project—Gāo's script, and the normative theatrical conventions of readily identifiable characters and a clear dramatic narrative—provided a wǔ impulse. Like the martial rituals of the dìyuán of old, *Biàn Hé Guānyú Biàn De Hànyǔ Yǔfǎ Tǎolùn* is remembered as having transformed the community that witnessed it—the 1990s Beijing arts

---

[64] Consecutive English translations of Wén Huì and Wú Wénguāng's accounts of their later work with the Living Dance Studio can be found in Huber & Chuan's 2013 *The Body at Stake: Experiments in Chinese Contemporary Art and Theatre*, 131–135, 135–144.

scene—even though ultimately, and sadly, it did not benefit the young perform-ers whose appetite for education had made it possible in the first place.

The performance created by Móu, Yú, Wén, Gāo, and all their students and collaborators had a unique and tacit relationship to traditional culture. Chinese martial arts in the late 20th century also nourished contemporary theatre more overtly, serving as both the collective practice of a theatre ensemble, and as a means of creating staging and choreography.

W. S. Rendra

Willibrordus Surendra Broto Narendra, better known as W. S. Rendra, was an Indonesian director, actor, playwright, poet, teacher, and activist. He staged his first piece of theatre in 1963, attended the American Academy of Dramatic Arts in New York City from 1964 to 1967, and on his return to Indonesia in that year founded the Bengkel Teater, or Workshop Theatre, in Yogyakarta, Java. In the early and mid-1970s he directed productions from the Western repertoire and his own original plays, as well as composing and performing his own poetry. Publicly critical of both the left-leaning revolutionary Sukarno regime that ended the colonial period and the rightist Suharto dictatorship that overthrew it, Rendra was monitored, arrested, imprisoned, and upon his release banned from performing from the late 1970s until 1985.

At the beginning of the 1970s, Rendra became a student of the Sino-Indonesian martial art *Siauw Lim Pek Ho Pay*, known now by its Indonesian name of Silat Bangau Putih, or White Crane Silat. He eventually made this art a central element of the continuing education received by the actors working in his theatre company and included its choreographies in his productions. While he is not well-known to Euro-American audiences or readers, in Indonesia Rendra was a leading theatre artist and acting teacher, as well as a celebrated poet (Adda 2022: 398–399).

The Persecution of Chinese Indonesians under Suharto

People of Chinese heritage living in Indonesia have long been the victims of violence and official discrimination, of which Suharto's 1965 coup and subse-quent dictatorship are but the most recent instance. Chinese Indonesians were among the groups targeted by death squads in the year-long period of gov-ernment-sanctioned sectarian and political violence that followed the putsch. State-sponsored hatemongering that characterized Sino-Indonesians as both communist infiltrators and wealth-hoarding exploiters was accompanied by laws that disenfranchised them. A *Basic Policy for the Solution of Chinese Prob-lem* banned all public Chinese cultural and religious expressions, including dis-play of Chinese characters, and closed all Chinese language schools. Chinese

Indonesians were pressured to adopt Indonesian names, a process that the dictatorship made both complicated and prohibitively costly for them to do officially. This effectively barred them from both higher education and the public service. Discrimination began to be relieved only in 2000 with the recall of the laws forbidding the practice of Chinese culture and religions, and the use of Mandarin in public. In 2002 the celebration of the Chinese New Year was made a national holiday. This persecution was decisive in how the adepts of Siauw Lim Pek Ho Pay presented their martial art to the public, and to W. S. Rendra's use of it in his artistic activities (Adda 2022: 399; Tan 2005: 795–808).

White Crane Silat

Siauw Lim Pek Ho Pay is the Romanized pronunciation of 少林白鶴派 in the Fújiàn Huà 福建話 or Hokkien idiolect of the Mǐn Yǔ 閩語 language group, named after the Mǐn River in China's Fujian province. The Mǐnnán Quánzhāng Rén 閩南泉漳人, or Hoklo people, trace their origins to Quánzhāng, an area in the south of Fujian. Present in Southeast Asia for centuries, the Hoklo or Hokkien group make up the largest Chinese community in Indonesia.

In Mandarin, the name of this martial art is pronounced *Shàolín Báihè Pài*, which means the White Crane imitative martial arts of the Shàolín sect. There are numerous schools of White Crane martial arts across Southeast Asia whose adepts trace their history to Fujian Province yet use the name Shàolín.[65] It is unlikely that these groups are directly descended from the martial arts practiced at the famous Shàolín monastery in Henan province. Rather, the myth of the alleged sack of the Shàolín monastery by Qing troops and the subsequent secret spread of its martial methods in rural southern China by five wandering adepts played a major part in the dramas acted out in the initiation ceremonies of the Tiāndìhuì 天地會 or Heaven and Earth Society, a fraternal association founded in Fujian in the early 1760s (Murray & Qin 1996: 5). For the martial arts of Fujian province, the name Shàolín more likely represents a historical relationship to the Tiāndìhuì. While known in popular tales as anti-Qing insurgent cells, the Tiāndìhuì were founded as mutual aid groups. Due to their importance to local communities, they spread to Southeast Asia along with the Hoklo people who settled there as traders and labourers.

White Crane Silat was formalized for public instruction as Siauw Lim Pek Ho Pay in 1952 by Liem Sin Tjoei (1925–1985), who also went by the Indonesian name of Subur Rahardja. He was referred to by his students as *suhu*, an alternate romanization of *saihu* 師父, the Hokkien term for a senior martial arts adept, pronounced *shīfù* in Mandarin.[66] Liem studied *kuntao*, 拳法 (*quánfǎ* in

---

[65] See Lee & Bernard 2021 for a Malaysian example, and Yang 1994 for a Taiwanese one.

[66] I do not know the Chinese idiographs that make up Liem's name. I speculate that they could be Lín Xìnzhū 林信珠, Lián Xìnzhū 廉信珠, or Lián Xìnzhū 连信珠. Thanks to Gey Pin Ang for helping me with the interpretation of the Hokkien names written in Roman script.

Mandarin) an alternate Hokkien term for wǔshù, with his father Liem Kim Sek for two years as a child. Liem senior died when his son was eight, and the boy was raised by his uncle, Liem Kiem Bouw, who was a Chinese herbalist and a kuntao teacher. In addition to his family's martial arts, Liem Kiem Bouw was said to have studied *Silat Cimande* with an expert named *Mpe*. Sutur, and he passed this on to his nephew as well.[67] The younger Liem studied further kuntao with one *Asuk* Yat Long.[68] Finally, he is reported to have learned from *Gusti Agung Gede* Djelantik Baliwangsa, who was king of the island of Lombok and of Kerangsem, a district on Bali.[69] Gusti Djelantik was reputedly an adept of silat, as well as of the mantras and yogas of Agama Tirta, the Balinese religion that incorporates Javanese, Indian, and Chinese practices (Redana, online; Adda, personal communication). White Crane Silat, perhaps in its movement vocabulary, and decidedly in the presentation of its sources, appeared as a combination of Chinese and Indonesian martial arts.

When Liem began teaching the martial synthesis that he referred to as Siauw Lim Pek Ho Pay in 1952, he registered his group as a physical culture association to avoid any perception that his school was part of a secret society or criminal organization. Both silat and kuntao were commonly thought to be related to the Javanese demi-monde, an understanding that he aimed to pre-empt in founding Persatuan Gerak Badan Bangau Putih, or the "white crane unified body movement association," commonly referred to as PGB. The association thrived in the years between its founding and the Suharto coup. The PGB had to close its doors for almost four years due to the persecution of the Chinese community by the rightist regime (Adda 2022: 401). From its reopening in 1969 to Liem's untimely death in a car accident in 1985, the PGB organization and its White Crane Silat flourished. Local groups were established in various Javanese cities, the decisive relationship with the Bengkel Teater began and developed, and an increasing number of visiting international students spread the school's influence around the world. Liem's son Gunawan Rahardja (b. 1958) inherited the leadership of the PGB from his father and remains the leader of the community today, and the *Guru Besar* or head teacher of White Crane Silat.

---

[67] Silat Cimande is one of the most widely diffused styles of silat in Indonesia. Oral history traces its founding to the late 1700s, when one *Pak* Kahir began to teach his approach, which soon spread all over West Java. *Pak*, short for *bapak*, is also an honorific that can mean "father," "mister," or "sir," as appropriate. "Mpe." is also an honorific term for a senior and expert personage.

[68] Some accounts of Liem's oral history report that at around the age of 20, he studied with a Chinese Buddhist monk recently arrived in Indonesia. Asuk is an honourific term meaning uncle, pronounced *ā shū* 阿叔 in Mandarin.

[69] *Gusti* or leader and *Agung* or great are honorifics indicating the royal status of a person from either the Satria or Brahaman castes of Balinese society, while *Gede* indicates that the person is the first son in his generation.

Structure and Movement

In December of 2018, I watched a Silat Bangau Putih class in Ubud, Bali which was led by *Dewan Guru Bapak* Irwan Rahardja, brother of the current head of the style.[70] My host was theatre artist and Silat Bangau Putih instructor Marco Adda (b.1975). In addition to the head teacher and Marco, five other students were present: an Italian PGB instructor who had moved to Bali, an instructor visiting from California, a student visiting from Germany, and two Indonesian students living in Bali. The class began at around 4:00 p.m. and lasted for just over 90 minutes. It took place in a pavilion without walls set on a smooth concrete pad, attached to a hotel complex. I sat cross-legged on the floor, as the training unfolded all around me. The temperature was around 33°C, and the humidity was over 75 percent. At the end of the class, a heavy rain poured down.

The students arrived, quietly and warmly greeted the teacher, and began to train on their own. The students practiced barefoot and wore light training clothes. Some had t-shirts with a PGB logo on the chest, but overall, there were no identifiable uniforms. The class had no explicit structure; rather, the participants all demonstrated a tacit understanding of what was to be done. They either practiced by themselves, or one on one with the teacher or an instructor, moving from repetitions of single movements to longer sequences. Toward the end of the period, the group gathered to watch pairs play a cooperative sparring game they called *tui cu*, 推手 (Mandarin: *tuīshǒu*, pushing-hands). Participation in the game appeared to be voluntary, with some students playing with several partners and some content merely to observe. After practice, the whole group sat on the floor of the training space to relax and chat, sharing hot black tea they had brought in a thermos. Some even smoked a few cigarettes. The relaxed yet serious and focused atmosphere of the training gave way to a welcoming, informal, and friendly one in its aftermath.

The movements I saw in this class were drawn from three families of southern Chinese martial movement. The students played long-armed crane movements that describe large ellipsoidal volumes in space, similar to those found in the Guangdong styles of Chói Lěih Fáht Kyùhn or Hahp Gā Kyùhn 俠家拳. They also practiced the stiffer, linear punching actions of the *Luóhàn* 羅漢 styles, where the heart of the fist usually points toward the ground and the line from shoulder to shoulder is often at a right angle to the line from shoulder to fist at the completion of a punch. The more experienced participants worked on the supple, elegant ground movements that I associate with the dog and snake, or *gǒu* 狗 and *shé* 蛇, movements of Fujian *wǔshù*, collectively referred to as *dìtàng* 地趟, tumbling and ground, or *xiàmén* 下門 "lower gate" methods.[71]

---

[70] The title *Dewan Guru* can be understood as "teacher's counsel," given both Irwan Rahardja's seniority as an adept and his brother's leadership of the PGB. *Bapak*, as noted, is a respectful term meaning "father," "mister," or "sir."

[71] See for example *Fukien Ground Boxing* (Cai 1993).

Figure 21: Marco Adda practicing a long-armed crane *jalan panjang* (tàolù) while the school's *Keilin Barong* looks on, in Bogor, West Java, at the Bangau Putih Headquaters, 2016.

The *tui cu* partner game involved extensive improvisation across a wide movement vocabulary. Again, tacit conventions seemed to determine its parameters rather than explicitly stated rules. Partners mostly maintained contact between the wrists of one or both arms, but the contact could be broken acceptably by implicit understanding. The goal of the game seemed to fluctuate between taking one's partner's space and compromising their balance. Hand-touches indicating a failure to defend against strikes were acceptable, but whole-body slams, headbutting, kneeing, elbow strikes, and ballistic throws were not performed, despite their near-constant availability due to the players' proximity to one another. In contrast, foot sweeps consequent to players overextending their upper bodies played a major role in the game, and the felled partners all recovered nimbly and with good humour from these trips, even on the polished cement floor of the training space.

Tuīshǒu played in northern Chinese Tàijí Quán, as well as the similar *róushǒu* 柔手 (soft hands) and *luànshǒu* 亂手 (messy hands) games played in *Bāguà Zhǎng* 八卦掌 and *Xíngyì Quán* 形意拳, incorporate an extensive movement vocabulary, performed in constant contact with a partner, in which a large ambit of improvisation is encouraged. While they share the same name, the pushing-hands exercises of most southern Chinese martial arts, Chói Lěih Fáht

Kyùhn, and Fujian Flying Crane *Fēi Hè Quán* 飛鶴拳, for example, use fewer movements and more restrictive parameters. Even the sophisticated *chīshǒu* 黐手 sticking hands practice of *Wihng Chēun Kyùhn* 詠春拳 does not, in my observation, usually give players the latitude that Silat Bangau Putih's tui cu does. Where tuīshǒu-like exercises in the Chinese martial arts aim to work on challenging players' balances, on moving their whole bodies out of position, or on misaligning their limbs to permit effective striking, it is rare to see all these parameters combined in a single game.[72]

Clearly, not all parts of the PGB association's curriculum were on display in the single class I visited. The group didn't train with weapons or practice any obviously contemplative exercises, for example. However, the shapes, trajectories, and syncopation of the martial movements being practiced were all familiar to me from previous training or exposure to Chinese martial arts. Interestingly, there was no sign of the tàolù named *Sān Zhàn* 三戰, or Three Battles. This choreography is found ubiquitously in the Shaolin White Crane martial arts of Fujian province and uses relatively few actions trained in a turned-in standing posture. The bent arms and open hands of the Sān Zhàn tàolù mime the shapes of a crane's wings, alternating between crisp and rapid strikes and slow-motion extensions where adepts create strength-building tension in their bodies by resisting their own movements. Sān Zhàn imparts a very specific quality of physical expression to its adepts, inflecting all their movements beyond the performance of a single tàolù. In contrast, the crane movements of Silat Bangau Putih favour extension, smooth movement done with minimal self-resistance, and relatively even timing. In this they recall the long-armed vocabulary of Guangdong crane movement, which employs more whipping than pressing in its execution.

Although Chinese and Indonesian martial movements have much in common, their syncopation and the details of how they coordinate players' bodies give them distinct aesthetics. While the movements of Siauw Lim Pek Ho Pay identified it to me as martial art of Chinese origin, the tui cu partner game seemed to show influences from Indonesian silat. Many silat styles use the convention of the mock fight to allow players to interact agonistically with minimal risk of harm. Students injured in training would be unable to tend to their daily work, let alone assist in community defence in situations of actual violence. Given the cost today and the historical absence of medicines such as antibiotics, of surgical procedures to repair torn or broken soft and hard tissues, and of protective gear such as padded gloves, mouth guards, shin guards or helmets, the conventions of a mimed fight are understandable.

The mock fight evolves from partner mirroring exercises, in which the players mimic one another's movements sequentially at a slow and even pace, gradually

---

[72] They are all present in the contemporary Chinese kickboxing sport of *Sǎndǎ*, which is played in a ring with ropes and a soft floor, by competitors wearing mouthguards, head-protectors, boxing gloves, and shin guards.

moving from reactive copying to proactive proposals of shapes that, in real contact, would fit into, defend against, or challenge one another.[73] Between skilled experts, the mock fight can include accelerations as well as brief moments of actual contact, the legitimacy of which is understood tacitly within the community of players. Like mock fighting in Indonesian silat, White Crane Silat tui cu uses a wide variety of movements, deployed freely while moving in the training space. Like the more focused push-hands games of the southern Chinese martial arts, it also develops touch response. These parameters make it a most versatile game, open to a wide variety of goals and trainable at many levels of intensity.

White Crane Silat and the Bengkel Teater

In the early 1970s White Crane Silat became key to W. S. Rendra and the Bengkel Teater in two important ways: It was the fundamental skill-building activity of the actors, and it also appeared on stage as a choreographic tool (Adda 2022: 411). Adept Max Palaar joined the Bengkel Teater in 1973, first as a songwriter, and then as the group's martial arts trainer (Redana, online). Palaar facilitated the use of White Crane Silat over the course of three productions created by Rendra that used European repertoire: *Antigone* in 1974, an adaptation of Sophocles' *Oedipus at Colonus* in 1974, and *Lysistrata* in 1975 (Adda 2022: 404). As the actors become more adept at silat, the nature of its appearance on stage evolved. In *Antigone*, the actors coordinated their performance of silat movements with their lines of text, in a composition orchestrated by Rendra. By the time they came to work on *Lysistrata*, the group had considerably more experience, and Rendra composed his staging using the actors' own proposals of stylized character movement and group choreography based on their personalized integrations of the movements of *Silat Bagau Putih*. Adda characterizes the result of this process of integration as "martial art-acting," a gestalt of martial art practice and its manifestation in the actors' performances, both of which had larger social implications. The Bengkel Teater shared their White Crane Silat with marginalized youth and women's groups in dedicated classes and, alongside their professional performances, their community outreach became a concrete manifestation of the resistance to the dictatorship implicit in their adoption of a major cultural tradition of the persecuted Chinese minority (Adda 2022: 398–399).

The martial game of tui cu held an important role in the genesis of the Benkel Teater's martial art-acting. The actors played a preliminary game referred to

---

[73] The mock fight and the practice of mirroring are known by many different names, particular to each of the many schools of silat that use them. I take these two useful terms from "The Search for the Tiger: Silat Harimau in an Austrian Transnational Context," Fatema Albastaki's presentation on Sumatran *Minang Silat* at the Martial Arts Studies Conference, Sheffield, July 2023.

using the English word "Feeling" as a preparation for the broader, more competitive parameters of full tui cu. Focusing on fewer movements, repeated cyclically using set breathing patterns, Feeling training developed the individual actors' fundamental coordination, timing with respect to their partners, and spatial perception. Feeling and tui cu were further supplemented by *Meditasi*, or meditation training, contemplative activities that used slow movement, coordinating breathing and visualization. The Meditasi included the visualization of the trajectories of individual movements in the mind's eye, as well as imagining movement within mentally formed geometrical shapes and the imaginal conjuring of natural elements such as water and fire. Adda proposes the *Agama Tirta* practices of Gusti Djelantik as a likely source of these methods, but they also closely resemble the cún xiǎng found in Daoist practice and in other Chinese martial arts in their combination of movement and breath control with visualization (personal communication).

Realized long before my formulation of spatial projection (see chapter 2), the process and procedures of Rendra's martial art-acting seem to have followed a similar trajectory, from foundation training in individual movements, through extended movement sequences, to improvised practices with a partner, to the perception of the entirety of the performance space. This overall process, along with the complementary uses of tui cu both as sensitivity training and as a compositional tool for performance, highlights what I suggest is a fundamental theatrical element of the Chinese martial arts, even when transformed by geographic and cultural relocation. Rendra's productions synthesized traditional practices with the Euro-American approaches to making theatre and selecting repertoire that he had learned in the United States. His use of Silat Bangau Putih can appear to have been an application of the Sino-Indonesian martial art in the production of theatrical performances with innovative aesthetics, created in consideration of the material and spiritual situation of their Indonesian audiences. Rather than being a novel combination of distinct art-forms, however, I believe that theatricality is a feature of both practices. Rendra used an older kind of theatre practice to facilitate the creation of a more contemporary one. The blurred combative, theatrical, and spiritual nature of the Chinese martial arts that can appear to be novel in Rendra's contemporary work is nowhere clearer than in the microcosm of traditional apotropaic puppetry.

Religious Celebration, Ritual, and Performance

Late in the 1990s PGB leader Gunawan Radharja began to restore the Chinese religious ceremonies of Siauw Lim Pek Ho Pay, which had been outlawed in the 1960s (Adda 2022: 401). Chief among these were the Lantern Festival and the Autumn Moon Festival, both of which are now celebrated by the members of the PGB and the community surrounding the school by the martial dancing of the *qílín* 麒麟 spirit-puppet.

The qílín is one of the four auspicious spirits first mentioned in the *Shījīng* 詩經, or *Book of Songs*, a Zhou dynasty collection of classic poetry and one of the five canonical books attributed to Confucius. The qílín is associated with the west, complementing the dragon in the east, the phoenix in the south, and the *bì xì* 贔屭, a tortoise-like creature in the north. Because it is sometimes represented with a single, central horn, the qílín has been described as a unicorn in English. Like the long, or dragon, which is a composite creature (see chapter 1), the qílín combines many creatures, and has been represented in many ways. It can have one, two, or even three horns. It has a lion-like mane and a beard, the body of a deer, ox, or horse, the scales of a fish, and the hooves of a horse. Brilliantly multicoloured, qílín are also depicted with flames adorning their coats and their feet. The qílín is seen as a harbinger of prosperity, appearing in times of great peace and harmony. Consequently, the performance of its dance is apotropaic, considered to bring good fortune while banishing bad luck. Like the more commonly seen performances, the *wǔ shī* 舞獅, or lion dance, and the *wǔ lóng* 舞龍, or dragon dance, the *qílín wǔ* 麒麟舞 dances are performed by students of the Chinese martial arts who use their martial movement to manipulate and animate these large whole-body puppets, accompanied by raucous percussion. In many communities, shopkeepers and residents express their appreciation for the luck-bringing passage of spirit-puppets like the lion and the qílín with donations of "lucky money" that recompenses the dancers and their school or raises money on behalf of local community charities.[74]

One of the earliest depictions of such spirit-puppets is a Tang dynasty pottery figure found in Xinjiang, near Turpan. Dating from between 618 and 906 CE, the figure shows a lion's head, seemingly carved out of wood, and a body created by a large cloth cape, from beneath which emerge distinctly human feet, wearing little shoes (Hu 1995: i). William C. Hu traces the relationship between ancient, apotropaic spirit-puppet dances and the Chinese martial arts to the early years of the Northern Song dynasty, 960–1127 CE. A martial arts expert from Lin Hai in Zhejiang province named Yáng Xiǎn Chuàng 楊顯愴 created a *zhèn* battle array choreography (see chapter 2) performed by a team of 30 of his students. He replaced the heavy wooden head of his local lion dance puppet with a larger one made of papier-mâché applied over a light frame, and added colourful fringes to the cape covering the performers. While one group of students performed solo and paired martial arts tàolù, a pair of lions would compete to ascend to the top of nine tables stacked as a pyramid, performing acrobatics and stunts en route. Yáng simplified the musical accompaniment of the dance, using only martial drums, gongs, and cymbals as signals that coordinated the performance of the battle array (1995: 116–121). Whether the many practices of Chinese martial spirit-puppetry all descend from this early

---

[74] As martial arts schools are often associated with the criminal demi-monde, this practice is also often frowned upon as a socially sanctioned excuse for the extraction of protection money (Amos 2020: 35).

documented instance, or developed in parallel in different regions is unclear, but spirit-puppet presentations have been martial expressions for almost a thousand years.

These puppets are considered to contain a spirit that is invited to take up residence during a ceremony of consecration. Still performed today by ritual specialists of the particular community involved, the rite is called the opening of the light, or *kāi guāng* 開光. Key to the ceremony is dotting the eyes and face of the puppet using a calligraphy brush loaded with cinnabar. Referred to using a term from painting, *huà lóng diǎn jīng* 畫龍點睛, or "painting the eyes of a dragon to bring it to life," the dotting allows the light of the spirit to enter the puppet, and subsequently become manifest here on Earth as the operator opens the eyes of the newly consecrated lion or qílín for the first time.

The consecrated spirit-puppet is treated as a celestial being, a status taken extremely seriously by the devotees of its community. Daniel Amos recounts the ritual involved in transferring the spirit of a qílín from a worn-out puppet and costume to a freshly prepared new one:

> After arriving at the anointed location for the ritual ceremony, a senior member of the cult, Master Chau's younger kungfu brother, who went by the English name Sullivan, assumed the central role in the ritual drama. His movements and actions became governed by the Qilin dance music as he became possessed and entered the old Qilin dance costume.
>
> When he entered the worn costume there was silence except for the groaning of the possessed man as he rolled on the ground inside the old Qilin and fought with the Qilin spirit, which was reluctant to leave the worn costume. After prolonged struggle, the possessed man emerged triumphant, threw off the old Qilin costume, and entered the new Qilin costume, which then became united with the Qilin spirit.
>
> When another disciple of the kungfu cult entered the tail of the new Qilin, the loud percussion music again commenced. The newly spirited Qilin began dancing toward a disciple holding the spirit box containing sacred text of the kungfu cult. The music prompted specific thematic movements from the dancers as the Qilin danced around the spirit box, bowing repeatedly in respect and worship. (Amos 2021: 34)

Amos describes the Hakka, Hong Kong-based martial arts association he joined and wrote about, the Praying Mantis Physical Exercise Association 螳螂健身會 (Mandarin: *Tángláng Jiànshēn Huì*), as a religious group, or "kungfu cult."[75] He characterizes their practice of the *Authentic Teachings of the*

---

[75] William C. Hu comments on the relationship between Hakka martial artists and the qílín in Hong Kong:

Jiangxi Bamboo Grove Temple 江西 竹林寺真傳 (Mandarin: *Jiāngxī Zhúlín Sì Zhēnchuán*) under their kungfu cult master Chau Kai-ming 朱啟明 (Mandarin: Zhū Qǐmíng) as a religion of the body, expressed by martial practice, for which the qílín and its dance serve as an embodied spiritual centre (2021: 2). As with the PGB in Java, the principal festivals over which Chau's Praying Mantis Physical Exercise Association qílín presides are the Lantern Festival and the Autumn Moon Festival.

The Lantern Festival takes place on the fifteenth day of the Chinese lunar year. It has many names in Mandarin Chinese: *Yuánxiāo Jié* 元宵節, or the celebration marked by the eating of *yuánxiāo* desserts, glutinous rice balls with a sweet paste filling; *Shàngyuán Jié* 上元節, or first *yuán* celebration; and *Shíwǔ Míng* 十五暝, or "fifteenth evening." The Autumn Moon Festival, *Zhōngqiū Jié* 中秋節—literally the "central sphere festival"—takes place on the full moon of the eighth month of the Chinese lunar calendar, at the approximate halfway point of the year. The activities and symbols of these festivals correlate the harmony and balance of circular, spherical, and cyclical forms with human thriving and the abundance of nature. The lamps played with by children during the Lantern Festival are rounded shapes, often inscribed with little riddles, the solving of which is rewarded with sweet desserts and treats. The full Autumn Moon is likewise celebrated with lanterns and with specially prepared *yuèbǐng* 月餅, or moon cakes. The themes of light, roundness, cyclical recurrence, and sweet nourishment offer concrete spatial and temporal reminders of the importance to human flourishing of the harmonization of self with nature, a fundamental value of Chinese religion (Cheng in Allinson 1990: 172).[76]

The Lantern Festival is pronounced *Cap Go Meh* in the Hokkien language of the founders of the PGB. On this day, the PBG Association's qílín—*kei lin* in Hokkien—parades to visit various Chinese and Javanese temples in the area to celebrate their deities. In the early years of the 21st century, this annual celebration has been massive, with hundreds if not thousands of participants, many coming from other parts of Indonesia, bringing their own community spirit-puppets to join in the festivities. The parade is led by the PGB kie lin and statue of the Chinese deity of kindness and mercy, Guānyīn. First the kie lin is awakened at the PGB headquarters in the Kebun Jukut district of Bogor, Java, from

---

Due to the congestion of Hong Kong, with martial artists from all parts of China concentrated in one small area, many of the Hakka Shih-hui in the urban areas wanted to avoid any possible conflicts and confrontations with others. They have substituted the Lion Dance with the Ch'i Lin 麒麟 popularly and most often called the Unicorn Dance by Westerners and as a Chi-kung-shih 雞公獅 (Rooster-shaped Lion) by other martial artists. By taking such actions, they have successfully been able to preserve all the old traditions while avoiding any conflicts with others in a most diplomatic move (Hu 1995: 270).

[76] Cheng contrasts the view that the purpose of knowledge is to harmonize the self with the world, which he feels is indigenous to China, with more recently arrived perspectives: a South Asian one from Buddhism that emphasizes the overcoming of the self, and a Euro-American one that emphasizes the overcoming of the world.

where it travels to the Vihara Dhanagun Buddhist Temple, some ten minutes away on foot from the training hall. Upon arrival, the kie lin pays its respects to Guānyīn, whose large, heavy, and fragile statue is raised onto shoulders of a group of Bangau Putih practitioners and carried through the crowds on its round of visits to neighbouring temples. While the affinity between Silat Bangau Putih and Guānyīn may be more recent, it is significant to note the long association between Guānyīn, the Shaolin White Crane martial arts of Fujian, and the Tiāndìhuì fraternities. The Tiāndìhuì was founded in the early 1760s in a building named the *Guānyīn Tīng* 觀音廳, or Guānyīn Hall, in the Gaoxi township of Fujian (Murray & Qin 1996: 5).

The Autumn Moon Festival, called *Pwee Gwee Cap Go* in Hokkien, is the occasion of evening rites particular to the practitioners of *Silat Bangau Putih*, as well as temple visits and prayers, offerings of specially formulated incense, and community social activities (Adda, personal communication). If the parading of Guānyīn led by the kie lin renews the space, or dìyuán, of the PGB, the rites of Pwee Gwee Cap Go, which honour the ancestors and seniors of the institution, situate it temporally in the xuèyuán:

> These special night-time functions involve reflection and meditation along with lighting candles as one of the symbols of life. That is: 18 candles for the 18 Pewaris Ban [the first circle of Inheritors], 18 candles for the 18 Pewaris Goan [the second circle of Inheritors], 41 candles for the Warga Perguruan [Citizens of the School] and various candles for PGB branches in Indonesia and foreign countries. (Atmadja, trans. unknown, online)

The members of the PGB refer to their qílín as a *kei lin barong*, combining the Chinese term with the Indonesian *barong*, a spirit-puppet associated with the culture of Bali (Adda 2022: 401). Some scholars speculate that the barong is an Indonesian adaptation of the Chinese lion spirit-puppet (Bandem & de Boer 1981: 119).[77] Whether these spirit-puppets spread by diffusion, or were developed by multiple cultures independently, the orthopraxic nature of Chinese religions lends itself to symmetrical correlations with other orthopraxic cultures, allowing for mutual comprehension and coexistence.[78] The traditional qílín is a consecrated figure responsible for spiritually significant actions; it is

---

[77] The metaphysical attributes of the Balinese *Barong* reveal the depth to which the practice of spirit-puppetry has been developed in Indonesia. Every Balinese is considered protected by a personal *Barong* spirit, the Barong Keket. In *Agama Tirta* newborns are accompanied by four revered spiritual brothers, the *hanya bercerita* who are embodied in the amniotic fluid, the blood, *the verbix caseosa*, and the afterbirth. The afterbirth is the most important and powerful brother and is associated with the Barong Keket, the personal *barong*. In Balinese esoteric religious lore, the *barong* spirit-puppet's appearance represents this connection: it has a shaggy body, stringy like the veins and arteries of the afterbirth (George 1991: 55 & Mershon 1971: 40).

[78] In Cuba, for example, where lion dancing is performed by a Chinese community with origins in Guangdong, the Chinese deity Guān Yǔ 關羽, a central figure honoured by

operated by martial artists, and its play is theatrical, combining ritual efficacy with entertainment. In its recent and local history, the qílín, like so many of the other elements of Silat Bangau Putih, was correlated with the practices and cosmology of Indonesia writ large, and of Java in particular. The PGB kei lin barong offers a microcosm of the triune, blurred-genre nature of the Chinese martial arts that informed and nourished the work of the Bengkel Teater.

Conclusion

The Chinese martial arts have had both tacit and explicit influence on late-20th-century Asian theatre artists. They have nourished training methods and performances, and provided more subtle cultural influences, whether explained after the fact by such ideas as the neutral actor state and martial arts-acting, or by artists letting their works speak for themselves. The relationship between the tacit and the explicit will be further developed in the next chapter, which looks at complementarity of ideas of the real and the unreal in Daoist and Chinese thought, and its consequences for martial arts and theatre-making.

Qing and later martial art schools, has been correlated with the Afro-Caribbean deity Shango (Alay & Hun, 2017: 22).

CHAPTER 5

Real yet unreal. Unreal yet real

若亡若存。若存若亡。

Ruò wáng ruò cún. Ruò cún ruò wáng

Introduction

In this chapter I examine what I call chimeras, recent practices and ideas made up of previously distinct, even incompatible elements. The chimera was originally a fantastical, fire-breathing beast described by Homer as part lion, part goat, and part snake. More recently, the term has been adopted to describe organisms created by combining the genes of two different species. While cultural practices can all be seen as the recombination of earlier, perhaps once-unusual combinations, chimeras here are recent constructions whose component elements can still be parsed. The overall chimera this chapter examines is the Euro-American concept of energy as used in discussions of Chinese martial arts and religions, and in contemporary cosmopolitan theatre.

To do this, I discuss two specific chimeras that are representative of larger cultural tendencies and have been sources of meaningful experiences and thinking. In the early 20th century, Sūn Lùtáng 孫祿堂 (1860–1933) created an intracultural interpretation of the relationship between Chinese martial arts and Daoist practices and cosmology that represents an important Chinese parallel to the development of the idea of energy in Euro-American, and later globalized, contexts. Jerzy Grotowski (1933–1999) applied an intercultural interpretation of energy as he located it in various non-European cultures in his last practical, theatre-related research project at the end of the 20th century.

Energy is an idea that has figured prominently in both 20th-century presentations of the Chinese martial arts in translation, and discussions of

How to cite this book chapter:

Mroz, D. 2025. *Resonant Space: Religion, Theatre, and the Chinese Martial Arts.* Pp. 93–134. Cardiff: Cardiff University Press. DOI: https://doi.org/10.18573/book11.g.
Licence: CC-BY-NC-ND

Euro-American theatre. Where it appears both in translations from the Chinese and in martial arts books written in English and other European languages, energy is proposed as a hypostasis, a subtle, mysterious substance underlying reality that can be harnessed to improve health and to manifest effortless fighting prowess. Beyond these instrumental applications, dealing in energy is associated with spiritual insight and authenticity.[79] Euro-American theatre artists have discussed energy along similar lines: it plays a role in audiences' experiences, in the stage presence manifested by actors, and in the relationship between artistic performances and personal spiritual growth.[80] In theatre, this view of energy has often been presented using examples from Asian martial arts, religions, medicine, and theatre.[81] Viewed critically, energy is a specific, esoteric Euro-American idea that has been used erroneously as a general term in descriptions of Chinese and other Asian cultural practices. Viewed creatively, however, recent discussions of energy that blend seemingly incommensurable combinations of ideas and activities have shown themselves to be productive, meaningful, and worthy of further discussion.

The Daoist phrase *ruò wáng ruò cún* offers us an ultimate poetic description of a chimera: its literal, English translation means "like death, like life," existence and non-existence equated, a combination of seemingly irreconcilable kinds that nevertheless can describe our experiences.

The terms *religionism* and *source amnesia* as used by Wouter Hanegraaf and Olav Hammer offer useful critical tools for the examination of chimeras (Hanegraaf 2013: 11; Hammer 2004: 180). Poly-ontology, multinatural somatic

---

[79] *Partes pro toto* examples of this trend include such popular books as Paul Dong & Thomas Raffill's *Empty Force* (1996), B. K. Frantzis's *Opening the Energy Gates of your Body* (1993), Al Huang's *Embrace Tiger, Return to Mountain: The Essence of Tai Ji* (1973), George Katchmer Jr.'s *The Tao of Bioenergetics* (1993), and Glenn Morris's *Path Notes of an American Ninja Master* (1993).

[80] Peter Brook (1925–2022) used energy generally to refer to the qualities of different kinds of Euro-American performances, contrasting such examples as the Elizabethan popular theatre of Shakespeare and the avant-garde late-20th-century dance of Merce Cunningham (1968). Eugenio Barba (b. 1936) used the term to describe the qualities of actors' behaviours in Euro-American and Asian theatre practices as they affect audiences' perceptions (1995: 49–79). Jerzy Grotowski used the word "energy" with more spiritual connotations, as we shall see.

[81] The writings of the late Phillip Zarrilli (1947–2020) were instrumental in legitimizing the idea of using Asian martial arts in actor training within the Anglo-American university system. While the intercultural combination of movement practices he proposed as techniques of actor training was a fascinating chimera, his engagement with Tàijí Quán was far more modest than his journeyman's commitment to the South Indian martial art *Kalarippayattu*. Zarrilli learned, then taught, a simplified *tàolù* of *Wú Shì Tàijí Quán* 吴氏太极拳 after a year's instruction under American theatre scholar A. C. Scott (1909–1985), who had taken public classes led by Cheng Wing Kwong 鄭榮光 (Yale: Jehng Wihng Gwõng, 1903–1967) in Hong Kong between 1947 and 1952 (Zarrilli 2009: 215, 219). Zarrilli's understanding of the Chinese martial arts was largely derived from popular books (2009: 72–76, 223–224). While I shall not be discussing his ideas here, his syncretic interpretation of Indian, Chinese, and Japanese concepts from different periods, presented as a phenomenology of energy (2009, 2020), is an example of the larger tendency I explore in this chapter in relation to Euro-American esoteric energy and the influential proposals of Jerzy Grotowski.

pluralism, and somatic mutability, described by David Palmer and Simon Cox, offer positive perspectives both on how these 20th-century chimeras might be understood to be productive, and on the function of practices whose originally chimeric natures have been obscured by precedent (Palmer 2021: 124–126; Cox 2022: 215).

Real yet unreal. Unreal yet real

The phrase "ruò wáng ruò cún" comes from *The Highest Supreme Jade Emperor's Wondrous Heart Seal Scripture*, the *Gāo Shàng Yù Huáng Xīn Yìn Miào Jīng*, 高上玉皇心印妙經, a short, anonymous discussion of Daoist meditation written during the Southern Song dynasty, sometime between 1127 and 1279 CE. In composing my poem from the Introduction, and in titling this chapter, I created an additional phrase by reversing the characters *wáng* and *cún*, compounding the ambiguity conjured by the original.[82]

Interpreters of the Jade Emperor's scripture suggest that this line refers to adepts' shifting perceptions in their meditations. Nèidān, which we will discuss further below, requires both physical and imaginal activities of its devotees. As practice develops, the student's perspective shifts. Are the sensations experienced in practice real qualities of the body and environment, or are the phenomena felt in meditation conditioned by cún xiǎng, by the received images the students have been taught to visualize and correlate with their feelings? Both can seem to be the case.

Combining "like death" with "like life," the phrase "ruò wáng ruò cún" recognizes our often-nebulous experience of meaning, as we change our minds about what is real and what is imagined, routinely revising our opinions about the nature of the world as we receive new information. "Ruò wáng ruò cún" has become a *chéngyǔ* 成语, a common idiom suggesting that "sometimes you remember, sometimes you forget."

Unlike contemporary Chinese languages, *gǔ wén* 古文, or ancient, literary Chinese most often uses one, not two logographs to indicate individual words. The extreme minimalism of this convention requires much of readers. Translator David Hinton's English rendering of the last line of the poem "Autumn Begins" by Mèng Hàorán 孟浩然 (689–740), reveals the degree of the interpretive work involved. Consider the space between the literal meanings of the individual words in the third line, and Hinton's translation in the fourth:

阶下丛莎有露光
jiē xià cóng shā yǒu lù guāng

---

[82] I was introduced to the phrase by Simon Cox, who inscribed it as part of the dedication he wrote in my copy of his book *The Subtle Body: A Genealogy* (2022). He felt it was a suitable theme for our conversations about Chinese martial arts and religions in both their historical and recent manifestations.

stairs below clump grass see dew radiance
At the bottom stair, in bunch grass, lit dew shimmers. (2008: xxi)[83]

Describing gǔ wén, Hinton explains that

> its grammatical elements are minimal in the extreme, allowing a
> remarkable openness and ambiguity that leaves a great deal unstated: prep-
> ositions and conjunctions are rarely used, leaving relationships between
> lines, phrases, ideas, and images unclear; the distinction between singular
> and plural is only rarely and indirectly made; there are no verb tenses, so
> temporal location and sequence are vague; very often the subject, verbs,
> and objects of verbal action are absent. (2008: xxi)

He continues, "in reading a Chinese poem, you mentally fill in all that emptiness, and yet it always remains emptiness" (2008: xxi). Rather than describing an assumed state of being, the line from Mèng Hàorán enacts an explicit
process of becoming in which the reader is causally involved. The space surrounding the four characters *ruò wáng ruò cún* similarly permits the blurred,
flickering complementarity of seemingly opposite realities, both in the phrase's
interpreted meaning and in the way in which the language in which it is written
operates. This flickering complementarity seems particularly useful in discussing the possible reality and the constructed nature of experiences of energy.

Religionism and Source Amnesia

Viewed in low resolution, such terms as Chinese qì or Sanskrit *prāṇa* encountered when practicing Chinese wǔshù and qìgōng or Indian haṭha yoga might
appear to share enough qualities that translating them all as "energy" seems
reasonable. In higher resolution, not only are such examples distinct, but the
term "energy" reveals itself to have pre-existing Euro-American meanings and
genealogies, descending from esoteric currents within Christian traditions
based in turn on interpretations of earlier Greek texts. Using "energy" as an
overall term can thus be described as a category error, akin to using the word
"red" where we mean to say "colour."

Such tendencies can be ascribed to religionism, a major mid-20th-century
view in Religious Studies described by Wouter Hanegraaf, which suggests

---

[83] The entire poem reads 不觉初秋夜渐长，清风习习重凄凉。炎炎暑退茅斋静，阶下丛莎
有露光。

Autumn begins unnoticed. Nights slowly lengthen,
and little by little, clear winds turn colder and colder,

summer's blaze giving way. My thatch hut grows still.
At the bottom stair, in bunchgrass, lit dew shimmers.

(trans. Hinton 2008: 149)

that low resolution similarities between different religious ideas reflect partial glimpses of a universal spiritual dimension:

> In the modern science of religion, the study of historical currents in search of an "inner" universal dimension is technically known as "religionism" … this agenda has strongly influenced the way in which religion has been studied after World War II, especially in the United States under the influence of Mircea Eliade and his school. (2013: 11)[84]

> [R]eligionism makes the mistake of ignoring religious diversity, historical change and any question of "external" influences because all it cares about is an experiential dimension that transcends history and will always remain inaccessible to scholarly research by definition. (2013: 61)[85]

Religionism assumes that different orthodoxies share the same ultimate referent, and in doing so presumes similarities that may not exist. The diverse experiences provided by orthopraxic religious expressions are seen as secondary to a presumed universal order that tacitly underlies them. Generalizations are not all inherently wrong, but religionism's *a priori* assumptions of universality have conditioned the conclusions of its scholarship, and consequently our common knowledge, in ways we are not always conscious of.

Olav Hammer borrows the term "source amnesia" from cognitive psychology to describe a key feature of new religions:

> In the case of religious bricolage, source amnesia typically takes place when a general term used in connection with an older tradition becomes associated with specific, modern reinterpretations. (2004: 180)

---

[84] Nile Green situates Eliade as a central religionist figure in the academic study of South Asian religions:
> Having their intellectual origins in theological notions of the universal, studies of Indian "mysticism" have generally failed to recognize the political dimensions to the physical and psychological acts of conditioning and control that comprise the full variety of Indian meditation systems. The most influential example is *Mircea Eliade, Yoga: Immortality and Freedom* (New York: Pantheon Books, 1958). Discussions of religion in South Asia have often failed to historicize these practices, in many cases assuming a simple continuity over long periods of time between, for example, Vedic references to Yoga and the famous Yoga practitioners of the colonial period and beyond. (Green 2008: 284–285)

[85] Through Eliade, academic religionism in the 20th century was influenced by the writings of an eclectic cluster of politically conservative amateur intellectuals. Authors René Guenon (1886–1951) and Frithjof Schuon (1907–1998) created the notion of Traditionalism, the belief that all extant and historical religions are partial remains of a universal and timeless revelation (Hanegraaf 2006: 1132). Eliade was an early adopter of Guenon's ideas, which were a decisive influence on his subsequent scholarship (Spineto 2001). Similar ideas about the universality of mystical insights in religion were expressed by the more politically progressive Aldous Huxley (1894–1963) whose *The Perennial Philosophy* (1945) was influenced by Vivekananda and Hindu Modernism, discussed below.

With time, a chain of transmission is built up, in which the latest spokes-persons may have a horizon in time that stretches no more than twenty or thirty years back, and in which anything older than this is considered to belong to a diffuse, ancient past. The question whether one's preferred doctrines are truly the result of an ancient tradition or were remade a few years ago by some creative religious entrepreneur becomes irrel-evant. The latest innovation and the ageless tradition are perceived to be essentially the same. (2004: 181)

Atemporal as they are, religionist presentations facilitate source amnesia by smoothing over the grafts made when concepts and practices are renovated, combined, or declared equivalent.

Poly-ontology, Multinatural Somatic Pluralism, and Somatic Mutability

While religionism has been largely superseded by later perspectives that treat religions as culturally relative discursive formations created by sociopolitical forces, its assumptions influenced 20th-century martial and theatre artists, and continue to inform Euro-American common knowledge. While clear theoreti-cal oppositions between the universal assumptions of religionism and the par-ticularism and relativism of later views appear in the abstract, they are even more complex in lived experience, as David Palmer points out:

It's possible to be engaging in a pragmatic ontology without knowing about an associated conceptual ontology, and it's possible to discourse on a conceptual ontology without engaging it in a pragmatic way. For exam-ple, to practice *taijiquan* is to transform one's body into an expression and experience of Chinese cosmology. However, it is not necessary to have any intellectual knowledge of this cosmology to do so. Conversely, Daoist cosmology is rooted in a specific experience of the body. Many people have intellectual knowledge of Daoist philosophy, without hav-ing ever practiced or experienced it in an embodied manner. (2021: 124)

Palmer characterizes these situations as poly-ontological: "The question of poly-ontological dynamics is to understand what happens when mul-tiple distinct ontologies interact and interpenetrate. Is there a logic to the interpenetration?" (2021: 125)[86]

---

[86] Palmer elaborates:

I refer to ontology in its general sense, which is a discourse on the nature and struc-ture of reality: What is reality, and what are the relationships between the basic com-ponents of reality? In this anthropological understanding of ontology, the Greek and Western discourse on the "nature of being" is only one of myriad discourses on what the world is made of, that exist in diverse cultures and religions. (2021: 124)

Simon Cox makes two bold suggestions about the consequences of poly-ontology. Cox is both a scholar and a Wǔdāng *Sānfēng Pài* initiate who lived in the Wǔdāng mountains from 2008–2013, where he studied under teacher Yuán Xiūgāng 袁修刚, becoming an ordained Daoist or *Dàoshi* 道士 with the formal lineage name of Kē Mào Zīqián 柯懋資乾. The curriculum he followed progressed through the numerous styles of wǔshù collected in the *Sānfēng Pài*, the traditional, low-risk partner games used to teach the application of both armed and unarmed movements, *Sǎndǎ* or contemporary Chinese kickboxing, various approaches to qìgōng, and *jìngzuò* or silent sitting mediation. These elements were presented as preliminary, then parallel training for the practice of nèidān, a meditative approach claimed to profoundly transform both adepts' physical bodies and the world that they perceive.

Cox's cultural environments can be seen as concentric rings of conceptual ontologies. Originally English-speaking, from the United States, he moved to China, eventually speaking, reading, and even dreaming in Chinese. Within China, however, he lived in a remote location, the space and time of which were organized in terms of the religious frameworks of one branch of contemporary Wǔdāng Daoism, distinct from both contemporary American and contemporary Chinese cultures. An accompanying pragmatic ontology was provided by demanding practices aimed at the enactment of cosmological and ontological visions of the *Sānfēng Pài*. These activities were intensive and durational: six years of training, 11 months a year, six days a week, six to 10 hours daily, which provided a deep immersion in the current manifestation of the dìyuán of Wǔdāng (Cox, online 3).

Cox explains that the combination of these practices and the environments in which he learned them demonstrated to him the possibility of "radical somatic mutability and multinatural somatic pluralism": our human embodiment can be profoundly changed, and with this change we can experience a completely different world from the one we lived in previously (2022: 215). More than reaching across a cultural divide, Cox speculates that his experiences and those of both his Chinese and non-Chinese classmates reveal a human potential to tune into other worlds, in this case using Daoist practice regimes tailored specifically for this capacity for transformation of the body in fundamental ways (Cox, online 3).

Rather than seeing all religious practices as glimpses of ultimate reality, somatic mutability proposes that intensive immersion in different pragmatic and conceptual ontologies reveals realities specific to those ontologies. Multinatural somatic pluralism suggests that these are distinct both from an individual's past experiences and from the experiences of pragmatic and conceptual ontologies revealed by practices of other cultural traditions. "Different cultural traditions give rise to different embodied beings," and the varieties of religious experience become gateways to different worlds, rather than different paths up a mountain that offers a single view from its peak (Cox 2021: 215).

The chimeras we shall examine below combine multiple conceptual and pragmatic ontologies. While they can be critiqued for religionism and for departing from the perceived purity of tradition, given a suitable intensity of practice, poly-ontology, multinatural somatic pluralism, and somatic mutability suggest that these chimeras might also disclose worlds, regardless of the genes and genealogies they combine. "Ruò wáng ruò cún, ruò cún ruò wáng" reminds us to tolerate the flickering we experience as we examine both misrepresentations and meaningful fruitions, and experiences presented as both spontaneously arising and constructed.

Sūn Lùtáng's Intracultural Chimeras

Sūn is remembered as an important 20th-century Chinese martial arts author and practitioner. Adept at Xíngyì Quán, he later created his own styles of Bāguà Zhǎng and Tàijí Quán. In the early 20th century, Sūn created a chimera by equating mastering the skills of Qing and Republic-era martial arts with the accomplishment of Daoist practice, recounting that he had experienced the Daoist phenomenon of *dān* 丹 as a result of practicing martial skills, or *jìn* 勁.

Sūn used three terms, *jìn* 勁, *qì* 氣, and *dān* 丹, to describe phases in a process of skill development, from the extroverted and martial, through the somatic and interoceptive, to the subtle and transpersonal. In chapter 8 of his 1924 book *Quányì Shùzhēn* 拳意述真, or *Boxing Concepts Explained*, Sūn describes his experience and equates it with the fruition of Daoist nèidān:[87]

> As I began the progression to "mysterious energy", after practicing the formal sequence [of Xíngyì Quán] I would finish with upright standing, trying to unify my spirit and energy. And every time I did that, I'd feel some slight subtle movement in my perineal area. At first it was barely perceptible. When doing my quiet standing after each day's practice, I'd sometimes feel it and sometimes not. But over time, the movement became stronger and more frequent, until it got to the point that as soon as I returned to standing at the conclusion of any formal drill, all I had

---

[87] Sūn is not alone in using Daoist terms in martial contexts in the early 20th century. The *Tàijí Quán Lùn* 太極拳論, or *Tàijí Quán* discourse, a text attributed to *Shānyòu Wáng Zōngyuè* 山右王宗岳 (*Wáng Zōngyuè* from *Shaanxi*) and likely composed in the later 19th century with the title added in the 20th, adopted the term *dāntián* from nèidān and earlier ritual sources to indicate the bodily and metaphorical centre from which Tàijí martial artists ought to move. It may have been inspired in this by *Yue Fei's Essential Requirements Treatise*, or *Yuè Wǔ Mùwáng Jiǔ Yào Lùn* 岳武穆王九要論, now associated with Xíngyì Quán, which is thought to have been written by Dài Lóng Bāng 戴龍邦 in the studio of Mǎ Xuélǐ 馬學禮 in 1750 (Szymanski in Jacobs 2023: xxiii). Wàn Lài Shēng 万籁声, author of the *Wǔshù Huìzǒng* 武術匯總 (1928), and Chén Xīn 陳鑫, author of the *Chén Shì Tàijíquán Huìzong* 陳氏太极拳匯總 (1935), are examples of the many Republic-era authors who used Daoist and Neo-Confucian cosmological terms to express the development of martial skill. Sūn's book stands out for his inclusion of a personal account his experiences. It was also a precedent for later accounts: Gù Rǔzhāng 顧汝章, for example, copied Sūn's text word for word, while prefacing it as a discussion of Tàijí Quán rather than Xíngyì Quán training (Gù 1936).

to do was concentrate for a moment, and I would feel a vectored energy discharge. I realized that this was the spontaneous energetic movement of the true yang-power, which is described in classical works on Taoist static meditation. (Meredith, online)[88]

This helpful translation was made by Scott Meredith, a Mandarin-speaking American Tàijí Quán teacher. It accurately relates Sūn's framing of his experiences in Daoist terms. Sūn explains how the training needed to acquire advanced forms of martial skill produced the sensations described in nèidān literature, which are associated with longevity, power, and spiritual insight.

In the first sentence of the excerpt, Sūn refers to practicing huà jìn 化勁, the skill of being able to change one's movements after they have begun. In the fifth sentence, he writes about feeling his qì 氣. In the final sentence, he equates his experience with writings about Daoist meditations, or dān shū 丹書.

The translator elects to render each of the three distinct terms–jìn, qì, and dān—as "energy." While such formulations as a "martial art movement skill, the proprioceptive sensations produced by breathing and the circulation of the blood" and the "transformational metaphor of Daoist practice" might be unwieldy, they provide vital information that the generic "energy" does not. The use of the English word energy for all these terms in a translation made in the 21st century is a significant choice that we will return to below.

Practically speaking, jìn is a skill, qì is a feeling, and dān is a metaphor—three different ideas that Sūn arranged in a developmental sequence, specific to his martial training.

Jìn

Prosaically, jìn means strength, but in the arts, it refers to the skill shown when demonstrating a particular quality of movement. In the Chinese martial arts, we find complimentary pairs of jìn. Fā jìn 发勁, the skill of emitting force, is understood in relationship to xù jìn 蓄勁, the skill of storing force. Duǎn jìn 短勁, or short jìn, is the skill of decelerating mass over a short distance, usually into the front foot. Zhǎng jìn 長勁, or long jìn, is the complementary skill of the accelerating mass over a longer trajectory, usually by pushing off the back foot.

Jìn can be literally descriptive—for example, dǒu jìn 抖勁 is a shivering, shaking quality, similar to the movement of a dog shaking water from its fur, while yōu jìn 悠勁 describes the quality of applying force by balancing the swinging movements of the arms. Jìn can also describe interactive situations more generally. Zhān nián jìn 粘黏勁 can mean literally sticking and following

---

[88] Sūn's original text, my emphasis: 余練**勁**所經者。每日練一形之式。到停式時。立正。心中神**氣**一定。每覺下部海底處。即陰蹻穴 處如有物萌動初不甚着意。每日練之有動之時。亦有不動之時。日久亦有動之甚久之時。亦有不動之時。漸漸至於停式。心中一定。 如欲泄漏者。想**丹**書坐功。

one's training partner's movements by maintaining uninterrupted physical contact, but also maintaining a constant, effective vigilance of them at a distance, proactively moving to limit their ability to initiate an attack. Similarly, *jué jìn* 覺勁, an awakened or conscious quality, is thought to allow one to proactively prevent an opponent's next move, seeing it before it occurs. Jìn can be unusually specific: *chòng jìn* 冲勁 describes the quality of relentlessly pursuing an adversary, which adepts should always demonstrate, even when practicing movements by themselves. *Hēi jìn* 黑勁 is the black-coloured or invisible movement skill of precisely dotting vital points on an opponent's body, causing them injury or even death with little obvious effort. There is even the skill of leading an opponent's movements without touching them, *líng kōng jìn* 靈空勁, spiritual, empty jìn or ethereal movement skill.

Jìn are not only found in the martial arts. The techniques of playing the Chinese seven-string zither, or *gǔqín* 古琴, include *dié jìn* 蝶勁, or "butterfly skill," which describes the movement of the hands when playing harmonics, or *fàn yīn* 泛音. *Shé jìn* 蛇勁 describes the snake-like movement of the hands when creating sliding ornamentations while playing stopped notes or *àn yīn* 按音.[89]

From the great variety of skills and movement qualities described, it should be clear that the meanings of jìn go well beyond such English definitions as strength, power, or energy.[90] In the martial arts, jìn are idiosyncratic, qualitative descriptions of style-specific skills rather than quantitative, univocal parameters like "power," which contemporary kinesiology defines and measures as strength over time.[91]

---

[89] Thanks to Simon Cox, who studied gǔqín under Daoist Mò Bái *lǎoshī* 墨白老师 in the Wǔdāng mountains of China, from 2008–2013 for this information.

[90] The character for jìn is relatively new, appearing only after the end of the Yuan dynasty (1368 CE.) It is composed of two logographs. The right side of a character typically indicates the meaning, while the left is a homonym of the pronunciation. The pronunciations referred to, however, are archaic, and spoken language varies widely geographically and has changed over time. Jìn is composed of *jīng* 巠, which refers to a manmade network of rivers and canals, on the left, and strength *lì* 力 on the right: 勁 = 巠 + 力. *Jīng* 巠 itself is made of *chuān* 巛, the character for rivers, and of the character for skill, or *gōng* 工, which depicts a Chinese carpenter's square, a tool of measurement used by the technically skilled. The line above the three horizontal chevrons of *chuān* indicates water flowing underground. It is very tempting to use all parts of the logograph for jìn in constructing its meaning: a powerful quality of movement as the result of skill which is not readily apparent as it flows invisibly below the surface. This might be illuminating, but it also may be simply a fortuitous coincidence of the logograph's history.

[91] Expert martial artist Christopher Bates describes the movements of Chinese martial arts as "exploring different ways of manifesting power into motion." He offers the example of Xíngyì Quán, which does this through five basic and 12 elaborated variations. Bates contrasts this approach with the Burmese martial art Bando, which he describes as using a single approach to generating power across multiple, divergent fighting strategies (Bates 2017: online). Manifesting power into motion is an elegant, accurate, and jargon-free way of explaining some of the nuances and skills of jìn.

Qì

Prosaically, qì means breath and air. It can refer to the phenomenology experienced by groups of trained specialists, as well as to a very wide range of common experiences. Qìgōng 氣功 players experience *qì gǎn* 氣感, "the sensations of qì," feelings of heat, weight, vibration, and mental expansiveness that accompany regular practice. *Wèi qì* 衛氣, or guardian qì, is the term used by doctors of Chinese medicine to refer to the body's ability to regulate the warmth and moisture of our skin, maintaining homeostasis and protecting us from illness. In daily speech, *tiānqì* 天氣 is weather, or sky qì; *diànqì* 電氣 is electrical energy; *xíqì* 習氣 is a habit or habitual qì; *yǎngqì* 氧氣 is oxygen, or nourishing qì; *àoqì* 傲氣 is arrogance, or proud qì; and so on. Finding a single English word, phrase, or concept that can encapsulate the multiple meanings assigned to even the single logograph 氣, let alone its contextual variants, is impossible: its usages cannot be summarized in a short paragraph. The many meanings of qì appear to have always been contingent on the context in which it was used, and it has been a contested term throughout Chinese history.

Michael Stanley-Baker's essay "Qì 氣: A Means for Cohering Natural Knowledge," chapter 2 of *The Routledge Handbook of Chinese Medicine* (2022), offers a thorough introduction.[92] In it, he describes the qì referred to in contemporary and historical Chinese somatic practices as "qi as a medium for self-cultivation" (2022: 27).[93] Perhaps the earliest extant example of qì used in this way is a text carved into a 12-sided ornamental jade block named the Xíngqì Míng 行氣銘, which dates from approximately 380 BCE:

> To circulate the breath (*xing qi*), breathe deeply so there is great volume. When the volume is great, the breath will expand. When it expands, it will move downwards. When it has reached the lower level, fix it in place. When it is in place, hold it steady. Once it is steady, it will become like a sprouting plant. Once it sprouts, it will grow. As it grows, it will retrace its path. When retracing its path, it will reach the Heaven area. The Heaven impulse forces its way downward. Whoever acts accordingly will live, whoever acts contrariwise will die. (Stanley-Baker 2022: 27)

Stanley-Baker points out that debates about whether qì was like a resource to be amassed or a natural process to become aware of were already taking place at the time of the composition of the *Zhuāngzi*, which in chapter 6 praised sages who can "breathe with their heels," yet in chapter 15 mocked the huffing and puffing of those practicing longevity exercises that imitated the movements of animals (2022: 28; trans. Ziporyn 2020: 54, 128).

---

[92] An open access publication: https://www.taylorfrancis.com/books/oa-edit/10.4324/97802037 40262/routledge-handbook-chinese-medicine-vivienne-lo-michael-stanley-baker-dolly-yang

[93] Thanks to Henry McCann, DAOM, LAc (Mǎ'ěr Bó, *Zhōngyī Bóshì* 馬爾博, 中醫博士), for this helpful suggestion.

The qì cultivation instructions of the Xíngqì Míng and the contemporaneous examples of the *Zhuāngzǐ* seem comprehensible to us today, congruent with some of the uses of the term qì in contemporary practices from China. Is this possible continuity an optimistic projection, or an indication that our experience of the phenomenology of our human embodiment is widely consistent? Both arguments could likely be made.

Dān

Dān 丹 indicates the colour red, and cinnabar or red mercury sulphide, which, while considered toxic today, was valued as both a pigment and a medicine in many periods of Chinese history beginning in ancient times, when it was used "to color the bones of the dead, as a means of ensuring them an eternal afterlife" (White 1996: 194). In esoteric institutional religions such as Daoism, *wàidān* 外丹, or dān from outside, is a metaphor for the practice of consuming an elixir prepared from rare and unusual substances in the pursuit of longevity and power. *Nèidān* 內丹, dān from within, an endogenous elixir created using meditation and physical culture, is claimed to produce not only longevity and power, but also insight.

Fabrizio Pregadio describes both wàidān and nèidān as "alchemy," a choice that is descriptive of the objectives, methods, and imagery of these systems, but also suggests equivalence with important currents in European esotericism. Because this chapter investigates the replacement of ideas from Asian traditions with a term drawn from European esoteric lore, I shall use the word alchemy parsimoniously to avoid confusion. Pregadio explains that nèidān

> aims to produce the elixir within the alchemist's person according to two main models of doctrine and practice: first, by causing the primary components of the cosmos and the human being to revert to their original condition; and second, by purifying the mind from defilements and passions in order to "see one's Nature." (2019: 2)

Nèidān writings refer to results of this process of reversion as jīndān, or the golden elixir, emphasizing the value of this endogenous electuary (see chapter 1.) The contents of nèidān texts are spread along a spectrum between "on the one hand, teachings on the Dao and, on the other, descriptions of physiological practices" (Pregadio 2019: 3).

Nèidān texts are also spread out over a long history, from their first complete expressions in the fourth-century *Shàng Qīng* 上清 Daoist scriptures to early 20th-century *Xiān Xué* 仙學, a modernist approach to nèidān developed to be practiced independently of Daoist initiation by contemporary reformer Chén Yīngníng 陳攖寧 (1880–1969).[94]

---

[94] A very lean list of influential *nèidān* texts by period could include:

From outside of the conceptual ontologies that provide the cultural frameworks of nèidān, its two principal ultimate aims might seem ineffable and unusual. The first, union with the Dào, is an objective that resists direct description
in unequivocal language. The second, present across a wide range of approaches,
is to use the cultivated medicine in the creation, nourishment, and training of a
spiritual embryo, or *shén tāi* 神胎, which can eventually depart from the adept's
body in order to explore different realities, as a means of assisting in the realization the Dào. Out of context, such goals might seem strange, but as nèidān
is understood as a process, some idea of how initiates have conceived of its
fruition is helpful to the discussions that follow.

From Jin to Dān

In proposing that dān could be produced by practicing the jìn of martial arts,
Sūn reversed centuries of lore, much of it humorously hyperbolic. Folk tales,
plays, and popular literature depicted adepts of nèidān as capable of astonish-
ing and funny feats not because they practiced wǔshù, but because they were
infused with powers that accompanied the actualization of dān. In a comic
episode in chapter 57 of the 1597 play *Sānbǎo Tàijiàn Xīyángjì* 三寶太監西
洋記, Zhāng Sān Fēng, a Daoist figure associated with nèidān since at least
1391 CE, defeats 24 imperial guards who disturb his sleep, fighting them in
a drunken stupor (Phillips 2019a: 42–46).[95] By the time he appears in *Huáng*

Jin Dynasty (265–420 CE)
- *Huángtíng Jīng* 黃庭經, 281 CE, attributed to Lady Wèi Huácún 魏華存 (252–334 CE).
  - The first nèidān practice manual, whose author claimed she had received it in a trance.
- *Bàopǔzi*, 抱樸子, by Gé Hóng 葛洪 (published 317–318 CE, revised 326–334 CE).
  - Contains legitimizing references to the *Huángtíng Jīng* 黃庭經 as a source of nèidān practice.

Tang Dynasty (618–907 CE)
- *Zhōuyì Cāntóng Qì* 周易參同契, attributed to Wèi Bóyáng 魏伯陽 (n.d.).
  - The earliest elements in this book date to 250 CE but the nèidān texts are likely not before 800 CE.

Song Dynasty (960–1279 CE)
- *Wùzhēn Piān* 悟真篇 (dated to 1075 CE) attributed to Zhāng Bóduān 張伯端 (approx. 987–1082 CE)

Ming Dynasty (1368–1644 CE)
- *Xìngmìng Guīzhǐ* 性命圭旨 (author unknown, published 1615 CE)

Qing Dynasty (1644–1912)
- *Wèishēng Shēnglǐ Xué Míng Zhǐ* 衛生生理學明指 by Zhào Bìchén 趙避塵 (1860–1942).
  - Known to Anglo-American readers due to its partial translation into English by Lu K'uan Yü (Charles Luk) in 1970 as *Taoist Yoga: Alchemy and Immortality*.

Post-Imperial Period (after 1912)
- *Zhōnghuá Xiān Xué* 中華仙學 (published in 1962) by Chén Yīngníng 陳攖寧 (1880–1969)
- *Wǔdāng Tàijí Quán* 武当太极拳 (published in 2014) by Zhōng, Yúnlóng 钟云龙 (b. 1962)

[95] Zhāng's biographical note in the *History of Ming*, or *Míngshǐ* 明史 (completed in 1739),
describes him as an eccentric but accomplished adept of nèidān, recording that he was summoned to court by the first Ming emperor in 1391 CE. Zhāng Sān Fēng appears in several periods, as noted in chapter 3, and he also been linked to the late 19th / early 20th-century martial
art of tàijí quán in multiple, contested ways. Early associations of a Daoist named Zhāng Sān
Fēng with martial training include ones found in the *Dàyì Xiànzhì* 大邑縣志, or Dayi Country

Zōngxī's 黃宗羲 (1610–1695) more dignified *Epitaph for Wáng Zhēngnán* 王征南墓志 in 1669, Zhāng's martial mastery has so developed that he vanquishes over 100 bandits in a single fight (Wile 1999: 53). Martial jìn has long been seen as a possible by-product of dān. The preparatory processes that students follow to prepare for the actual practice of *nèidān* have also informed the conceptual ontologies of martial arts practice (see chapter 1.) Sūn's account of jìn producing dān is, however, new and departs significantly from the methods and assumptions of other 20th-century approaches to nèidān.

The tradition of the *Wǔdāng Dàojiào Sānfēng Pài* requires its students to practice silent sitting, or jìngzuò 靜坐, so as to be able to remain comfortably in meditation for four hours continuously, before they begin to feel and manipulate the sensations of *yào* 运, the medicine whose appearance precedes the creation of the elixir or dān.[96] Comfortable quiet sitting for four hours is considered to produce an extremity of stillness. As sitting for long periods of time is very demanding, intense martial training that strengthens the lower back and develops both the explosive strength and the flexibility of the legs is done in tandem with jìngzuò, which is practiced for a full hour every day for three years before the student's capacity to sit for four hours is checked.[97]

In the *Sānfēng Pài*, the first step when the four-hour mark has been achieved involves the student lying down on their back and paying attention to the many sensations occurring just below the surface of their skin, between the tip of the tailbone and a point on the back between the vertebrae opposite the navel. As the sensations become stable and identifiable according to the metaphors used in this tradition, the student can bring their attention to spots higher up their back, gradually completing a circle that loops up the back and down the front of their bodies. The strange sensation of a thick vapour or liquid flowing within the body associated with this circle is a first glimpse of the medicine, and its circulation is called the *yùn yào* 药运, or the "transportation of the medicine."

This circle is also called the *xiǎo zhōu tiān* 小周天, or the "small circuit across the sky," a term used in many traditions of nèidān.[98] The process of moving the felt sensation of yào between the tailbone to points on the back to dredge a

---

Chronicle, toward the end of the Yuan dynasty, where he is remembered for his horseback riding and his archery (Estrella Sanchez 2011: 7 & Wong 2010: 28–37).

[96] Thanks to Simon Cox, *yì shī yì yǒu* 亦師亦友, my teacher and friend. A clear and practical summary of this practice is found in the chapter on Daoist inner alchemy, *Dàojiā Nèi Dān Gōng* 道家內丹功, in Zhōng Yúnlóng's *Wǔdāng Tàijí Quán* 钟云龙。武当太极拳 (2014).

[97] Cox suggests that such sitting must always be comfortable. Beginners are encouraged to use blankets and pillows to create support and to extend and rub their legs if numbness arises, continuing to practice in a more comfortable position until feeling returns to their limbs. Robert Coons, reporting on another Quánzhēn tradition of nèidān, also emphasizes the importance of beginning in comfort (2015: 21).

[98] *Tiān*, or sky, usually rendered as heaven, refers here to the medicine passing over the top of the head, the way the stars wheel overhead across the night sky. The circuit is small, as it only passes up and down the front and back of the body. In a later phase, the large, or *dà zhōu tiān* 大周天, the circuit passes over the head and includes channels created in the arms and legs.

channel through which the medicine is to move is referred to as the implementation of *huǒ hòu*, or "fire timing"火候 (literally *fire waiting*), which describes the segments of the circular path through which the medicine passes.

The sensation of circulation felt after four hours of stillness has been achieved and the pathway established through basic fire timing is called the *shuǐ zhōu tiān* 水週天, or water circuit. In the *Sānfēng Pài*, it is firmly distinguished from the sensations of the *huǒ zhōu tiān* 火週天, or fire circuit, that often accompanies the cún xiǎng of contemporary qìgōng. The fire circuit is not considered a major attainment. While it follows the same path up the back and down the front of the body, it is comparatively easy to create and feel. In many qìgōng and martial practices that use the fire circuit, qì is imagined rising along the back as the arms are raised, passing over the head, and continuing down the front of the body as they are lowered.

Nèidān in the *Sānfēng Pài* works first on what is called the *mìng* 命, or real body, before working on the imaginal body, or *xìng* 性. In this approach, the student must regulate the mìng by becoming quiet and still before the metaphors of the xìng can be acted upon. It relies mostly on sensation, and uses very little visualization.

Considerable austerity accompanies nèidān in this tradition. Adepts retreat from civilization, living in remote shelters and isolated caves, fasting in silence.[99] An orthodox practitioner might be surprised by Sūn's claims, wondering how an urban-dwelling householder with a family and martial-arts students, whose kinship ties include regular social functions that likely involve eating meat and drinking alcohol, could possibly experience the stillness and quiet considered necessary to create dān. Sūn's experiences might very well be attributed to the easily felt sensations of the fire circuit by an orthodox representative of the *Sānfēng Pài*.

There are, however, less-severe practices that might more closely resemble Sūn's account. In Zhìnéng Qìgōng 智慧氣功, a contemporary reformulation of the clan tradition of nèidān of the Liú 劉 family of Tianjin, Hebei, the cultivation of mìng and xìng are combined. Students experience this combination as using their imaginations to amplify the various sensations created by their practice, which is done in a standing position. It is comprised of a very long sequence of complex small movements, which also has a quietening effect on the student's body and thoughts (Mroz 2011: 78–80).

While moving slowly or holding still positions students project their attention both out into a visualized cosmos and along precisely described channels in the limbs and torso, returning regularly to the three principal locations where medicine is accumulated. These places—the *shàng, zhōng,* and *xià dāntián* 上, 中 and 下丹田—or the upper, middle, and lower "fields of the elixir" are linked

---

[99] Nida Chenagtsang characterizes similarly demanding practices in the Tibetan tradition as "professional yogas, ones that cannot be taught to the general public because of the intensive trainings they require" (2020: 3).

by the *zhōng mài* 中脈, a channel that passes vertically through the centre of the body, running from the pelvic floor to the top of the head. The locations and dimensions of the dāntián that students are to imagine, as well as the sensations associated with them, are transmitted orally by their teacher. As it does not involve extended sitting, Liú family Zhìnéng Qìgōng seems more immediately accessible. It also does not assume the intense martial preparation that the *Sānfēng Pài* nèidān does. It does, however, include squatting and stretching exercises to develop the lower back and legs of students who lack previous martial training. Foundational practice of Zhìnéng Qìgōng also demands at least an hour a day for three years after the entire sequence of movements has been learned before the initiate is introduced to the later practices of condensation and circulation.

Historical Attributes

While the way Sūn related nèidān to martial practice is novel, the link between martial movement training and the expression of wondrous powers is not. The pragmatic and conceptual ontologies of wǔshù have existed for millennia, combining martial ingenuity or qiǎo, upright and filial conduct or *xiào*, and wūshù, or sorcery.

The qiǎo of the Chinese martial arts goes back to the *Zhuāngzi*. In chapter 30, the sage describes his swordplay:

> Zhuāngzǐ said, "This is a swordplay that displays false appearances to the opponent, leading him on with the lure of gain, thrusting forth only after he does, but preceding him in landing the blow." (trans. Ziporyn 2020: 251)[100]

The xiào of wǔshù hearkens back to the wandering *xiá* 俠, the Chinese martial heroes today associated with theatre, literature, and cinema. Stephen Teo reminds us that:

> Sima Qian's *Shi Ji* (Records of History), written between 104–91 BCE during the reign of Han Wudi (the Martial Emperor) contains two chapters, "Biographies of Knights-Errant" ("Youxia liezhuan"), and "Biographies of the Assassins" ("Cike liezhuan"), which are usually cited as the historical records of remarkable personalities broadly described

---

[100] The language of the Zhuāngzǐ is so flexible that Ziporyn can offer an alternate interpretation that even more fully articulates a Daoist conceptual ontology:

莊子曰：夫為劍者，示之以虛，開之以利，後之以發，先之以至。

Zhuāngzǐ said, "What wields this sword unsheathes empty and open, but grinds keen and sharp; follows in starting out but precedes in arriving" (2020: 251).

as xia and their feats of chivalry and loyalty in the Warring States and Qin periods (2009: 17).

In the preamble to "Biographies of Knights-Errant," Sima Qian identified righteousness (yi), trust (xin), meritorious service (gong), tidiness (jie), and tolerance (rang), as the ethical principles guiding the behaviour of xia (2009: 18).

The xiá are remembered as common, working people whose martial calling led them to adopt Confucian virtues of "chivalry, altruism, benevolence and justice for the common good" (2009: 18).

The non-ordinary martial methods of the wū are likewise ancient. Powers derived from war magic (see chapter 3) have used martial movement since at least the Song dynasty. Marcia Butler notes how adepts incorporated complex rituals into their own bodies. Recorded in the *Wǔjīng Zǒngyào* 武經總要 (1044 CE), a Song dynasty manual of war magic, the Three Cosmographies, or *Sānshì* 三式, claimed to offer adepts the amazing ability to travel in space and time, taking their troops along with them. Butler refers to contemporary cinema to summarize the gnomic languages of Song dynasty military magic texts:

> In modern times, the "Three Cosmographies" have become popularized in Hong Kong martial arts movies—in which the hero draws a circle on the ground, scribes a writ in the air, "paces the void" and then disappears by climbing through a rip in space-time. (2007: 155)[101]

The theory of these rituals correlated such cosmographic representations of space as the *Luòshū* (see chapter 1, 2, and 3) with the particularities of the Chinese calendar, which measured time by coordinating two different cycles, the 10 *tiāngàn* 天幹, or celestial stems, and the 12 *dìzhī* 地支, or earthly branches:

> These cosmograph techniques exploit the rather odd phenomenon of a time-tracking system that employs ten Heavenly stems crossed with twelve Earthly branches yet produces only a sixty-year, rather than one hundred and twenty-year, cycle. This meant that there were unused stems and branches at certain systemic intersections. By using cyclically impossible stem/branch combinations, metaphysical correspondences, and universal forces in conjunction with ritual performance, doors between series of nested universes opened at certain "time" locations. (Butler 2007: 175)

---

[101] The Three Cosmographies are the Six Water Cycles: *Liùrén* 六壬; the Supreme One *Tài Yǐ* 太乙; and the Hidden Period *Dùnjiǎ* 遁甲 (2007: 155). Butler suggests that the Hidden Period cosmography might be traceable to the earliest nèidān practices from the Six Dynasties (220–589 CE) transformed and instrumentalized (2007: 202).

A magical operation from the *Wǔjīng Zǒngyào* that Butler translates as "The Jade Maiden reverses and closes the potential circumstance" contains both mathematical, written ritual preparations to magically reunite separated wings of an army, and physically enacted methods to beat a hasty exit. In the first example:

> This method relies on using tallies and enacting the scheme for finding the Heaven Gate and the Earth Door where the Jade Maiden is located. The head commander enters through the Earth Door and comes out the Heaven Gate; by obtaining the Jade Maiden's assistance, this will unite the army so that the enemy will be defeated. There will be nothing that will not bring certain victory. (trans. in Butler 2007: 185)

While in the second:

> If the strength of the troops is flagging and it is desirable to retreat, call out praying to the Jade Maiden and go out the Earth Door. Holding a knife in the left hand, draw backhanded [on the ground] cutting through the Earth arteries; this will close the Earth Door. Still with the left hand, take hold of an inch of grass; shielding one's middle half [with it], without turning back to look, go out [the gate]. Neither human nor demon will be able to perceive or follow [your path]. (trans. in Butler 2007: 201)

Butler comments that "there is a tension between the magical authority of writing and the efficacy of the performance through gestures, incantation, and the manipulation of (magical) objects" (2007: 201).

Through both diffusion and reinvention, the writing of spells and talismans and the performance of magic martial movement became attributes of the Chinese martial arts early on, and such practices were well-established by the late 18th century. In her history of Eight Trigrams Uprising, an 1813 rebellion by a heterodox jiào in Zhili, Hebei, and Shandong provinces, Susan Naquin notes the martial art and war magic of an adept named Liú Yùlóng 劉玉隆:

> In 1803 Liu learned the Chin-chung-chao (Armor of the Golden Bell) technique of fighting from a chance acquaintance (they met in a teashop at a fair in Shantung). A few years later Liu borrowed a book containing the various talismen and chants of the Golden Bell system, which he studied and used to cure illnesses. (1976: 320)

Meeting the head of a martial jiào in 1908 in Baoding city in Hebei province, and becoming his disciple,

> Liu's new teacher had taught him the Jung-hua Assembly's system of yogic meditation, and combining these techniques with his skills in various

forms of fighting and his ability to make charms that could cure illness, Liu Yü-lung began to make a reputation for himself. He combined the martial with the meditational aspects of the White Lotus tradition and, returning to central Chihli, began to take disciples. (1976: 320)

The attributes of ingenious fighting skill, altruism, and esoteric knowledge have been associated with Chinese martial arts and those who practice them for millennia.

Sūn's Contributions

With the jìn-to-dān process Sūn described in his account, he appears to have added a fruition of nèidān—feeling the spontaneous movement of *dān* in his body—to the conceptual ontologies of Chinese martial arts practice. In chapters 1 and 2, I suggested alchemical transformation as the key metaphor that structured the curricula, pedagogy, and phenomenology of the Chinese martial arts. Earlier syntheses had already combined ingenious combat skill, moral rectitude, and war magic. As *jìndān* spread in the early centuries of the common era, the Chinese martial arts adopted its process as a structural inspiration for martial training, and fostered lore associating its adepts with martial feats. Sūn went beyond this in equating his personal martial arts experiences with the actualization of dān. Even if we imagine that his jìn-to-dān process is an ingenious fǎn, or reversal, like the ones that already constitute much of nèidān training, his idea remains novel. His actual practices, the original curricula of Bāguà Zhǎng and Tàijí Quán that he developed, added new pragmatic ontologies proposing variations of the Chinese martial arts whose practice could lead to the experience of nèidān.[102]

While the Chinese martial arts have included Daoist cosmological references and stories of magical powers for millennia, Sūn's novel association of a particular Daoist practice with a distinct history with the training of jìn in Xíngyì Quán, Bāguà Zhǎng, and Tàijí Quán has largely been folded into 20th-century common knowledge, creating source amnesia and the impression these martial arts were originally developed to produce the specific outcome of nèidān. This common knowledge view has been spread by the diffusion of the Chinese martial arts worldwide and their translation and articulation in mid-century

---

[102] The phenomenon I describe as spatial projection in chapters 1 and 2 bears some resemblance to Sūn's experiences, beginning as it does with martial training and producing a pragmatic ontology which I have understood and expressed in terms of a Daoist conceptual ontology. None of the martial practices I've been introduced to personally descend from the ones developed by Sūn, and I speculate that the phenomenology of spatial projection might derive from the altered spatiotemporal perceptions that are the heritage of war magic in today's Chinese martial arts. Nevertheless, I cannot escape feelings of "ruò wáng ruò cún" when I consider the similarities between Sūn's account and my own.

Euro-American religionist terms by both Western and Chinese authors using Euro-American frameworks to express themselves.

Scott Meredith's translation of Sūn's chapter 8, above, demonstrates the Euro-American use of energy to translate the distinct terms of jìn, qì, and dān. More recent popular translations by Paul Brennan and Chen Faxing also use the word "energy" to denote jìn, qì, and dān in the same exact places (2013: online; 2023: 604, Kindle location 7338). Where does this use of the word "energy" come from? It comes from Europe and America.[103]

Euro-American Esoteric "Energy"

20th-century Euro-American esoteric energy can be traced back to the "magnetic fluid" posited by Frans Mesmer in the late 1700s (1779: 6). All living things contained and were suspended in this invisible substance, and those adepts who could manipulate it claimed to produce extraordinary effects, namely the healing of others. Mesmer hoped his idea would join the ranks of such successful philosophical and scientific theories as Descartes' substance dualism (1641) and Newton's gravity (1687), both of which combined Christian theology with the study of the physical world. Mesmer's ideas can be seen to harken back to Aristotle's original use of the term *energy* in his 350 BCE *On the Soul* or *Peri Psychēs*, where he examined the movement of the breath, or *pneuma*, in people and animals. Mesmer's iteration departed from observation, creating not only a theory but also a therapeutic intervention that directly manipulated energy. Despite the great initial popularity of his healing methods, Mesmer's ideas did not receive institutional acceptance, but though they died out in early scientific circles, they remained of interest to more marginal and esoteric thinkers.

Among them was French occultist Éliphas Lévi (Alphonse Louis Constant, 1810–1875), who recast Mesmer's magnetic fluid as the "astral light," a subtle,

---

[103] Euro-American scientific concepts were translated into Chinese in the late 19th century and subsequently adopted into 20th century Chinese-language nèidān texts outside of the context of martial arts, in a separate genealogy from Sun's writings.

Late Qing imperial officials sponsored the translation of technical and scientific literature from Europe and America: *British sinologist John Fryer (1839–1928) moved to China in 1861, became head translator of the Jiangnan armory, founded Shanghai Polytechnic and inaugurated China's first scientific journal Gezhi Huibian 格致汇编 in 1876. It was through Fryer's works in introducing electromagnetism and thermodynamics to China that western ideas such as energy* 能量 *and fields* 场 *arrive in translation* (Cox, 2024: 13).

For example, Chén Yīngníng's *Zhōnghuá Xiān Xué*, mentioned in note 94, incorporated scientific ontology, describing *qi as a continuum of ether (以太), neutrons (中子), electrons (dianzi 电子) atoms (原子), molecules (分子), cells (细胞), body (肉体), and semen and blood (精血)* (Cox, 2024: 13). Chén's *Xiān Xué* was a new approach to nèidān that aimed to create practice groups made up of edcuated urban householders, perhaps inspired by the *huǒjū* 火居, 'fire-dwelling' Daoists of old who married, had children and lived among the people they served, distinct from the later *yǐnjū* 隱居, celibate recluses inspired by Buddhist monasticism. It seems likely that the *Dàodéxuéshé* described by Jung's protégée Erwin Rousselle and discussed below, was a part of Chén's project.

non-ordinary substance permeating the cosmos. He combined Mesmer's more materialist idea with his personal, idiosyncratic, Christian Cabalist and Catholic interpretation of the much older *Corpus Hermeticum*. Assembled by Marsilio Ficino (1433–1499) and Ludovico Lazzarelli (1447–1500) in the 15th century, the *Corpus* is comprised of medieval Byzantine versions of allegedly pre-Christian Greek texts originally dating from 100 to 300 CE.[104]

The 17 texts included in Ficino and Lazzarelli's Latin translation transmit some of the teachings of the pre-Christian, Greco-Egyptian deity Hermes Trismegistus in dialogue form. The cosmology presented in the *Corpus* articulated normally hidden correspondences, and its conceptual ontology described occult relationships that occur at the most fundamental levels of reality, direct links in a great chain of being. The correlations presented were morphological. In such a view, for example, the black bile humour of my body and the planet Saturn are directly connected by substantial resonances—distance and scale are no obstacle to this bond. The zeitgeist of the 1700s, decisively influenced by Descartes' differentiation of mental and physical substances, made this kind of direct relationship seem naive, and materialist metaphysics demanded the creation of such proposals as Newton's gravity, Mesmer's magnetic fluid, or Lévi's astral light.[105]

Lévi was a key figure in the development of modern esoteric thought. His *Dogme et rituel de la haute magie*, published in two volumes in 1855–1856, sought to rehabilitate magic as a lost science, comparing pagan and Christian ontologies. His astral light maintained the planetary influences suggested in the *Corpus Hermeticum*, while adding a more modern, substance-dependant explanation for their effect (Josephson-Storm 2017: 104).

Lévi's framing of esotericism as a lost science influenced Ukrainian medium Helena Blavatsky (1831–1891), who, along with her American associates, founded the Theosophical Society in New York City in 1875. Blavatsky's 1877 book *Isis Unveiled: A Master-Key to the Mysteries of Ancient and Modern Science and Theology* proposed a sprawling correlation of esoteric ideas, presenting both European and Asian examples. Blavatsky claimed to have visited Tibet, where she studied with adepts from whom she received her unique formulations of Eastern religious concepts. Blavatsky associated her invented Asian cosmology with Mesmerism in the late 1800s, giving it an evolutionary teleology (Baier 2012). From the 17th century to the late 19th centuries, these ideas

---

[104] Ficino referred to a *prisca theologia*—ancient theology—a very early instance of what would eventually be claimed by perennialism, traditionalism, and implied by academic religionist thinkers: the existence of an original theology that underpins all religions, given to humans by a single, supreme deity. Further back, this idea finds some precedent in the *interpretatio graeca*, the tendency of the ancient Greeks to create correspondences between their own gods and those of the peoples they encountered—of Zeus with the South Asian Indra or Hermes with the Egyptian Thoth, for example.

[105] In the 1600s it became apparent that the *Corpus* dated from the second to third centuries CE and did not present any pre-Christian teachings, shaking confidence in its claims (Yates 1964: 2).

moved from being obscure esoteric interests to popular (if alternative) ideas. Mesmer, Lévi, and Blavatsky represent important nodes in the network that distributed them.

In the early 20th century, Western esoteric ideas were given further legitimacy by Carl Jung (1875–1961), who interpreted European alchemy as an expression of the human psyche and its energies (1932; 1956). Jung also used Asian ideas to fuel his speculations, interpreting Chinese nèidān and Indian tantra as models of psychological transformation.[106]

Jung commented extensively on Richard Wilhelm's *The Secret of the Golden Flower*, a Christianized translation of the *Tàiyǐ Jīnhuá Zōngzhǐ* 太乙金華宗旨, a 17th-century Daoist nèidān manual. The *Tàiyǐ Jīnhuá Zōngzhǐ* was produced in two versions by two different groups of devotees of the Daoist immortal Lǚ Dòngbīn 呂洞賓 through spirit writings channeled by mediums, in 1688 and 1692.[107] Jung's transformation of the *Tàiyǐ Jīnhuá Zōngzhǐ* is exemplified by his commentary on the phrase Wilhelm translates as "turning in a circle about oneself." This refers to adepts' circulation of the *yào*, or medicine, they have created, but for Jung it is a psychological process, in which practitioners direct their own conscious faculties of observation inward toward their psyches, integrating their lighter and darker natures (in Wilhelm 1931: 101).

Jung continued his imaginative adaptations of Asian ideas using John Woodroffe's translation of Pūrṇānanda Yati's *Ṣhaṭ-cakra-nirūpaṇa*, the explanation of the six cakras, co-authored with Atal Bihari Ghose under the shared pen name of Arthur Avalon (Taylor 2001: 149). This English-language account of a chapter from a 16th-century North Indian Tantric text was the pretext for Jung to present his own proposals in the lectures transcribed in his 1932 *Psychology of Kundalini Yoga*.[108]

Jung used Woodroffe and Ghose's text to create a psychological metaphor where primal impulses found in the lower body evolved toward more subtle and sophisticated ones located in the head. The evolution of the human species was recapitulated in the psychic and physical structure of a single person. Somatic equivalencies–appetites in the belly and pelvis, feelings in the heart, reason in the head–represented evolutionary progression (Leland 2016:

---

[106] Jung also commented on W. Y. Evans-Wentz's *Tibetan Book of the Great Liberation* (1954), which reconfigured the *Rig-pa ngo-sprod gcer-mthong rang-grol*, a Tibetan text describing *Dzogchen* meditation attributed to the eighth-century Himalayan Buddhist culture hero Padmasambhava but revealed centuries later. Jung correlated Evans-Wentz's Theosophical, neo-*Advaita*-influenced creation of a "Cosmic All-Consciousness," an idea not found in the Tibetan original, with his own psychological models (Evans-Wentz 1954/2000; Reynolds 1989: 109–115).

[107] Later translator Thomas Cleary described Wilhelm's work as a "garbled translation of a truncated version of a corrupted recension of the original work" (1993: 5).

[108] Blavatsky's ideas were popularized by her many students. Charles Leadbeater's text *The Chakras* (1927) preceded by his earlier essay on the same topic *The Inner Life* (1910) was particularly influential on 20th century energy. The similarities between Jung's *The Psychology of Kundalini Yoga* (1932), and Leadbeater's ideas are striking, although Jung never mentions him directly.

300–301). In constructing his metaphors, Jung naturalized the ideas in the *Tàiyǐ Jīnhuá Zōngzhǐ* and the *Ṣhaṭ-cakra-nirūpaṇa* and assumed that they referred to generally present features of human embodiment and development, rather than to imaginal constructions only experienced by initiates.

The popular and scholarly networks that followed Blavatsky and Jung diffused these ideas widely, successfully, and anonymously.[109] The resulting complex is a principal source of Euro-American common knowledge of East- and South Asian religious practices today, characterized by source amnesia about

---

[109] Some of them even became sources for 20th century Asian thinkers. Early 20th century Theosophical and Jungian accounts of Chinese *nèidān* and Japanese archery or *Kyūdō* 弓道 were decisive in the writings of Japanese philosopher Yuasa Yasuo 湯浅 泰雄 (1925–2005). In a chapter devoted to *Ki and the Body in the Martial Arts and Meditation Methods* (1993: 69–98), Yuasa develops ideas found in Eugene Herrigel's (1884–1955) *Zen in the Art of Archery* (1948) and Erwin Rousselle's (1890–1949) account *Spiritual Guidance in Contemporary Taoism* (1934).

Herrigel's influential book was an account of his studies with the eccentric adept Awa Kenzō 阿波研造 (1880–1939) sometime between 1924 and 1929. Japanese historians do not remember Awa as a Zen initiate, and his presentation of traditional archery was unique: *When one considers the disparity between actual kyðdō and the description of Japanese archery that Herrigel presented, however, it is impossible to uncritically accept his book as a reliable account* (Yamada, 2001: 3). Herrigel appears to have derived his ideas about Zen from the mid-century scholar of Buddhist literature D.T. Suzuki 鈴木大拙 貞太郎 (1870–1966) (2001: 13). Suzuki's account of Zen was personal, idiosyncratic and oddly Euro-American: *...Suzuki takes Zen literature out of its social, ritual, and ethical contexts and reframes it in terms of a language of metaphysics derived from German Romantic idealism, English romanticism, and American transcendentalism* (McMahan, 2008: 135). Suzuki and his American wife joined the Theosophical society in 1920 and opened their own branch, Mahayana Lodge, in Kyoto in 1924. Suzuki's response to Blavatsky's fabulations was magnanimous and he folded her inventions into his own charismatic presentations.

Rousselle, advised by Jung and Wilhelm, travelled to Beijing in the late 1920s, where he had the good fortune to attend a group practice of the *Dàodéxuéshé* 道德學社, the Society for the Study of the Virtue of the Dao. An English translation of Rousselle's account was published in 1954 in the Jungian Eranos Yearbook. Rousselle described his ritual of admission into this Daoist studies society and sketched a practice which resembles *nèidān*. His presentation was Jungian, Christian, and European: He equated Daoist *xiūshēn* 修身 or embodied training and practice with the process of *individuation*, an unrelated Jungian term (1954: 84). He explained that his Daoist preceptors had admonished him to *walk in the paths of Christ, understood in a very profound and ultimate sense* (1954: 90). He described his "Daoist initiation" using Greek terms for effect: *As in Eleusis, all mystery cults are transmitted through sacred actions (dromena), words (legomena), and symbols (deiknumena)* (1954: 62).

Rousselle's essay is an important document of early 20th century history that demonstrates the religionist assumptions of the period. He created false equivalencies between culturally unique Chinese ideas and Western religious terms which he delivered using a condescending, omniscient tone. His presentation of Daoist practice was at best oblique.

Yuasa, who had access to both Japanese written scholarship on Daoism and to living exponents of the Japanese martial arts nevertheless foregrounded the European fabulations of Herrigel and Rousselle. His writings on energy and the martial arts combine of the ideas European thinkers such as Bergson and Merleau-Ponty with the less obviously European views of Asia conjured by Herrigel and Rousselle. Rather than an insider's account of Asian conceptual and pragmatic ontologies written in the language of European phenomenology, Yuasa created a Japanese, Theosophical and Jungian chimera.

when and by whom its assumptions were established, and religionist contextualization which presumed that distinct pragmatic ontologies shared a common conceptual ontology.[110] The genealogies of Euro-American esoteric energy braid together marginal, popular, and scholarly presentations with spiritual, materialist, psychological and evolutionary characteristics.[111] To better understand how these genealogies informed the influential work of 20th-century theatre artist Jerzy Grotowski, we need to examine the historical Asian religious traditions from which they are at least in part derived.

Chinese and Indian Conceptual Ontologies

Euro-American ideas of energy inspired by Asia came by their chimeric combinations in part due to low-resolution similarities between the imaginal cartographies of the body used in the practice of nèidān and tantra. Adepts of both traditions were taught to associate the sensations experienced in practice with imagined reservoirs and channels within their bodies. The dāntián mentioned above in relation to nèidān seem correlate to the cakras, empty wheels that adepts of tantra filled with imagined deities, mantric syllables, symbols, colours, and elemental qualities such as air, fire, or water. Both could be described as sophisticated heuristic devices, models created in practice using a combination of the imagination and the felt senses to viscerally experience the conceptual ontologies these traditions proposed. These Chinese and Indian body maps share a historical relationship.

Body maps featuring centres and channels seem to have been a part of Chinese internal alchemy before similar conceptions appeared in India. It is likely that the idea of internal alchemy travelled from China to India in the second century CE, accompanying the importation of red mercury sulphide, an important substance in Chinese external alchemy and medicine which was also used as a pigment in art and artisanry (Samuel 2008: 278–279, 281). Cinnabar, literally "Chinese powder" or *cīnapiṣṭi* in Sanskrit, is very rare on the

---

[110] Sixt Wetzler, PhD, student of the late Burkhard Gladigow (1939–2022) reports that "Prof. Gladigow often mentioned the 'Elektrifizierung der Religionswissenschaft,' the electrification of the study of religion in class." What he meant by this was a tendency in the late 19th/early 20th century to describe non-Christian religious ideas by the means of "energy"—implying that the non-Christian cultures themselves thought in such terms, where they probably didn't. The discussion of Polynesian "mana" was a prime example (Wetzler, personal communication).

[111] Energy has been extremely successful and compelling in fiction, which has had a powerful effect on our tacit assumptions. In 1871 Edward Bulwer-Lytton published a novel entitled *The Vril: The Power of the Coming Race* about the discovery of a subterranean, antediluvian people, the Vril-Ya and their amazing *vril*, a healing, psychic, and telekinetic power. Bovril, the salty meat-extract paste first developed to feed Napoleon III's troops in the 1870s, gets its name from a combination of the word "bovine" with the then-popular term "vril": a healing elixir indeed (1972: 13). In the late 20th century, George Lucas's *Star Wars* (1977) offered us the Force, and the Jedi and Sith who competed for its powers, the popularity and influence of which now appear to considerably exceed that of Bovril!

Indian subcontinent and was imported from Hunan, China by sea to the coasts of present-day Tamil Nadu in the south and to Gujarat in the north, as well as along the Silk Road, through Himalayan Pakistan and Afghanistan in the west, and Assam in the east (White 1996: 61, 63).

During the period when Chinese body maps seem to have been introduced into India, China was enthusiastically embracing Indian Buddhism, and with it the Sanskrit language. The likely transformation of Chinese dāntián into Indian cakras would have been a small, esoteric event when compared with the monumental Chinese encounter with Indian Buddhism. In 401 CE Yáo Xìng 姚興 (r. 394–416 CE), the second emperor of the Later Qin dynasty, installed the influential Kashmiri Buddhist adept, teacher, author, and translator Kumārajīva or Jiūmóluóshí 鳩摩羅什 (344–413 CE) as National Preceptor in the capital of Chang 'an, institutionalizing an aristocratic and popular appetite for Indian Buddhism that would only continue to grow in subsequent dynasties. This powerful Indian influence decisively affected the development of subsequent Chinese religious practices and cultural expressions. It had a vital and long-term effect on language as

> words of Sanskrit origin not only stayed in the Buddhist literature, but some of them also entered all aspects of people's daily life, affecting ordinary Chinese people's thinking, or even constituting the core of their moral values and mentality. (Shi in Wang & Sun 2015: 238).

Linguist and historian Xiangdong Shi suggests that this influence is still felt today, and "that Sanskrit-influenced Chinese has become an indispensable part of modern Chinese" (2015: 243).

The massive scale of this Indian influence on China led to many common knowledge assumptions attributing Indian origins to indigenous Chinese cultural practices, which in turn might make my suggestion that Indian cakras were inspired by Chinese dāntián seem unusual. For example, since at least the 17th century the semi-legendary Buddhist patriarch Bodhidharma, or Dámó, who is remembered in China as Indian, has been credited with the creation of martial arts, physical culture, and meditative practices first developed by Chinese adepts and later associated with the Buddhist Shǎolín temple (Shahar 2008: 12–19). This perception persists today, found in popular 20th and 21st century qìgōng manuals by Chinese authors who attribute Chinese practices to Bodhidharma, and suggest that Indian yoga was the source of Chinese nèidān (Wong 1993: 11; Yang 2006: 191–192). The precedent for such folk genealogies is longstanding.

Many of the early Chinese aristocrats who patronized Indian Buddhism suspected that Indian adepts had mastered methods of achieving immortality. In 646 CE, Chinese courtiers offered a Sanskrit translation of the Daoist *Lǎozǐ Dào Dé Jīng* to the king of Kāmarūpa—now Assam—purportedly in exchange for information concerning immortality formulas created by Indian alchemists (White 1996: 62). In 649 CE, an Indian scholar named Nārāyaṇasvāmin was

captured and held in the Chinese court allegedly because he knew how to create an elixir of life, and in 664 CE, an Indian physician named Lokāditya was
summoned to the Chinese court to serve as an alchemist (White 1996: 62).
However, Indian potentates also suspected that their Chinese visitors knew
about alchemy and immortality. In 520 CE the king of Udyāna in the Swat
region of present-day Pakistan is remembered to have interrogated Sòng Yùn
宋雲 (n.d.) and his companions, all Chinese Buddhist visitors to his court,
about Daoist medicine, science, and about "the silver and golden palaces of
the Immortals" (Needham 1954: 207, 209; White 1996: 63). In an enduring
example of the bi-directionality of alchemical inspiration, a founding ancestor
of a lineage of Siddha Yoga in Tamil Nadu named Bogar, thought to have lived
sometime between the third and fifth centuries CE, is remembered as either a
Chinese adept who came to India to teach alchemy and medicine, or as a South
Indian alchemist who travelled to teach in China.[112] Regardless of his historicity
and geographic origin, in the late 20th century Bogar was still worshipped at
the site in the Palani Hills of Tamil Nadu where he is said to have practiced and
taught alchemy (White 1996: 61).

Placing texts together on a timeline, the Chinese creation of nèidān with its
maps of the dāntián predates the invention of tantra and its system of cakras in
India. Perhaps the earliest use of the term dāntián to refer to imaginal centres
within an adept's body is found in the *Huángtíng Jīng* in the early third century
CE (see note 94). The earliest written references to cakras in relation to the
practices of *tantrikas* appears to be Bhavabhoti's *Malatt-Madhava*, an eighth-
century play about Saivite ascetics.[113] Body maps of centres and channels thus
seem to have appeared in China about 500 years before they did in India. As
Geoffrey Samuel notes:

> When it appears in India in the 8th century, the elaborate internal struc-
> ture of the subtle body, with the series of cakras along the central chan-
> nel, has no real precedent in Indian material, for all that the language in
> which it is described is entirely Indic. (2008: 281)

Future research may reveal that the consecutive creation of Chinese and
Indian body maps were independent developments. For now, I believe the
evidence suggests that while they developed into distinct conceptual and
pragmatic ontologies, the early Indian systems were indebted to the older
Chinese ones.[114]

---

[112] Needham 1956: 285 and Velan 1963: 18 suggest a Chinese origin, while Bagchi 1930: 584–587
and Filliozat 1968: 78 prefer an Indian one.

[113] "The group of six cakras (shat-cakra) is first mentioned in dramatist Bhavabhoti's play Malatt-
Madhava, which is dated to the eighth century CE" (in Feuerstein, ed. 2013: 84).

[114] Joseph Needham went much further, stating that the "'Taoist department' of Buddhism was
Tantrism" (1956: 425). While I feel that cakras developed from dāntián, determining all the
Daoist influences on Indian Buddhist tantra would be a much more ambitious project.

Heuristic Devices and Geographical Metaphors

Regardless of their genealogies, like the dāntián of nèidān, the cakras of tantra were not discoverable latent universal structures.[115] Rather, initiates created their cakras using their imaginations, correlating their phenomenological experiences in practice with a conceptual map of the body transmitted by more experienced adepts in their tradition. As heuristic devices the cakras provided "both a structure to aid practitioners in directing their sensations, and a grid through which associations could be built up with other elements of the symbolic world within which the practice was taking place" (Samuel 2008: 289). In the history of South Asian tantra, there have been dozens, possibly hundreds of such grids, containing different numbers of cakras (White 1996: 367). Which one was transmitted depended on the practice being taught. Such maps did not express universally accessible human experiences of embodiment. Rather, they facilitated uncommon human experiences that only occurred within the sociology of each group of initiated religious practitioners.

Where they did refer to more commonly accessible experiences, the maps used in nèidān seem inspired by a hydrological metaphor. South China is moist and verdant, while the north is far more arid. Irrigation of the northern plains has been a civilizational preoccupation for millennia. This macrocosm was expressed microcosmically in nèidān, in which adepts sought to raise the cool, watery qualities of their kidneys to cool the fires of their hearts.

In contrast, Indian body maps reflect South Asian geography. The three principal channels found within the body prescribed by many tantras are a microcosmic transposition of the three rivers of the Ganges delta—the Ganges, the Brahmaputra, and the Meghna. Adepts of tantra's imaginal journeys within adopted the metaphor of pilgrimage. Tīrtha, meaning ford or crossing place, also indicates sites of pilgrimage, the physical seats or pīṭha of deities, which were represented in adepts' visualized worlds as cakras where the channels of the South Asian body maps met (Feuerstein 2011: 34; Leland 2016: 77).

From Collective to Personal Ritual

In Indian and Chinese history, nèidān and tantra were part of a long process whereby large group rituals involving temple architecture, costumes, music, offerings, and a wide variety of ritual specialists, not to mention congregants, were gradually transformed into ones that adepts could perform in their imaginations, allowing them to practice in small groups or alone.

Beginning in fourth-century CE the Shàng Qīng 上清 school of Daoism replaced the collective practices of the earlier Tiān Shī Dào 天師道, which began around 200 CE, and those of the Líng Bǎo Pài 靈寶派 from around 400

---

[115] Contemporary nèidān adept Yáng Hǎi 楊海 explains "The Elixir practice was not Fa Xian (discovered) but Fa Ming (created) 丹道非发现也，乃发明也。" (Yáng, online).

CE, with cún xiǎng visualizations to be performed individually. The *Shàng Qīng* transformed earlier rites of heterosexual intercourse used to produce the *shén tāi*, or spiritual embryo, into solo practices (Valusi 2022: 445–446). Similarly, in India, in the 10th and 11th centuries CE, both Shaiva and Buddhist tantra began to change into internalized, solo practices, transforming their collective and often sexually transgressive ritual forms into visualized ones.[116] Developing from actual to imagined rituals, and from imagined rituals to energetic abstractions, these practices removed themselves from both overt theatricality and group activity. Historically, the more developed the role of qì or prāṇa, the more individual the practices seem to have become.

Layered Ontologies

Similar-seeming body-maps, practices, and phenomenological experiences disclosed distinct worlds due to the assumptions that supported them. Views contextualizing both the reasons for undertaking practice and explaining its results at different phases of training were transmitted tacitly and explicitly to initiates. The channels and reservoirs of nèidān and tantra were themselves overlaid on distinct pre-existing conceptual ontologies. In China this was the body's life seen in terms of the five organs of the liver, the heart, the spleen, the lungs, and the kidneys, which interacted over five phases of inspiration, growth, flowering, fruition, and decline. Each phase in the cycle was named for substances whose generation enacts a particular quality: wood, fire, earth, gold or metal, and water.[117]

When Chinese body maps arrived in India, they were orthopraxically integrated into a view of the body based on sheaths or *kosas*, layered one on top of the next: the physical form, the breath, the senses, the intellect, and a final, causal, and most subtle spiritual layer. This fivefold account of embodiment can be traced to the *Taittirīya Upanishad*, dating from the sixth century BCE, substantially predating tantric maps of cakras and nāḍīs.

Optimistic and Pessimistic Views

In the historical religious practices of both India and China we find at least two contrasting worldviews. For example, the early nèidān of the *Shàng Qīng* school of Daoism and the tantras practiced in Indian Vajrayana and Shaivite communities

---

[116] The sexual rites of tantra were considered socially transgressive as they occurred outside of marriage and had non-reproductive, individually ecstatic purposes.

[117] The Han dynasty chronicle the *Shǐjì* 史記 *(Records of the Historian)* attributes this view, called *yīnyáng wǔxíng* 陰陽五行 or "complementary polarity and five phases," to a philosopher named Zōu Yǎn 鄒衍 (305–240 BCE) whose original writings are lost. The yīnyáng wǔxíng cosmology is a structural system that expresses complementary polarities and cyclical change (Saso 1990: 3).

proposed different descriptions of an optimistic cosmos, operating on a spon-taneous and generous creative principle. Quánzhēn 全真 Daoism (from 1200 CE), much of historical Buddhism in both India and China, and 19th-century Modern Indian Vedanta held more pessimistic views of human life, which was characterized to different degrees by continuous suffering in a cycle of reincar-nations governed by hierarchies of virtue and stern laws of cause and effect.

In all these examples the experiences of phenomena such as qì or prāṇa were not an end in and of themselves. Rather they were concrete means to experi-ence a view of reality, pragmatic ontologies performed in close relationship to conceptual ontologies. With these relationships and distinctions in mind, we shall examine sophisticated, late-20th-century intercultural artistic chimeras.

Jerzy Grotowski's Intercultural Chimeras

Jerzy Grotowski is remembered as both an influential European theatre direc-tor and as one of the late 20th century's most significant innovators in theatre aesthetics and actor training. Grotowski created his internationally celebrated productions between 1962 and 1969, after which he stopped directing new theatre and dedicated himself to a different kind of activity.

Beginning in the late 1970s, Grotowski observed interactions that he arranged between specialists in non-Western religious physical and musical prac-tices and an international array of students and actors. In *Theatre of Sources*, he expressed his interest in conducting practical research into the sources of the methods different cultures have developed in pursuit of what, citing Mircea Eliade, he referred to as "techniques of deconditioning" (in Schechner & Wolford 1997: 225).

> It is not a synthesis of techniques of sources that we are after. We search for sourcing techniques, those points that precede the differences. Let us say that there exist techniques of sources. But what we search for in this Project are the sources of the techniques of sources, and these sources must be extremely unsophisticated. Everything else developed after-wards, and differentiated itself according to social, cultural, or religious contexts. (1997: 233)

In 1986 he was offered a long-term home for his endeavours in Pontedera, Italy, where he founded the Workcenter of Jerzy Grotowski.[118] The activity he undertook there with his collaborators, which his friend director Peter Brook subsequently named "Art as Vehicle," was the creation of "Actions"—ensemble

---

[118] Later renamed the *Workcenter of Jerzy Grotowski and Thomas Richards* to include Grotowski's principal collaborator.

performances emphasizing acapella singing, explicitly dedicated to the transformation of the participants' energies (in Richards 1995: 119):

> Art as vehicle is like a very primitive elevator: it's some kind of basket pulled by a cord, with which the doer lifts himself toward a more subtle energy, to descend *with this* to the instinctual body. This is the *objectivity* of the ritual. If Art as vehicle functions, this objectivity exists and the basket moves for those who do the *Action*. (1995: 124–125)

Grotowski explained that unlike theatre, which aims to affect the perceptions of its audience, the performances created during the Art as Vehicle project did not need an audience, as they aimed to transform the perceptions of the performing artists themselves (1995: 120). However, while they were not necessarily intended for an audience, the Actions of Art as Vehicle were composed like theatrical performances. The relationships among the performers and the order of and transitions between the songs were developed based on the primary phenomenological experiences the performers had of singing individual songs, each of which was attributed with human characteristics and qualities, as though each were a character in a drama (1995: 127).

Like Sūn Lùtáng, Jerzy Grotowski contributed substantially to the pragmatic and conceptual ontologies in which subsequent artists and thinkers participated. Art as Vehicle was a practical, rather than a discursive, activity. Nevertheless, in presenting his project to the world, Grotowski also articulated a conceptual ontology. Unlike Sūn, whose tàolù and writings comprised a substantial and clear artistic portfolio, Grotowski's chimeras were more ephemeral. Teachers of Sūn-style martial arts continue to transmit his curriculum, and his books are available in Chinese and in translation. The actual practice of Art as Vehicle is not easily seen: the Workcenter continued its activities after Grotowski's death in 1999 until 2022, when its directors moved on to the next phases of their artistic lives, going their separate ways. Its performances are no longer practiced or presented, and the video archives of its activities are rarely screened. While its influence can be detected in the subsequent work of the many artists who participated in its activities over the 36 years of its life, the practice referred to by Grotowski in his conceptual articulations is no longer being done in the same form.

While Grotowski did write about his project, he preferred to lecture. Many of his texts about his work are translated, edited transcriptions of talks or interviews he gave. Both his artworks and his publications generated a very large body of secondary writings authored by his collaborators, by scholars directly involved with his project as observers, by theatre specialists and enthusiasts who witnessed Art as Vehicle, and by participants in practical workshops offered by the Workcenter over the years. To understand the role the Euro-American concept of energy played in Grotowski's thinking, I shall examine some of his writings and statements from the period just before his death in the late 1990s.

Personal Connections and Questions

While I was never directly involved in any of Grotowski's activities, many of my teachers, colleagues, close friends, and professional acquaintances were. Their accounts, and their ways of making and thinking about theatre, have also informed my thinking. Without exception, they felt that their experiences with Grotowski had been professionally formative and personally meaningful.

Director, actor, and teacher Richard Fowler, with whom I studied intensively in the 1990s, took part in Grotowski's Theatre of Sources in the summer of 1980, prior to beginning his decade as an actor at the Odin Teatret in Denmark. With Grotowski's collaborators, Richard learned the fundamental movement and voice training he later taught and used himself as an actor, methods that were decisive in his subsequent work in Denmark and Canada, and in my own apprenticeship (Brask 1992: 150–177).

I met actor, teacher, and director Gey Pin Ang in 2011 when she came to Ottawa to teach as a guest of Les Ateliers du corps, a practical theatre research project I was leading at that time (see chapter 6). Gey Pin, whom I esteem as my "older sister" or lǎojiě 老姐 in both theatre and Tàijí Quán, took part in a project of Grotowski's named Objective Drama in the 1980s and early 1990s, and later participated in the activities of the Workcenter (see note 54). These experiences were decisive in her long and productive artistic career. Gey Pin presented some of her performance *Feast of Yóu Shén* (遊神—wandering spirit) as part of her teaching in Ottawa. For me it was a powerful example of how much meaning a soloist can evoke in the minds of an audience, comparable to the solos I had seen by such senior accomplished performers as the late Ōno Kazuo (1906–2010), Tom Leabhart (b. 1944), and Teshigawara Saburō (b. 1953).

My late friend Lisa Wolford Wylam (d. 2011) was both personally close to Grotowski and renowned as a scholar of his work. I met Lisa in the spring of 1996, at Survivors of the Ice Age, a theatre festival of Canadian and American works organized in Winnipeg, Canada by Primus Theatre and Richard Fowler. Lisa wrote the foreword to *The Dancing Word*, my book on the use of Chinese martial arts in the creation of contemporary theatre (2011). In our many long and meandering conversations, she shared her detailed knowledge of Grotowski's work with me.[119]

---

[119] To these I would add Téo Spychalski, who had worked with Grotowski in the 1970s in Poland and later became the artistic director of Le Groupe de la Véillée in Montréal. Richard introduced me to Téo, who was very generous: he gave my young collaborators and me the keys to his then-brand-new theatre space during the quiet summer months of 1996. We worked all hours in the vast, empty building. Through Lisa I met Raymond Bobgan and Holly Holsinger

My curiosity about Grotowski's use of the term "energy" is in many ways a response to a comment of Lisa's. In 2008 Lisa and Kris Salata, along with Richard Schechner, co-edited an issue of the American theatre journal *TDR/The Drama Review* dedicated to Grotowski's work. In a gesture characteristic of her generous friendship, she wrote:

> When I discuss the subtler dimensions of the work of Art as vehicle with my friend Daniel Mroz, a director who has made a prolonged study of Asian meditative and martial disciplines, he comprehends instantly that Grotowski's articulation of a transformation in quality of energy from dense to light, *tamasic* to *sattvic*, is neither metaphoric nor nebulous, but rather refers to concrete processes that can be activated by means of embodied practice. (2008: 135)

Lisa was a far more accomplished and visible scholar than I, and I remain touched and grateful that our conversations were a point of reference for her. Her comment followed Grotowski's lead, expressing the phenomenology, structure, and objectives of Art as Vehicle using South Asian terms. While I'd seen live performances created by Grotowski's former students and collaborators that were influenced by their time at the Workcenter, I first saw the 2006 video *Action in Valicelle*, which documents one instance of Art as Vehicle in performance, when the Workcenter broadcast it on the internet in 2021. I experienced the Action I saw as totally defined by the performers' powerful singing of Afro-Caribbean songs.[120]

Given what I've explained above about Euro-American esoteric energy and the traditions of China and India, Lisa's equation of the Daoist process of transforming qì into yào and yào into dān with South Asian concepts like tamasic and sattvic, and with the performance of songs from yet further cultural sources, seems to me to be a bridge too far. And yet the pragmatic and

---

who had studied with Grotowski during his Objective Drama project and who make theatre in Cleveland, Ohio. Lisa also introduced me to Mario Biagini, one of Grotowski's principal collaborators in Art as Vehicle, with whom I had several informative conversations, and who directed the performance *I am America* I attended in New York City in 2010. Led by Lisa and Polish Grotowski scholar Kris Salata, I helped run the practice as research working group at the American Society of Theatre Research from 2009 to 2014. Participants included director and teacher Jim Slowiak, one of Grotowski's major American collaborators from the Objective Drama project, and scholar and artist Ben Spatz, who has also written about Art as Vehicle (2015) and who has become both a friend and colleague. In August 2016 I participated in the Collective Mind, a theatre workshop in which attendees observed Eugenio Barba, assistant director to Grotowski from 1962 to 1965, leading the final rehearsals of the Odin Teatret's original production *The Tree*. At Eugenio's request, I edited the English text of the multi-lingual production, and assisted Danish and Indonesian actors with their English pronunciation.

[120] *Action in Valicelle* is rarely screened. Readers can get some idea of the nature and quality of the Workcenter's singing in these excerpts from their public performance *The Living Room* (2017): https://www.youtube.com/watch?v=abvov7z5W6c (archived here: https://vimeo.com/806112082/b6edc5cadb).

conceptual ontologies of Art as Vehicle were centrally important and meaningful to the social group that created them, Lisa among them.

Art as Vehicle was an intercultural chimera: written accounts of its structure and phenomenology used South Asian ideas, the actual practice seemed derived from Caribbean and African sources, and the principal, credited creators and performers were Euro-American theatre artists.[121]

Seen from without, it produced a unique acapella music theatre whose qualities could be readily appreciated by non-initiates.[122] One didn't need to have practiced it oneself, nor to understand that the participants were transforming an esoteric energy to find the ensemble singing which was performed while moving in compelling relationships and configurations, evocative and meaningful.

What can the ideas of poly-ontology, multinaturalism, and somatic mutability reveal about the worlds Art as Vehicle disclosed to its participants? How were its conceptual and pragmatic ontologies determined by the religionism and source amnesia that can be found in Grotowski's thinking?

Grotowski's Energy

Grotowski's earlier general discussion of East Asian martial arts and theatre revealed that he had observed Chinese martial arts and theatre, for example, quite accurately. Discussing them in terms of energy, however, I think he confused jìn, the skill of displaying specific qualities of movement, with the many possible meanings of qì, resulting in an opaque presentation:

It is not by chance that in the Orient, among the arts, martial arts included, great emphasis is placed on energy, and that techniques are discussed in terms of energy. Great Western actors know how to improvise while keeping up a flow of action. They can even be using a written script, without changing it, while improvising the actions

---

[121] Haitian artist Maud Robart collaborated with Grotowski from 1977 to 1993, including six years spent in residence at the Workcenter. A significant artist in her own right, Robart co-founded a rural arts community in Haiti with artist Jean-Claude *Tiga* Garoute (1935–2006) in 1973. Their collaboration led to the development of the *Sen Solèy* arts movement also known as *le movement Saint-Soleil*, and to the post-naïve school of Haitian painting. Robart introduced Grotowski to Haitian *Vodou*, and taught songs and her interpretation of a dance called the *yanvaloo* to the participants in his projects. He taught her his version of Stanislavsky's actor-training approach, and helped her master the *exercises plastiques*, a movement training developed by his earlier collaborators in Poland in the 1960s (De Marinis 2017). Robart is not mentioned by Grotowski in his major writings, but her contributions are well-documented in secondary sources.

[122] By music theatre I refer to contemporary theatrical works in which the integration of music, performing, and staging is key to the way the performance conjures meaning for its audience, distinct from repertoire-based genres such as Euro-American musical theatre or opera. Examples might include performances and projects created, directed, or led by Laurie Anderson, Heiner Goebbels, Meredith Monk, or Harry Partch.

(in Stanislavsky's sense of the word). In the Orient, it is much more a question of improving the applications of energy, of discovering forms as energetic functions. The elements, the forms/details, are very precise—to the point where they become movement, gesture, and vocal signs. But within this framework, the order of the details can be rearranged in a subtle manner, the rhythmic accents changed, the duration of the "stops" between the details modified, and an even greater complexity achieved. The actor is able to observe "how things are going," "how it is done," and discover the surprises of the moment (even give himself some surprises). The forms are rediscovered as channels. Energy flows in its own way, indefinable. (1996/1989, trans. Schaeffer, in Pavis 1996: 237).

If techniques, or *shì* 式, are discussed in terms of jìn, as named skills considered necessary to a successful performance rather than as energy, what Grotowski wrote becomes more accessible.[123]

Lán cā yī 拦擦衣, or block touching coat, is the second technique found in the first tàolù of my branch of Chén Tàijí Quán. It is often used to knock down a training partner who has attempted to close distance, covering their step by throwing a left-handed punch to the chest, neck, or jaw. To defend, my right arm reaches out and then retracts a little while rotating on itself, shaving along the line of my partner's incoming left jab, modifying its trajectory slightly. As contact occurs, I place my right foot behind my training partner's front, left foot and re-extend my right arm across their chest. The rotation of my arm drives the mass of their torso to the right, while my right foot and leg immobilize their lower body for a moment. They stagger or fall due to the imbalance I have created between the relative positions of their chest and left leg with respect to their forward momentum. The skills I'd rely on when using lán cā yī against a training partner are huà jìn 化劲, or changing skill, to reposition their incoming punch, and *liè jìn* 列劲, or splitting skill, to separate their centre of mass from their point of support on the ground.[124]

Grotowski's concluding metaphor of "forms rediscovered as channels" can be made more concrete through this example: the choreography of the movement lán cā yī is a conduit for the consecutive performance of huà jìn and liè jìn. If my training partner is more experienced than I, I might be forced to attempt a different jìn to defend myself against their superior ability; the same conduit can thus also contain different expressions of skill than the two I mention. When capably done, deviating the incoming force and knocking one's partner down occur as a single beat, rather than as two discrete phases. The subdivision

---

[123] For nuance, where martial technique can be seen in the formalized repetition of a movement, combative skill is found in the satisfactory completion of an often unintentional, responsive action. Thanks to Richard Bailey for clarifying this idea.

[124] The huà jìn of Chén Tàijí Quán refers to a different movement skill than the huà jìn of Xíngyì Quán mentioned earlier in this chapter.

of the entire process into precise movement qualities creates the possibility of greater complexity, as Grotowski suggested. The conceptual subdivisions of jìn within my execution of the overall technique allow me to parse the interaction more finely. I observe how things are going and adjust accordingly as Grotowski described, in a way that also recalls Gāo's neutral actor state (see chapter 4.)

The last line of Grotowski's paragraph about "energy flowing in its own way" might refer to an idea like qìfēn 氣氛, the overall atmosphere or surrounding qì of a situation. A performance or a martial bout is a process of becoming, an ongoing communication between performers and their audience, or between agonists and any witnesses, within a particular environment. The interaction of these elements creates shifting impressions that the nebulous qìfēn captures well. Reinterpreted, Grotowski's statements can be made clearer, and more representative of Chinese martial arts and theatre; however, skill and atmosphere are ideas that suffer from being conflated with energy.[125]

Grotowski discussed his specific conception of the body's energy in his Art as Vehicle project in an interview about the early 20th-century spiritual teacher G. I. Gurdjieff (1867–1949.) Describing his own work, Grotowski said:

> [W]here one approaches the more complex issues, the so-called inner work, I avoid as much as possible any verbalization. I avoid, for example, verbalizing the question of the centers of energy which we can locate in the body. I mean it when I say "which we can locate in the body," because it is not so clean-cut. Do they belong to the biological domain or to one that is more complex? The best known are the centers according to the yoga tradition, those called chakras. It is clear that one can in a precise way discover the presence of centers of energy in the body: from those that are most closely linked to biological survival, then sexual impulses, and so forth, to centers that are more and more complex (or, should one say, more subtle?). And if this is felt as a corporal topography, one can clearly draw up a map. But here there is a new danger: if one starts to manipulate the centers (centers in the sense close to the Hindu chakras), one begins to transform a natural process into a kind of engineering, which is a catastrophe. It becomes a form a cliché. Why do I say "like" the chakras? Because the tradition of the centers exists in different cultures. Let's say that in the Chinese culture it is more or less linked to the same tradition as in India. But it existed also in Europe. In the text of Gichtel from the seventeenth century, one can find for

---

[125] Grotowski also had some familiarity with Japanese theatre and martial arts, traditions that display similar diversity to Chinese ones in their interpretations of the logograph 氣 or ki in Japanese. Even within the same martial art, karate dō 空手道, we find recent and divergent variations. Tanaka, for example, uses it to refer to "the concentration of power focussed in one point" (2001: 27). Ushiro, however, uses it to indicate the "depth of thought, the consciousness that enables simultaneous, multidimensional movement" (2008: 5). Grotowski's comments might be interpreted quite differently in the context of Japanese theatre and martial arts.

example drawings that are very instructive from this point of view. If all of this is verbalized, there is also a danger of manipulating the sensations which one can artificially create in different places of the body. So I prefer a less fixed terminology, even if in precise work one can discover here something very precise and fixed. (in Needleman, 1996: 92–93)

In this dense paragraph, Grotowski suggested that centers of energy in the body are discovered—for example, the chakras (*sic*) of yoga. He put them on a developmental spectrum; he described "manipulating" them as "engineering" and a "catastrophe"; and he explained that similar traditions of energy centres appeared in India, China, and Europe. These four statements allow us to extrapolate his sources, offering insight into the effect of religionism and source amnesia on the conceptual ontology he proposes.

Discovery and Authenticity

Grotowski wrote that one can discover "centres of energy" in the body and offered the Hindu chakras as an example. As noted above, in the Indian and Chinese traditions body maps were not discovered but constructed within a particular sociology of practice. While these maps were attached to phenomenological experiences, novices were primed to make those associations through both socialization and instruction.

While he condemned manipulating the energy centres, opposing nature to engineering, the Indian and Chinese traditions he mentioned as examples are best described as manipulative. Grotowski also seemed aware of this. He explained both in writing and in his late lectures why the participants in Art as Vehicle sang Afro-Caribbean songs rather than using the mantra that were closer to his South Asian example of cakras:

Why do I speak of mantra and then move toward the song of tradition? Because in the work which interests me, mantra is less applicable, given that the mantra is far from the organic approach. On the contrary, the traditional songs (like those of the Afro-Caribbean line) are rooted in organicity. It's always the song-body, it's never the song dissociated from the impulses of life that run through the body; in the song of tradition, it is no longer a question of the position of the body or the manipulation of the breath, but of the impulses and the little actions. Because the impulses which run in the body are exactly that which carries the song. (1995: 129)

Organicity: it is also a term of Stanislavski. What is organicity? It is to live in agreement with natural laws, but on a primary level. One mustn't forget, our body is an animal. I am not saying: we are animals, I say: our body is an animal. Organicity is linked to a *child-aspect*. The child is almost always organic. Organicity is something which one has more of when one is young, less of as one gets older. Obviously, it is possible to prolong the life of organicity by fighting against acquired habits, against the training of common life, breaking, eliminating the clichés of behavior. And, before the complex reaction, returning to the reaction which was primary. (1989: 16–17)

Using constructed Asian imaginal structures like cakras as examples in a general description of a project predicated on organicity as Grotowski sketches it, even when individual procedures such as mantra recitation are offered as an anti-organic contrast category, is ambitiously chimeric. The historically linked dantian of nèidān and cakras of tantra are already quite distinct from each other; how much more so would any Afro-Caribbean practices be? Grotowski's organicity conjures an atavism that seems incompatible with all the Asian traditions I have practiced.[126] My teachers of martial arts, nèidān, and indeed contemporary theatre and dance were at pains to emphasize the intentionally constructed nature of these activities.[127]

The view of the transformation of energy Grotowski explained and his projection of it onto the historical traditions of India and China is, to me, an application of religionism. Anxiety about authenticity is inherent to a religionist perspective, attached as it is to participation in a comprehensive if ineffable underlying schema. Poly-ontology, multinaturalism, and somatic mutability suggest that one ultimately might not be able to tell the difference between what is natural and what has been engineered, as each discloses distinct worlds. This is a very worrying prospect for a view of religious experiences that requires them to share a common and ancient general structure to be authentic.

19th- and 20th-Century Sources

Grotowski characterized the energy centers he speaks of as evolving from primal impulses towards subtle ones. In the yoga and tantra of South Asia before

---

[126] Historically, actual combinations of yoga and theatrical performance seem to have been rare. Theatre scholar, yogi, and martial artist Sreenath Nair, PhD speculates that a lost practice named *svara-vayu*, where actors used specific breathing methods to render their performances more compelling and credible, might have been the result of the synthesis of South Indian Siddha Yoga with the religious theatrical performance genre of *Kudiyattam*. Kunjunni Tampuran, the King of Kodungalloor (1858–1926), who was reputed to have been the student of a Siddha yogi and a capable adept himself, was also a performer of Kudiyattam. He apparently applied his yoga training to his performances with exceptional results, but due to a lack of apt students, this unique approach was lost (2007: 129–135).

[127] Chén Zhōnghuá, for example, routinely scolds his students when we move in free and flowing ways that we personally find comfortable. Correct Tàijí Quán movement does appear free and flowing, but he reminds us that it is something that one would never perform naturally. It is hard to achieve voluntarily, let alone spontaneously, reversing as it does our habit of hand-dominated movement and replacing it with movement initiated from the legs and large muscles of the back.

the late 19th century, cakras were empty imaginal spaces that adepts populated with practice-specific deities, letters, symbols, and qualities. The correlation of the cakras with the evolution of human ontogeny and phylogeny is a Euro-American, religionist idea—developed, for example, in Leadbeater's *The Chakras* and Jung's *The Psychology of Kundalini Yoga*—and adopted in late- and postcolonial India, as a consequence of Hindu Modernism.[128]

This movement aimed to create an organized presentation of the many kinds of South Asian religious practice collected by the 18th century colonial term Hinduism, making them visible in India and abroad as a world religion comparable to Christianity, Islam, and Buddhism, practiced as they are in multiple nations and cultural settings. Reformers reframed yoga and its related conceptual ontologies, making them acceptable to the Indian 19th-century status quo (De Michelis 2004: 156–159). In keeping with both Indian middle-class conservatism and Victorian prudery, these modernist presentations omitted the sexual, antinomic and asocial components of *yoga* and *tantra*:

> Much effort was given by people such as Swami Vivekananda into reconstructing yoga, generally in terms of a selective Vedantic reading of Patañjali's *Yogasutra* (de Michelis 2004). The effort was largely successful, and many modern Western practitioners of yoga for health and relaxation have little or no knowledge of its original function as a preparation for the internal sexual practices of the Nath tradition. (Samuel 2010: 336)

While the claim that the distantly related, second-century CE Patañjali *Yogasutra* was the Ur-text of haṭha yoga is still widely accepted common knowledge, James Mallinson proposes that the source text for haṭha yoga is the 11th-century CE Vajrayana Buddhist *Amṛtasiddhi*, attributed to the *mahasiddha*, or Buddhist adept, Virupa (Mallinson 2016).[129] The practice recorded in this text was adopted and adapted by various Indian traditions, including the *Naths* mentioned by Samuel.

Vivekananda and other reformers interpreted the Patañjali Yogasutra to formulate and promote a quietist, developmental, prāṇa-centred ontology whose

---

[128] Grotowski also referred to the images created by Johann Georg Gichtel (1638–1710) which seem to show a European version of the body's energy centres. Gichtel's diagrams illustrate an idealized relationship between the individual's body and the divine cosmos. They are metaphorical expressions of Gichtel's Christian mysticism, and do not appear to have been part of any practice or method involving the imagination of energy or of a particular body-map (Hammer 2004: 187). Gichtel's drawing that most resembles Indian cakras appeared on the cover of Leadbeater's *The Chakras* in 1927, where it was offered as a visual example of the universality of the energy centres.

[129] According to David Gordon White, the aphoristic Patañjali Yogasutra contains but four verbs, making it a very plastic document indeed (2014: 10). While it inspired influential commentaries and translations in the 500 years following its creation, it languished in obscurity for a further 700 years until it was rehabilitated by Vivekananda in the late 19th century (2014: xvi).

fruition was definitively not pursued using sexual rites, actual or imaginal.[130] This reformed vision

> proposes a cosmology in which *prāṇa* (as understood by Vivekananda) plays a central part, describes soteriological aims and methods in terms of power and control over "gross" and "subtle," "internal" and "external" aspects of the cosmos, and predicates the achievement of freedom or liberation by way of an "accumulation" or "concentration" of *prāṇa*, which will speed up the adepts on their evolutionary path towards the ultimate goal. Vivekananda's interpretation of these teachings is heavily influenced by the mesmeric beliefs popular in North American milieus at the time. (De Michelis 2004: 151)

The evolutionary teleology and the naturalization of the cakras and their energies added to Indian yoga in the late 19th and early 20th centuries also found their way into British popular literature. Writing under the pen name of Paul Brunton, Raphael Hurst (1898–1981) introduced these two novel ideas to Western readers:

> Transfer the Darwinian theory to the realm of human character; accept the Brahmin teaching that there is a spiritual evolution running parallel with the physical one ... If you want the best proof—first-hand experience—of these spiritual truths, then you must persistently follow up a course of Yoga practices. I assure you that the human body is really capable of higher functions than those we commonly know; that the innermost parts of our brain centres are associated with subtle worlds of being; that, after proper training, these centres can be energized until we become aware of these subtler worlds; and that the most important centre of all enables us to obtain divine consciousness of the highest order. (Brunton 1935: 30, 244).

Awareness of all these developments does not reduce the importance of earlier scholarly and current common knowledge understandings of yoga or prāṇa. These ideas have been extremely significant in the creation of personal and cultural meanings. But while the conceptual and pragmatic ontologies of Hindu Modernist yoga are composed of earlier elements, they are not old, and we can no longer understand them as simply traditional. Their proposed quietist

---

[130] Unlike the very visible and active Vivekananda, the few advanced contemporary adepts of meditative disciplines I know of rejected authority, celebrity, and contact with the public. For example, Guō Gāo Yī 郭高一 (1900–1996), the nèidān expert who led the restoration of Daoist martial arts in the Wǔdāng Mountains from 1984 until 1989, quickly tired of institutional politics and retired to practice in a remote cave, where he lived out his days in contented solitude (Shuì, trans. Cox, online 4).

fruition reflects the preoccupations of the historical period in which they were formulated, rather than ancient or perennial views.

The historical studies that explain the development of what Grotowski believed about yoga due to source amnesia, and that outline the religionist assumptions of the mid-20th-century scholarship he embraced, were written after his death. In the 1990s he was in failing health, and very busy with both the Workcenter and his sadly brief appointment as *Professeur au Collège de France, titulaire de la chaire d'Anthropologie théâtrale* in 1997 (online). It would be unforgiving indeed to expect him to have known these things.[131]

Critical Response

Grotowski's conceptual ontology naturalized the idea of energy and energy centres. These were ancient and found across many cultures. They could be used to facilitate a more profound vision of the world. He used the term organic to describe his approach to using a naturalized energy to create the experiences about which he speculated, exemplified by the free movement of the body while singing. He made this idea clearer using the contrast category of anti-organic, exemplified by the practice of mantra recitation in India. He did not specify which mantra practice, in what period, or done by which people, but he did list controlled breathing and composed postures as the features that make it anti-organic.

Given my experience and my review of current scholarship—historical, philological, and anthropological—his account is confusing to me. Energy and energy centres are not natural kinds, they are European terms used recently to describe concepts and practices created in Chinese and Indian cultures after 200 CE. Discoveries of similar-seeming energies and energy centres in other cultures, including examples from medieval and Renaissance European mystical texts where we find diagrams of discs connected by lines, are superficial resemblances highlighted by religionist scholars and their precursors and by creative religious entrepreneurs. In the case of Tibetan, Japanese, and Southeast Asian examples, such similarities seem due to diffusion, adaptation, and rediffusion of Chinese and Indian sources.

Constructs such as qì, dāntián, prāṇa and cakras are specific components of practical and conceptual ontologies that Grotowski characterizes as anti-organic. Energy and energy centres cannot appear upstream generally as

---

[131] Polish theatre scholar Grzegorz Ziółkowski suggests that Grotowski's interest in Asian religions was an anti-status-quo position, linking it to his enthusiasm for European modernism and the Polish Romanticism of Adam Mickiewicz, and his admiration for the American counterculture of the 1960s and 1970s. Modernism's search for alternatives to normative European regimes of thought and belief led Grotowski toward Romantic ideas (personal communication). However, Grotowski's ideas about India and China were so reflective of the mid-20th-century, Theosophical and Jungian Euro-American status quo that the possibly rebellious character of his interest is not immediately apparent.

natural kinds independent of cultural influence while also being constructed later downstream, originating as they did in the intentions of practitioners in two specific cultural histories.

Grotowski's pragmatic ontology, the Actions of Art as Vehicle, linked Afro-Caribbean songs in a theatrical montage. This combination of singing and movement was impeccably performed. I do not know how it felt to perform it. From the accentuated anterior pelvic tilt and lifted torso that the performers all displayed, affecting the sequencing and quality of all of their movements, to the markedly blissful state that seemed to inhabit them all as a kind of baseline from which they departed and returned, *Action in Valicelle* looked to me very unlikely to feel like the Chinese, Indian and Tibetan martial and religious practices I've experienced in either long-term training or short-term study, or to produce their specific fruitions.

Creative Possibilities

From the outside, Art as Vehicle developed a uniquely compelling kind of music theatre. From within, it appears to have offered participants an experience of their own somatic mutability and the multinatural possibilities of embodiment, as they themselves changed and saw into the embryonic new worlds created by their practice. For me, the creative heritage of Grotowski's intercultural chimeras is found in an original and compelling approach to singing that does not need to depend on a necessarily Afro-Caribbean repertoire.[132] It transformed bodies and disclosed new worlds for both participants and direct observers, and for people like me, who saw a video of *Action in Valicelle* and attended performances of the music theatres developed by alumni of the Workcenter.

Conclusion

Sūn Lùtáng's early 20th-century intracultural chimeras tightened and specified the existing relationship between martial arts practice and Daoism, attributing

---

[132] Future scholars of Grotowski's work and artists following in his wake may feel the need to further examine the use Afro-Caribbean songs in this project, a complex choice given the history of Euro-American colonialism, its practices of slavery, and its many cultural misappropriations. Mario Biagini, the associate director of the Workcenter, left the organization in 2021 prior to its closure in 2022. Recognizing this fraught aspect of *Art as vehicle* he wrote:

> I also understood that I don't want to sing songs from the African Diaspora anymore as I have been doing since 1986. I know hundreds of songs. They wake me up in the morning like birds. But now, after 35 years spent studying these extraordinary creations of human beings who have been deported and exploited and who are still oppressed, I know enough. I know there is a lot I don't know and that I will never know. After 35 years of work in a field I didn't choose from the start, I now understand that I am not obliged to continue and have decided to stop (2022: 191).

the outcome of nèidān or jīndān directly to the long-term and serious practice of tàolù. Jerzy Grotowski's late-20th-century intercultural chimeras furthered the idea that the phenomenology of theatre and religion, usually parsed into separate categories, might be understood together.

In both cases the conceptual ontologies they proposed were chimeric. Sūn's proposal that the movement skill of jìn could produce dān fortuitously resembles Grotowski's idea that movement he characterized as organic could produce a fruition developed in traditions he characterized as anti-organic. Both combined distinct conceptions, and both used ideas now constructed as energy.

The pragmatic ontologies they both proposed disclosed new worlds to subsequent artists, creating new, if embryonic experiences of embodiment, and new sociologies of practice. Sūn's curriculum has become a visible component of today's Chinese martial arts, and his ideas decisively contributed to the perception that Xíngyì Quán, Bāguà Zhǎng, and Tàijí Quán have special common characteristics and a Daoist orientation. Grotowski's work developed a compelling approach to acapella song, rewarding for participants as an activity in its own right and meaningful to audiences when received as a performance. His focus on what I call Euro-American esoteric energy legitimized and offered a concrete example of the application of procedures both theatrical and religious in the practice of contemporary performance.

The last two chapters of this book present my own experiences applying the Chinese martial arts in the creation of contemporary theatre and dance as a director, teacher, dramaturg, and facilitator. These reflections are more phenomenological than historical, yet they are nevertheless informed by the parameters present in all my examples thus far: the relationships established within a group of artists—martial or theatrical; their chosen daily practices; the performances created—artistic or ritual; and the relationships between this collective activity and the transformations experienced individually by each of the participants.

Introduction to Chapter 6

In the spring of 2009, I was awarded a three-year Research/Creation Grant by the Social Sciences and Humanities Research Council of Canada, an initiative that offered artists working within the Canadian university system generous funding for practical artistic research. I used this grant to create Les Ateliers du corps, a studio of committed emerging artists who met regularly to practice Chinese martial arts as an approach to performer training. This sustained practice served as the basis for aesthetic innovation in the creation of original theatrical performance.

From 2009 to 2012 Les Ateliers offered its participants ongoing training in *Chén Shì Tàijí Quán* and Zhìnéng Qìgōng. We also practiced European early music and folk songs, vocal training for spoken English and French, and the

Figure 22: Mary Catherine Jack, Tracey Guptil, Emmanuelle Lussier Martinez & Amelia Schembri (front) getting ready to rehearse *Circe/Landfall*, Les Ateliers du corps, June 2010 (photo by Daniel Mroz).

extended vocal technique of harmonic overtone singing. We hosted several guest teachers who taught short introductions, and longer intensive workshops on a variety of subjects. At the end of each year's work, we created and presented an original piece of theatre, scripted for us by American playwright Michael Geither. We presented *Circe/Landfall* at the Canada Dance Festival (2010), *Shah Mat* at the Ottawa Dance Directive (2011), and *And Treat the Distant Peoples with Kindness* at the University of Ottawa (2012). Appendix C provides a full list of the participants in the project, while Appendix D gives links to full videos of Les Atelier's three performances. In 2011, filmmaker Jean-François Dubé created *Liberté [in Motion]*, a short documentary about our work which is also linked in Appendix D.

Les Ateliers owed its inspiration to an ideal of artistic practice I absorbed in my apprenticeship with Richard Fowler, that new forms of theatre emerge from the sustained work of a group of artists. Theatre historian Mirella Schino referred to this 20th-century experimental orientation as *laboratoriality* (2009: 24). Theatre scholar Ben Spatz developed a very precise contemporary articulation of this idea in *Making a Laboratory*, a book published after the project of Les Ateliers was completed. Defining an experiment as an event where "a precise relationship is set up between initial conditions and the derivation of a trace via an experimental moment" (2020: 30–31), Spatz proposed that

> The most basic experiment would then take the form: *Let's do X and see what happens*, where "X" is the opening cut and "see what happens" is the closing cut. I will therefore call "laboratorial" a *particular kind of rigor* associated with the implementation of *inscription* at both cuts. According to that definition, "Let's do X and see what happens" would be experimental but not laboratorial, because its opening and closing cuts are not archivally traced. An experiment becomes a laboratory when both cuts are traced or inscribed archivally, so that those not present can have access to both "what was done" (the opening cut) and "what happened" (the closing cut). (2020: 32–33)

In the final year of the project, Colin Lalonde, who had participated in the first two years of the studio, returned to assist me as apprentice director. Chapter 6 shares Colin's perceptions of "what was done," and "what happened" in the final phase of Les Ateliers' work preparing and performing *And Treat the Distant Peoples with Kindness*, a performance inspired by Gavin Menzies' speculative, fantastical history *1421: The Year China Discovered the World* (2002).

Our performance told the story of Niccola de Conti, an Italian traveller who met the Chinese admiral Zhèng Hé 鄭和 (1371–1433), whose fleets had allegedly mapped the entire world almost half a century before Columbus's first Atlantic voyage. De Conti's exciting life and the tragic deaths of his family were set against a broader story of early Ming dynasty exploration and trade.

In Menzies' telling, the second Ming emperor Zhū Dì 朱棣, the Yǒnglè 永樂 Emperor (r. 1360–1424), instructed his admiral Zhèng Hé to "treat the distant peoples with kindness." A Chinese fleet of massive treasure ships, or *bǎochuán* 寶船, carried gifts and technological wonders which they offered as gifts, hoping to put the peoples they encountered in the emperor's debt. Zhū Dì's expeditions allegedly bankrupted the empire. He died in 1424 and his impoverished successor sealed China's borders, burned the giant ships, destroyed the maps, and erased the logs of the voyages from history.

Playwright Michael Geither combined ideas from Menzies' fantasy with ones from *Le Voyage aux Indes (1414–1439)*, a 2004 French translation of the historical accounts of de Conti's travels. In our story, Niccola de Conti saw the Chinese treasure ships during his travels in Indonesia. He met Zhèng Hé, who gave him maps and an explanation of how to calculate latitude at sea, a central problem for maritime navigation of the time. De Conti got married in India and converted to Islam. With his wife and daughter, he settled in Cairo, only to lose his young family to a cholera epidemic. Broken-hearted, he returned to Europe, where Poggio Bracciolini, the papal secretary, after extracting from him a painful confession, took the world maps de Conti had acquired in Asia and sold them to the European monarchs, beginning the waves of conquest that moved west across the Atlantic.

Colin Lalonde incorporated his directorial work on this production into the thesis project of his master's degree in international performance research at the University of Warwick. In this chapter, he describes our work together.

CHAPTER 6

And Treat the Distant Peoples with Kindness

By Colin Lalonde, MA, MA

[T]he theatre has always been an enclave: a handful of men and women united by a rigorous craft of cultivating a garden which, in the eyes of others, seemed exotic or a utopia. In reality all of them, from Stanislavski to Grotowski, have erected a fortress with walls of wind, at the same time an island of freedom and a shelter from the spirit of time.

–Barba 2010: 202

Preface

I met Daniel in 2009 when I was a student in the undergraduate movement and voice class he taught in the Department of Theatre at the University of Ottawa. I was a little older than most of my classmates, having previously completed a three-year professional actor-training program in my hometown of Montréal. I was struck by the rigour of Daniel's class, by how clear his instruction was, and by the focused energy that he required of acting students. Many of my fellow undergraduates were surprised by the intensity of the experience, but for me it was both a revelation and homecoming. I recognized standards of precision I had been introduced to in my professional training, and I saw for the first time a wider range of creative possibilities for the actor than I had previously imagined. Later that semester Daniel invited me to participate in a special project he was working on. While I didn't know about the history of European laboratory theatre at the time, and the whole thing seemed a bit mysterious, I accepted his invitation because I'd enjoyed his class. As time went by, I became obsessed with our work. I dedicated over 1000 hours of training to Les Ateliers du corps,

How to cite this book chapter:
Mroz, D. 2025. *Resonant Space: Religion, Theatre, and the Chinese Martial Arts.*
   Pp. 139–152. Cardiff: Cardiff University Press. DOI: https://doi.org/10.18573
   /book11.h. Licence: CC-BY-NC-ND

I wrote about the project in graduate school, and I meditated on my experience long after the conclusion of our project and my graduate studies.

I joined Les Ateliers du Corps in 2010. I worked as a performer and co-creator in 2010 and 2011, then took a leave of absence in the fall of 2011 and the winter of 2012 to move to the UK for graduate school. In the spring of 2012, I returned to serve as the apprentice director for our final performance, *And Treat the Distant Peoples with Kindness*. I also documented our creative process through recordings of rehearsals, interviews with the participants, and journals, an archival process upon which I based my subsequent MA thesis.

The memories, interviews, videos, and reflections I have assembled in this chapter are a palimpsest. I have written, erased, and overwritten my recollections of the events I narrate for clarity and effect, hoping to evoke some semblance of the magic we experienced at work in 2012. The reality was much messier than what I describe, made up of the artistic proposals and personal perspectives of each of the participants. Like the final performance, our creative process was a beautiful, structured, and yet tangled knot of multiple inputs. Our time in the studio preparing *And Treat the Distant Peoples with Kindness* was ripe with a multitude of meanings. While we shared this unusual rehearsal experience with one another, our preparatory work in the studio was never seen or interpreted by an audience. Now, at the removal of over a decade, I hope I can invite readers into at least a part of our process.

Introduction

In this chapter I offer three examples of how our working methods at Les Ateliers du corps widened our creative possibilities and contributed to our artistic agency, while also extending some of this agency to the audiences of *And Treat the Distant Peoples with Kindness*.

In our rehearsals, Daniel and I led a process in which we combined and juxtaposed individual compositions made by our collaborators to create a larger, more intricate and evocative tapestry. We hoped to create a performance that would preserve the qualities of the actors' individual expressions, while combining them to tell a larger story. In developing an ensemble performance from the fragments of original material created by each participant, Daniel proposed an autonomous and rigorous creative process for individual actors. This working method generated a cooperative, accountable relationship among the performers by making the creation of meaning into a collaborative exercise. This does not mean that the process was an idyllic, seamless experience of self-actualization and mutual understanding. It was technically difficult and even frustrating at times. The process was rife with challenges as the performers attempted the difficult task of preserving their personal associations and the integrity of the fragments they had created while integrating them into a larger whole guided by us directors. The creation of the Overture, the first scene of the piece, the Conclusion, its last scene, and the "Torture scene," a key moment halfway through the play, reveals a different facet of this experience.

Creating the Overture from the Performers' Physical Scores

The making of the first scene in *And Treat the Distant Peoples with Kindness* exemplified the artistic chaos our approach created in rehearsal, and the almost magical way it evoked new meanings for the actors as they combined their work. The opening scene was not a part of the script Michael Geither had written for us. Daniel and I assembled it from the individual fragments that the performers had begun making in the winter of 2012. We wanted to create a fascinating, mysterious overture that would evoke the major themes of the play while introducing the audience to the style and aesthetic conventions we were using. We also wanted to underscore the importance of the actors' individual proposals. By beginning the performance with the work that had been slowly developing all winter, we gave the participants' contributions a decisive role.

While we included a collage of texts that foreshadowed the story to come, variously evoking longing for a loved one, the difficulties of loving someone, the symptoms of cholera, and the realities of travel by sea in the 1400s, the Overture was crafted to immerse the audience in a new, fascinating, if not easily comprehended world, before the exposition of a recognizable plot and characters that followed it.

The Overture: https://vimeo.com/908004606?share=copy

In chapter 2, "Spatial Projection," Daniel describes the process of creating and combining physical scores, the pre-arranged movement patterns created by individual actors which the director combines into an eventual performance:[133]

> Physical scores resemble tàolù as their mimed movements evoke interactions with unseen elements … Solo scores are palimpsestic, evoking unseen elements which inform the visible causality created when two solos are integrated into a duet. The actors simultaneously preserve the felt senses of their original solos, while also accommodating the context created by their new stage partners. This layering ideally creates a live version of magic realism, where the invisible world of dreams and the imagination is always present at the edges of the action.

---

[133] The term "pre-arranged movement patterns" was originally coined by Hunter Armstrong, a former American serviceman, adept of Japanese martial arts, and director of the International Hoplology Society, to refer to solo and partner martial training characterized by set movement (Armstrong 1988). Daniel adopted and adapted this idea in his first book to create an English term for the choreographic activity shared by Chinese martial arts and contemporary theatre at one remove from the jargon of either discipline (Mroz 2011: 21).

To build their scores for *And Treat the Distant Peoples with Kindness*, the actors with whom we collaborated developed choreographic, spoken, and sung compositions that were, at least initially, meaningful only to them. They used an image, a theme, or a concrete task, and some included a text or a song. They all had to go off and create a repeatable short performance for which they were totally responsible. Each score was created as a whole; it contained within it an event, a fully formed image; an expression with a beginning, middle, and end. In their first iterations, these scores were pure explorations of each actor's interests, expressing a world of personal associations that could only ever be fully understood by the performer who created it.

The central piece of the Overture was a duet Gabrielle Lalonde and Katelin Richards had begun making in the winter of 2012.[134] Gabrielle created her material using Ghérasim Luca's poem "Le Rêve en action" (1953) and a folk song in old French from the isle of Guernsey. Katelin used William Carlos Williams' "The Descent of Winter" (1928/1970) to create her movements.[135] As Katelin and Gabrielle already had almost three years of experience of Daniel leading the process of creating duets from distinct solos, he suggested that they themselves negotiate how to make their scores co-exist in the same space and time, with minimal input from him. Katelin described the resulting situation:

> "You kind of have three different versions, you have your version which is the solo material … and then you have the version which is the solo and [someone else's] solo in the same place. And then you have a duet between the two solos where it's actually working, as in pause, speak, move, pause, whatever. Instead of just 'Arrgghhh' [doing hand motions of two things coming together]." (in Lalonde 2012: 35–36)

Gabrielle described her experience of this encounter:

> "When I was told I would be combining this with Katelin's work I started one of my [scores] and she incorporated pieces of hers. But we were always altering them in order to … we realized that we developed after doing it time and time and time again without making too many rough decisions, without sitting down and deciding 'Ok, this is where it's going to be cut.' It was mostly instinctual. But specifically realizing that when we were combining them the thing we were adding was the relationship, was the contact. So making sure that we are in the same space together, that we are reacting to each other's actions, that we are aware of the other person's breathing or movements or speed or all of those little elements that get put together. So we spliced our two solos,

---

[134] While we share the same last name, Gabrielle and I are not related.

[135] Daniel suggested the Luca to Gabrielle, who chose the Guernsey song from *Les Travailleurs de la mer*, a recording of early music by Andrew Lawrence-King and the Harp Consort. Katelin proposed the Williams herself.

adding in that element of reaction and movement and then later added on top of that a layer of the [spoken] poetry [that had originally been the source of inspiration for the scores]." (in Lalonde 2012: 36–37)

Initially this combination created a chaotic situation, which Katelin referred to when interviewed as "just 'Arrgghhh'" while banging her hands together! For several months, the two women improvised their duet differently every time they practiced. Sometimes there would be large passages from Richards' text; sometimes there would be more of a dialogue between the two poems. They tried many things with the text: they didn't want to just "hammer it down the first time" (Lalonde 2012: 37). After much tacit negotiation and practice, the two actors set a repeatable duet that incorporated both their movement work and a collage of the texts of their two source poems.

We confronted Gabrielle and Katelin's duet with yet another chaotic situation by incorporating the duet composed by performers David Benedict-Brown and Sean Sonier into the Overture. David and Sean had joined the project in the winter of 2012, and as they were much less familiar our working methods, they created their first physical scores using variations of the martial games described in chapter 2, assisted by Gabrielle and Kaitlin. David recalled his experience of disorientation and reorientation as he built his initial material:

"It was challenging at first, like I mentioned in the previous interview, I realize what it is now, and it was being given almost total creative control over our specific little units that we created. Because I'm not used to that; I'm used to having structures handed to me and interpreting within that. So straight creation like that is always daunting ... and that was interesting because one would think it would be freeing. But at first it wasn't freeing because it was more enclosing than the structures that I was used to. Just not having ... real grounding in any kind of world or reality. I remember asking Daniel, 'What do you want?' He was like, 'What do *you* want?' and I was like, 'Ohhh...' it was a kind of 'eureka' moment." (in Lalonde 2012: 69–70).

David and Sean combined their two solo scores with a geometric walking pattern Daniel had suggested to them. Daniel placed David and Sean on either side of Gabrielle and Katelin's duet. We added a text about cholera spoken by Sean, and a text about travel by sea performed by David. The four performers then had to negotiate all the new elements that this added to their work, finding ways to make the whole co-exist in the same space and time.

Gabrielle described this process:

"In the beginning they seemed like they were very independent of us. They were doing their own thing connected together across the room. And we were on the inside already very connected with our script, with our movements. And I remember telling you about this, the one rehearsal, just a few days ago, where all of a sudden, connecting words and impulses with the two solos from the men who were, kind of, just physically more on the outside of the space. All of a sudden things make sense and we are in a relationship. Even though I don't really acknowledge them, even though they don't really work with us directly. But meaning sort of unfolds out of itself. Which to me is a magical moment; where all of a sudden I have an action and someone says a word and all of a sudden that action takes on a new role or has a new meaning that I never thought of before." (in Lalonde 2012: 45)

The signs and relationships in the Overture were generated via simultaneous, multiple, and independent processes. Over time, the scores in the montage began to interact in subtle and overt ways. On the physical level, the actors' kinaesthetic responses to one another became clearer as they rehearsed and were able to perceive more fully what their colleagues were doing. On a personal level, the associations, memories, and images that played out in each participant's mind further influenced their timing and the way they spoke their lines. Although Daniel and I directed the final montage in which the scores interacted, the method we used to create the whole meant there was no single author and no final, correct way of interpreting the poetry of the scene.

Our choice to begin with the actors' own material gave them the confidence to navigate the chaos inherent in our process of montage. As Sean recollected:

"We created the whole thing together which I think is very satisfying ... it's a great feeling to create something and be proud of what you created. And I guess for me the most satisfying thing was how involved and how engaged I was in it. And I think because of how Daniel brought everything together he didn't drop us, like I was so involved and engaged that it just didn't fall flat in the end. It actually brought us somewhere, which is a great feeling and I think that's what's satisfying." (in Lalonde 2012: 67)

Multiple Dramaturgies in the Conclusion

The creation of the initial materials upon which the whole production was based fell largely under the control of the performers themselves. They were also responsible for many important editing and sequencing decisions. Given how decisive the actors' choices were, what did Daniel and I do as directors?

Daniel and I created a chaotic artistic situation of our own to reckon with. We confronted the story, music, and staging we were interested in with the reality of our collaborators, their individual abilities, dispositions, preoccupations, and the material they had made, while trying not to subsume one into the other. Our decision-making process was an attempt to coordinate our experience of the fascinating, idiosyncratic performance proposals created by our collaborators, with the text, songs, and staging ideas we had brought to the project. Because of this commitment, we had to negotiate between two qualities of meaning, one visceral and the other narrative, with every decision we made. The visceral attraction of the actors' proposals seemed to require one kind of dramaturgy, while our work with music, staging, and the script Michael Geither had written at our request felt like it required another.

Dramaturgy is a much-used term. Guy Cools describes it as

> the organisation of the actions of the performance, the "weaving together" of the different, often multi-disciplinary threads of the work. It is understood that dramaturgical thinking and strategies contribute to the quality of the work, its readability and accessibility. (2019: 43)

Cools' idea covers both an older use of the word in which it refers to the understanding of the literary structure of a piece of dramatic repertoire and its place in history, and a more contemporary one suggested by Marianne Van Kerkhoven:

> The type of dramaturgy I relate to, and which I try to apply both in theatre and dance, follows a certain "process": we consciously choose material from various origins (texts, movements, film images, objects, ideas ...); the "human material" (actors/dancers) clearly prevails over the rest; the performers' personalities and not their technical capacities is [*sic*] the creation's foundation. The director or choreographer starts off with those materials: in the course of the rehearsal process he/she observes how the materials behave and develop; only at the end of this entire process do we gradually distinguish a concept, a structure, a more or less clearly outlined form; this structure is by no means known at the start. (1997: 20–21; and in Cools 2019: 43)

Our work on the Conclusion of *And Treat the Distant Peoples with Kindness* demonstrated to me the challenge of distinguishing concepts and structures related to narrative in a process where human material had provided the foundation on which the piece was built. On July 31, 2012, in a personal journal, I wrote:

> Today we were working on the ending, and it became quite stressful. The composition Daniel was making and I was advising on was not working out. It was seeping energy, what we had built to that point was only being lost in the last few minutes. He tried many different things, none of which were working. The performers were patient with him and [me], but you could tell that the unsure nature of our work was

Figure 23: Cardinal Bracciolini, played by David Benedict-Brown, drinks the ocean (photo by Laura Astwood).

wearing on them. The work they were doing was physical and took quite a bit of energy, so the meandering around creatively grasping at straws must have been disheartening for them … After we had finally found something that felt good, Daniel sat down next to me with a sigh. I told him that was stressful and strange. He said, "It's like doing two things; you're trying to create tension and kinaesthetic responses, while also making meaning." This exchange really stuck with me. It is really a very simple thing to say, but it also encapsulates the director's role in this kind of work. (Lalonde 2012: 48)

In this rehearsal, Daniel knew what he wanted to build toward. Just as the Overture had introduced all the elements of the performance in a condensed form, we hoped to refer to the texts, choreographies, and music developed over the course of the piece in the Conclusion. We had already discussed the final image that we wanted to create, the character of Cardinal Bracciolini, played by David, drinking from a large paper boat that had been a major prop in the production.

The boat was our way of evoking giant objects and vast spaces on stage. We had originally used it in our 2010 production *Circe/Landfall*. Built by performer Brandon Groves, it was a large version of a child's paper boat. It was made of a moisture-resistant paper used for architectural drawings and its shape was reinforced by fine wire. We filled it with an iridescent blue sports drink. When lit from the side, a microcosmic ocean could be seen sloshing around inside. For Daniel, the image of Cardinal Bracciolini guzzling down the liquid in the boat evoked the single-minded greed that characterized the European conquests of North America, and suggested the hubris of imagining one could drink the ocean.

We also wanted to reiterate an important musical element we'd introduced earlier. One of the proposals Daniel and I had made was that the ensemble learn acapella songs from a 19th-century American Mennonite song book. Published in Virginia, USA in 1832, the *Harmonia Sacra* is a compendium of hymns and anthems in English. The lyrics of its many songs celebrate Christian faith and ideals we would understand today as colonial. We hoped to end the show with a song named "Social Band," which juxtaposed what we felt to be overtly destructive and colonial lyrics with a joyous and celebratory tune.[136]

While we had all the performers' original materials, and all the scenes of the production up to this point to sample from, we didn't know how to put them together. How would the song be introduced or even sung? Could its lyrics be spoken? How would David get to the boat and pick it up? What would lead to his drinking from it? And most importantly, could we reuse the simultaneous, dissonant singing of two of our *Harmonia Sacra* songs to inform the final image, mixing in more percussion? We had a fragmentary glimpse of our destination: it was at least theoretically foreseeable, yet the path that would get us there was unforeseeable.

Eugenio Barba's book *On Directing and Dramaturgy: Burning the House* had come out in 2010. Reading it, I related the in-the-moment difficulties we were having creating our Conclusion to the three levels of dramaturgy he had distilled from a lifetime of experience: the organic, the narrative, and the evocative:

> At the level of organic or dynamic dramaturgy I worked with physical and vocal actions, costumes, objects, music, sounds, lights, and spatial features. At the level of narrative dramaturgy, I worked with characters, stories, texts, events, and iconographic references. The evocative dramaturgy had a different nature from the other two. It was a goal. It designated the work necessary to make the same performance reverberate differently in the spectators' biographical caverns ... The organic dramaturgy is the performance's nervous system, the narrative dramaturgy is its cortex, and the evocative dramaturgy is that part of us which lives in exile within us. The organic dramaturgy makes the spectators dance kinaesthetically on their seats; the narrative dramaturgy releases conjectures, thoughts, doubts, evaluations, and questions; the evocative dramaturgy makes us live a *change of state*. (2010: 10–11)

---

[136] The entire *Harmonia Sacra* is available online, and the two songs that I discuss below, "New Monmouth" and "Social Band" can be found here https://www.harmoniasacra.org/151.html and here https://www.harmoniasacra.org/268t.html.

While working out how to create our Conclusion, I felt that Daniel and I went back and forth between Barba's narrative and organic levels of dramaturgy while paying close attention to what was being evoked in us as we watched. At the core of our problem was that the organic level was not producing an adequate kinaesthetic response in either of us. The tension we desired was lacking. We were the most sympathetic viewers possible for the piece, as we deeply wanted to be kinaesthetically affected by the performance, but our staging attempts left us unmoved. We experimented by asking the actors to spiral in various circular patterns, variations on ones used in a prior scene in which they had sung "Social Band" and "New Monmouth" simultaneously and cacophonously.[137] We played with different staging positions in the space for the final image with David and the boat, and we varied how the performers sang "Social Band."

We were also struggling with the narrative level, wondering if we should accompany the imagery with more information using textual exposition. We asked Katelin to speak a line that described the Chinese treasure ships but also foreshadowed the later European voyages to North America: "When their sails are spread, they are like great clouds in the sky." We also asked David to speak the last lines of the final verse of "Social Band": "Oh, let your thoughts delight to soar where earth and time shall be no more."

In the end we realized that we had made our attempted Conclusion too literal and leaden. The narrative level of dramaturgy was already strong enough and did not need further clarification. We decided to let the image of David drinking from the boat speak for itself, flavoured only by the other performers singing the final verse of "Social Band." The actors performed their original scores alone, frenetically, in semi-darkness, no longer in visible relationship to one another. Their frenzy and isolation underscored both the personal tragedy of de Conti and his family, and the human tragedies to come in the colonial era. Drinking off the contents of the boat in one long draught right after performing his demanding choreography left David out of breath. His panting was the last sound heard in the play, after the lights came down.

The Conclusion: https://vimeo.com/908005491?share=copy

This chaotic rehearsal brought home to me the complexity and tensions that accompany working in the open-ended way that we had chosen. Implicit in our final decisions about the Conclusion was our belief in evocative dramaturgy, in the ability of spectators and performers to infuse their own meanings into the montage we had made. When we let the image of the boat speak for itself, we hoped that we were allowing spectators to create their own meaning. We believed that in relating what they were trying to know (the meaning of the

---

[137] See 35:10—35:58 in the full video of *And Treat the Distant Peoples with Kindness*, linked in Appendix D.

image of drinking from the boat) to what they already knew (the meanings they had already attributed to the boat, the character of Bracciolini, the song "Social Band," etc.) and reflecting upon what this meant for the piece as a whole, our audience members would synthesize the choreography, music, and plot we'd offered them into a much more personal experience, greater than the sum of its parts. Rather than didactically telling them what to think about the final image and attributing a specific sense to it, we allowed it to be infused with the multiple meanings that might be conjured by all participants in the performance— performers, directors, and spectators alike. Our audiences' responses to our attempts to create such an open experience were fascinating in their variety. This was particularly noticeable in their reactions to a stylized scene of torture that occurred in the middle of the performance.

Soliciting Spectator Authorship in the Torture Scene

A chair, a string, a wooden wheel, a song, lines of text, and some muscle contractions: this was our recipe for torture in the summer of 2012. When combined in the imaginations of our audience members, these ingredients produced very different reactions. Individual spectators' accounts of the nature and severity of the torture ranged widely, even though they had all seen the same performance. Somehow these mundane objects, sounds, and movements inspired visceral responses in a bunch of people sitting together in a dimly lit room, even if they didn't all interpret or remember them in the same ways.

The Torture scene was the principal scene of *And Treat the Distant Peoples with Kindness*, placed about halfway into the piece. Compositionally, this scene was simple. Cardinal Bracciolini, played by David, interrogated de Conti, played by Sean. David moved about the space manipulating the mundane objects mentioned above, while Sean mimed the effects of being tortured. The text of this scene is found in Appendix B.

The Torture scene: https://vimeo.com/908005760?share=copy

Many spectators spoke to me about this sequence afterwards. I am not exaggerating when I say that it had conjured different images for each person I spoke with. Hearing so many different accounts made me understand how the collaborative generation of meaning in our process had also involved our audiences. While they understood the scene's overall narrative, the diversity of their reactions to the scene made me appreciate that every spectator had become a collaborator in the generation of meaning. It also offered me the opportunity to experience what I think Barba meant by evocative dramaturgy.

Of course, there was no torture occurring on stage. Instead of attempting literally to present the torture of de Conti, Daniel, the performers, and

I developed a combination of elements that we hoped would evoke very personal dramaturgies in our spectators, hoping that they, too, would collaborate in the process of generating the scene's meaning.

At the organic level of dramaturgy, we used the materiality of the objects: the firm wooden quality of the wheel and the chair, the way the wheel rolled on the ground and lay flat when on its side, the delicate, clean white lines of the string which contrasted with the black stage and backdrop, the way Sean's robes flowed in space and David's shirt and pants did not, and so on. We also used the kinetic quality of the movements: the delicate way David held the string, placing it slowly and precisely, the quick, jerky force he used when moving the chair, and the sudden muscle contractions Sean employed in response to David's movements. We further shaped the soundscape using contrasting elements: the harmonies of Katelin and Gabrielle's song, the quiet questioning tone David used, the rising intensity of Sean's voice, his pained laughter, and the sudden silences. We switched the lighting states from warm reds to cool blues, punctuating David's actions. This tapestry of organic dramaturgical elements had a somatic impact on both the performers and spectators.

The narrative level of dramaturgy in the scene included representational imagery, identifiable characters, and the actual text for the scene. Bracciolini's mitre was an obvious sign of his position. De Conti's attempts to provide information to stop the torture led only to continuing questioning by Bracciolini, which slowly revealed his unique knowledge of navigation. Gabrielle and Kaitlin, who played de Conti's deceased wife and child, provided the music for the scene, suggesting that de Conti's family were singing to him from beyond the grave. The narrative level of dramaturgy provided spectators rational waypoints to connect and interpret in terms of the established plot. These dramaturgical layers occurred simultaneously in the real time of the performance, supporting one another and offering different stimuli for spectators to interpret and respond to.

I remain fascinated how much the scene affected me in rehearsal and in performance given that the fictional nature of the torture was not hidden, but rather emphasized. The actors assembled the "torture devices" from the harmless objects that had already been used in previous scenes. I was fully aware that Sean's hand was in no danger when David placed it inside the handle of the chair. Yet Sean's physical contractions and the contortion of his face nevertheless produced a strong kinaesthetic response in me. The narrative elements enhanced this organic input. The imaginary situation of Bracciolini torturing de Conti further focused my response to what was occurring in the real space occupied by the performers and spectators. In the terms I've used above, I already knew the story of de Conti. I was *trying to know* why Sean appeared to be suffering. Because of the open way we'd created and staged this scene, my imagination was set in motion by all these elements. I was actively involved in creating the scene for myself from the elements provided. Due to this active participation, I believe that I put the organic and the narrative elements together in a way that affected me more strongly than a realistic depiction of the same events might have. My speculations were born out in conversations with our audience members after the performance. I heard interpretations of the torture scene that ranged from the overtly political to the intensely personal. The scene evoked memories for some and considerations of ethics for others. For a few it simply advanced the narrative of the piece without eliciting a strong response.

Two instances stand out among our audience's reactions. I think that these are examples of evocative dramaturgies, and they brought home to me the idea that the ultimate authors of *And Treat the Distant Peoples with Kindness* were the audience members themselves. A friend who came to see the performance shared that he was incredibly disturbed by the torture scene, and it stuck with him for days afterward. My friend described the moment when Sean had one foot in the wheel and was leaning back tensely while his right arm hung slack as the "image of a man choking on his own teeth," recalling text from earlier in the piece spoken by David, describing the vicious acts of colonization in India perpetrated by Vasco da Gama. For him, a man with a grounding in history and political science, the scene became a microcosm of the cruelty of the European colonial projects. He felt sick to his stomach as he kinaesthetically responded to Sean's physical tension, tied it to the narrative of the play, and considered the whole in light of his extensive knowledge of colonial history. The combination evoked an emotionally potent experience, the specifics of which we could not have predicted.

At another performance I heard laughter in the audience, a response we had not experienced before. I wondered, could it be anxious laughter? Was it excited, malevolent? It turned out to be none of the above. Someone had brought their son, no older than 11, to the show. The boy's laughter came from a simultaneously thoughtful and authentically simple place. Like most, he understood the scene to be about a man being tortured by another, more powerful man. But he also saw Bacciolini's funny hat, the rinky-dink string-chair-wheel-torture-device, and a bunch of adults very seriously pretending together in a darkened room. Both observations were true. While the idea of torture was disturbing, the adults' credulous engagement with such obvious make-believe was funny.

Overall, our pragmatic decisions seem to have accomplished our dual goal of telling a collective story while preserving the proposals of our actors. From an artistically chaotic working situation with unpredictable outcomes, we seem to have communicated a plot that was globally understood, and that generated visceral responses and associations that were particular to each audience member.

Conclusion

In presenting examples of how our work widened our creative possibilities, contributed to our artistic agency, and shared that agency with our audiences, I've been reminded of the many artistic proposals we solicited and edited together, and of just how many things happened in consequence.

Our working method of combining the actors' original compositions with the narrative given shape by Michael Geither's script gave us two sets of materials to work with. We experienced these as distinct visceral and narrative elements and found ourselves coordinating two different kinds of dramaturgy. Our commitment to preserving and foregrounding the scores of our collaborators established a conceptual space between these two sets. I speculate that it was this space that permitted the resonances and personal interpretations felt and made by our audiences. Gǎnyìng, which Daniel mentions in the Introduction to this book, is not a term we used at the time, but reflecting on this process and all its elements leads me to conclude that such resonance is perhaps the best overall descriptor for what we hoped to create for our audiences, and the invisible, spatial ingredient that allowed this production to function as it did.

Colin Lalonde holds an MA in International Performance Research from the University of Warwick and the University of Arts in Belgrade as well as an MA in Public Policy and Public Administration from Concordia University in Montréal. He was a member of Les Ateliers du Corps between 2009 and 2012 and went on to found Studio Porte Bleue in Montréal in 2013, where he wrote and directed multiple performances including While Rats Eat Pie *and* The Binaries Between Us. *He is a policy analyst for Immigration, Refugees and Citizenship Canada, a department of the federal government of Canada.*

CHAPTER 7

Space is Time. Time is Space

勢即時, 時即勢

shì jí shí, shí jí shì

Introduction

Wǔshù has determined how I experience space and time, providing a view that underpins my work as a theatre director and teacher of acting and directing, as a teacher of martial arts for dancers, and as a facilitator and dramaturg for choreographers. Where chapter 2 and chapter 6 describe the process and procedures of directing, in this chapter I discuss the impact of Chinese martial arts training on my work as a facilitator and dramaturg. To elucidate this experience, I share a phenomenology of space and time informed by the Chinese martial arts, describe two key elements of martial movement training that arise from this, and recount my work in creative processes in which I served as a facilitator and a dance dramaturg.

A Phenomenology of Space, Time, and Change

My perception of space is possible due to differentiation: If I cover my eyes with my hand, all I see is a blurred shape. As I move my hand away from my face, its contours appear. The space between my eyes and my hand allows me to perceive it. Differentiation allows me to understand my shape, and my position with respect to my environment. My understanding of time is possible because of alternation: my recurring inhalation and exhalation, the contractions and expansions of my heart, or the cycle of day and night give me regular parameters within which I can situate the present moment. Both differentiation and

---

How to cite this book chapter:
Mroz, D. 2025. *Resonant Space: Religion, Theatre, and the Chinese Martial Arts.*
    Pp. 153–176. Cardiff: Cardiff University Press. DOI: https://doi.org/10.18573
    /book11.i. Licence: CC-BY-NC-ND

alternation appear because of changes in my body and my environment, all of which happen due to movement.[138]

Examining movement from the perspective of temporal alternation, I notice that I usually experience changes in the shape of my body in three phases. The smallest complete unit of muscular action that I would use to change the shape of my body involves some combination of the muscles lengthening, pausing, and shortening—three parts. I usually experience the displacement of my body by parsing it into two phases, one for each footfall, with a complete step occurring in a unit of two. The spatial qualities of my changing shape and position become temporal qualities of twos and threes. I can likewise examine the effect of my deceleration, suspension, and acceleration within the three-count of shape-changes and the two-count of locomotion to better understand the temporal sequencing that links my movements together to form more complex actions. I can also reverse this and parse locomotion into three and manipulation into two. As the flux of muscular activity is mostly unconscious, my parsing of action and locomotion into units of three and two is a helpful first step in making the timing of my movements clearer to myself.

Overall, my understanding of space, time, and change arises from my experience of my body and my environment, and I experience these abstract ideas as differentiation, alternation, and movement. My general movements of locomotion and manipulation can be felt in temporal phases of two and three. The quality of these phases can be felt in my movements of deceleration, suspension, and acceleration.

While chapter 2 introduced how the Chinese martial arts parse space, teachers of wǔshù have also addressed time both in terms of the microcosm of tactical interaction, and the macrocosm of lifetime training. Like the spatial grids, volumes, and principles described in chapter 2, these microcosmic temporal parameters have allowed me to better parse and remember what I'm experiencing in the studio when working as a facilitator and dramaturg. The larger macrocosmic ideas have allowed me to adjust my comments and suggestions for collaborators with different degrees of artistic experience.

Tactical Time in Wǔshù

Across the Chinese martial arts, the timing of interactions between training partners, competitors or antagonists is broadly divided into three kinds

---

[138] I learned the correlation of space, time, and change with differentiation, alternation, and movement in 2008 from the late Liú Míng 劉明, né Charles Belyea (1947–2015), who was a teacher of the Bā Tiān Mén Dào 八天門道, a jiào that he claimed to have learned from a Taiwanese hermit whose family name was Liú (Belyea & Tainer 1991: 4). Liú Míng was also an initiate of the Dzogchen school of Tibetan Buddhism, which he had studied under such notable teachers as Namkhai Norbu (1938–2018) and Tarthang Tulku (b. 1934.) As the phenomenology of space is a hallmark of Dzogchen teachings, it is quite possible that his presentation is syncretic. His pithy correlations between space and time are also summarized in a pamphlet entitled *Sleep, Dream, and the Dao of Night* (2007: 1). For more on Liú Míng see Phillips 2008: 161–176.

of responses. An ideal response is proactive, preventing a training partner from initiating aggressive movement. A later response intercepts aggressive movement before it can be completed. The most common response is reactive, attempting defense after a partner's incoming action is complete. The time these categories describe is qualitative rather than objective, predicated on the phenomenology of the interactions they produce.

American wǔshù teacher Tim Cartmell described these three experiences of time using the metaphor of defending against being shot at by an archer.[139] *Jìntóu* 勁頭, catching the head of the initiative, is like dodging the fired arrow and then attacking the archer. *Jìnwěi* 勁尾, catching the tail of the initiative, is like holding the arrow tip just as the archer pulls his bow to a full draw but before he releases it. *Jiélán* 截攔, to intercept and obstruct, is like attacking the archer just before he releases the arrow.

Xíngyì Quán teacher Zhū Guāng 朱光 of Beijing described similar kinds of timing to his students in the UK. In *xíng* 形, or shape-based timing, I respond after my partner has completed their movement. In *qì* 氣 or breath-based, timing, I intercept their movement before they complete it. In *yì* 意 or intentional timing, I proactively attack to prevent them from moving in the first place. Xíng timing is thus described because I perceive the shape of my partner's body and react accordingly. Qì timing refers to breathing as I see or feel the inhalation that signals my partner's impulse to move and intercept them. In yì timing, I read the gestalt of the situation and determine my fellow player's intention before it manifests as a breathing impulse or a physical action.[140]

The intervals that these metaphors describe feel quite distinct from each other. If I have the skill to behave proactively, my exchange with my partner feels very brief, as they don't have the opportunity to move. If I can respond actively, the exchange feels that much longer, as they signal future movement and I move first in reply. When I can only react, the number of movements involved is multiplied as both my partner and I move, creating an exchange that requires more time to complete.

Seen from the outside, these three experiences of time combine to determine the changing shapes of the two bodies interacting and of the shifting volumes of the negative space that surrounds them. While, in the abstract, space and time appear to be equal complementary concepts, in a personal phenomenology conditioned by Chinese martial training the experience of space seems to dominate, determining as it does the sense of time conjured by different physical interactions. Physicist John Wheeler's summary, "Matter tells space-time how to bend; space-time tells matter how to move," which tellingly uses the verbs bending and moving, is a pithy expression of the perspectives on

---

[139] Cartmell remembers learning these metaphors from one of his early Tàijí Quán teachers, perhaps Lín Ā Lóng 林阿龍, in Taiwan in the 1980s (personal communication).

[140] I learned this classification from Graham Barlow (UK), who learned it from Damon Smith (UK), himself a student of Zhū Guāng, PhD, who founded and led the Tai Chi and Hsing Yi Society at the University of Leeds from 1989 to 1998 while conducting post-graduate work in Civil Engineering (Hamilton 1998).

space and time that are inculcated by Chinese martial training (Misner, Thorne & Wheeler 1973: 5).

As a facilitator and dramaturg, parsing time subjectively and spatially allows me to see how rudimentary meanings are created in the physical interactions of dancers and actors that I observe. These subjective timings create patterns to which I can attribute the fundamental human responses of attraction, aversion, and indifference, giving a meaning to the behaviour of the performers I observe that goes beyond the tactical intentions of martial artists at play. Sharing my interpretation of their movements with the artists I'm watching permits them a wider range of future creative options, as they understand more clearly how their initial choreographic proposals are being interpreted.

Lived Time in Wǔshù

The unit of three is also used in Chinese martial arts to describe the phases of personal practice over a lifetime. The late Taiwanese wǔshù teacher Zhōu Bǎofù 周寶富 (1951–2013) explained that it takes three years of study to incorporate the fundamental vocabulary of movements, a further five years of practice to be able to employ them spontaneously, and then ten years to properly explore their possibilities:

> What does "small achievement in three years, middle achievement in five and great achievement in ten" mean? Rather than thinking of it as time, it is better to think of it as a guide to the proper proportions of training. Three plus five plus ten equals eighteen. By the time a child reaches eighteen years of age he should be an adult. These eighteen years of education are a necessary and inevitable process. Three years of basic training, five years of understanding and ten of experience. This proportion is also known as "practice 3, think 5, search 10." Of course, these numbers will vary according to the specific abilities of the student, but the proportions will not be far off. (Zhōu online)

Zhōu's "practice 3, think 5, search 10" resembles the wǔshù expression *xué liàn huà* 学练化—to learn, practice, and transform, a pithy description of the stages of development through which the would-be adept passes (Wong 1976: 81). In my experience, the cycle of *xué liàn huà* repeats itself many times over the course of an artist's life. Completing the 18 years Zhōu describes does not interrupt an artist's need for practice, reflection, and further searching. Experienced creators who accomplished their 10 years of searching long ago are very different from emerging artists, and these broad phases allow me to situate the artists I am advising and hopefully speak with them in a way that best suits their projects. As a primary witness of the art being created in the studio, I am hoping to see moments of transformation. Where these seem absent or obscured, xué liàn huà offers me a useful way of framing my questions and observations: Does the work require some fundamental attribute that needs to be learned? Does it simply require more practice? Is there some way of facilitating a transformation that is not quite happening yet?

Movement Patterns and the Transformation of Space-Time

When I assist artists creating new work, my objective is not to share my own aesthetic preferences, but rather to help the people I advise to see the possibilities available in the material that interests them. I do, however, carry a personal preoccupation with me into the studio that influences the way in which help my collaborators. Because I have been conditioned by the Chinese martial arts, I am attracted to moments in the sketches of working artists that seem to offer the potential for transformation, or *huà*, by which I mean two kinds of decisive changes in the performer's body that alter witnesses' experience of the space and time of the performance they are watching. My perception of these two kinds of change comes from my training, which has sensitized me to key movement patterns I refer to as the *pulse* and the *maelstrom*.

All the Chinese martial expressions I have seen use combinations of two different kinds of movement patterns, or *lì* 力. Prosaically, lì refers to strength. When it appears as part of a martial arts term, it describes how a particular kind of power is produced. While still referring to movement quality, it is a more literal descriptor than the many jìn discussed in chapter 5. The two movement patterns that I believe generally characterize the Chinese martial arts are *zhěng hé lì* 整合力, power produced by integrated movement, and *júbù lì* 局部力, power produced by sectional movement, which I first introduced in chapter 1.[141] Described very simply, zhěng hé lì is like jumping on a balloon on the ground where the whole mass of the body arrives at once. Júbù lì is like throwing a ball, which takes place in phases from the wind-up to the release of the ball.

In more detail, Chén Tàijí Quán players, for example, raise and lower their hips vertically to create power. The dropping of one hip presses the leg below it into the ground, provoking an opposite reaction force that can emerge from almost any point on the body, manifesting as zhěng hé lì. Many small actions and decisions are needed to produce the effect of integrated movement. Chói Lěih Fáht Kyùhn, in contrast, requires that players keep their hips level during movement. The horizonal disk of the waist is the principal link in a series of actions that create júbù lì. Players push off their back legs to add force to the

---

[141] I have chosen these two kinds of complementary lì to explain the relationships between movement quality and time, but they are not absolute parameters. Among the many other examples of lì found in Chinese martial arts, we could also include *luó xuán lì* 螺旋力, power produced by spiral movement, and *yāobó lì* 腰膊, power produced by waist and shoulder movement. Like the many jìn, different kinds of style-specific lì abound.

rotation of their hips, which they shift toward their supporting leg while rotating their torsos, moving their arms, and allowing the power created by the initial push off the ground to be expressed through the hands. These, however, are ideal parameters. In sparring and partner games, Chói Lěih Fáht Kyùhn players occasionally differentiate their hips vertically, and Chén Tàijí Quán players sometimes make horizontal shifts. [142]

As their practice matures, players can tacitly discover zhěng hé lì as they refine their júbù lì, and vice versa. While it may not be as precise as the skill developed by explicit training in each approach, the process of unconsciously converting sectional movement to integrated movement, for example, can begin with the intention to apply one's mass more effectively. Expert martial artist Ellis Amdur offers a clear description of refined júbù lì:

> You push off the back foot and then pull with the front—it is a pulse, without moving either foot. The force travels through your body into your weapon. Your arms transmit force; they do not express it. (2023: 32)

If one traces the pushing and pulling of the feet up to the hips and adds the requirement that while the hips can move vertically, one up and one down, they should not move side to side or back and forth, one will have turned sectional movement of the sort found in Chói Lěih Fáht Kyùhn into the integrated movement found in Chén Shì Tàijí Quán, placing the two approaches on a single spectrum.

The refined expression of zhěng hé lì creates a pulse that instantly changes the shape and the tone of the body of the player who manifests it. The refined expression of júbù lì creates a maelstrom of winding tissues in the body of the artist who displays it. Pulses change the curves of space-time almost instantly, while maelstroms reshape them more gradually, creating intensity and suspense. Subjectively, pulses seem to speed time up, while maelstroms slow it down.

These two movement patterns present separate coordination issues for the martial artist using them. For zhěng hé lì the challenge is to be able to change

---

[142] The late sports scientist Mel Siff (1944–2003) suggested that contemporary elite athletics in China owed much to traditional concepts. Siff's account of what he calls Chinese "basic power sequences" is a pithy, kinesiological description of the *wài sān hé* 外三合, the three outer or visible harmonies, a concept in Chinese martial arts that links the movement of the hips and shoulders, knees and elbows, and the ankles and wrists. The wài sān hé are used in different ways in the production of júbù lì and zhěng hé lì:

> The Chinese pair up equivalent joints in the upper and lower body. Trunk rotation in all three planes is regarded as fundamental to all movement. Then, the upper body joint closest to the trunk is the shoulder, whereas the lower body joint closest to the trunk is the hip. Therefore, actions of the shoulder and hip joints are regarded as equivalent. Similarly, the elbow and knee joints, and the wrist and ankle joints, are analogues of one another. Finally, the carpals and the metacarpals, and the tarsals and metatarsals of the foot are equivalent in action.

> On the basis of these upper-lower body analogues, the Chinese have developed basic power sequences. (Siff 2016/1995: 272).

shape in motion, retaining control of the position of one's mass. For júbù lì, the challenge is not to leak power as the body moves sectionally. In zhěng hé lì the exponent is a sort of "smart bullet," able to change shape and trajectory enroute to an opponent's body. In júbù lì the player is more like a gun or a launchpad and is less able to change ideas once a strike has been launched.

Getting interrupted upstream on the body is not often a problem for adepts of zhěng hé lì, as they can rapidly reposition the "dot" where they will eventually express force by changing the distribution of muscular tone within themselves with little or no adjustment to the configuration of their body. An adept of zhěng hé lì could move the point where they express their force from one part of their fist to another, or to their forearm, hip, shoulder, or shin, adapting to their opponent's defensive movement without much change in the shape of their body.

Getting interrupted upstream on the body is a much larger problem for players using júbù lì, as potentially powerful punches are not at all strong up near the shoulder, and a light brush to misalign the torso can cut the momentum of a strike substantially. Júbù lì adepts are often very skilled at folding their limbs and rotating their waists and thoraxes to adapt to changing circumstances, creating maelstroms of spiralling limbs.

In the first video example below, my teacher Chén Zhōnghuá performs *Pào Chuí* 砲捶 or Cannon Hammers, the second tàolù of the Chén Tàijí Quán system, a choreography that is full of the powerful pulses of zhěng hé lì. In the second example, my grand-teacher Chiu Kwok Cheung performs the *Daaih Sahp Jih Kyùhn* 大十字拳, or Large Ten-Character Fist, the second tàolù in his Chói Lěih Fáht Kyùhn curriculum. This choreography presents many very rapid displays of júbù lì, and is so named because of the large plus-sign its footwork describes on the ground, which in Chinese is the character for the number 10: 十.

Chén Zhōnghuá performing *Chén Tàijí Quán Pào Chuí*—a whole-body pulse of zhěng hé lì is clearly visible at 0:13–14: https://vimeo .com/912349999?share=copy

Chói Lěih Fáht Kyùhn adept Chiu Kwok Cheung performing the *Daaih Sahp Jih Kyùhn*—the maelstrom of júbù lì is particularly visible at 0:21–26: https://vimeo.com/914012873?share=copy

Pulse and Maelstrom in Performance

Pulses recurve space-time all at once, while maelstroms sculpt it more gradually, allowing us to see the changes being effected. A pulse creates surprise, while a maelstrom builds suspense. After a pulse we ask ourselves "what just happened?" During a maelstrom we ask, "what is going to happen?" The moment of suspension following either kind of movement is a node of stillness that can reset our perception as spectators. The artist can use such a suspension to provide the audience with new information without disorienting them or losing their attention. This effect is common in cinema: in a hard cut, an event concludes and another begins without the introduction of any transitional material. In a smash cut, an initial action is abruptly suspended, and a new action is introduced. These cinematic examples might seem unusual for theatre and dance, which traditionally unfold live and in real time. Director Anne Bogart describes how she sees these kinds of changes operating in theatre:

> Shortly before German playwright Heiner Müller died, he visited Columbia University to speak with graduate theater students. After a long, brilliant, eloquent, complex talk, a bright-eyed young student raised his hand with the question: "Mr. Müller, do you have any advice for a young actor?" There was a moment of silence. "Yes," replied Müller generously, "because you have a body, you do not need transitions."

> This advice could require a lifetime to understand and digest, but at the same time it helps to crystallize the notion that we don't *always* have to think our way from one state to another. So often we want to understand why a character goes from A to G, but we discover that in simply going from A to G, in simply putting it in our bodies, in simply *doing* it, there is a kind of understanding that emerges, an understanding beyond reason and psychology. (Bogart & Landau 2005: 185)

The kind of leaps Bogart describes can be used by performers to move a piece from scene to scene or to change the quality of what they are doing within a shorter fragment of a performance. While the transformation of the on-stage action can be supported by altering elements such as the set, the lighting states, and the sound cues, like Müller and Bogart I feel that the transformation of the performers' bodies is the primary source of change on stage. The *huà* of the body preserves continuity while also allowing the introduction of new information, stimulating audiences' imaginations while retaining their attention.

The pulse and the maelstrom are the fundamental perceptual experiences that I bring with me into the studio. While I want to be available to all the proposals the artists I'm advising make, pulses and maelstroms are inherent to my way of parsing movement. Making them explicit to myself allows me greater clarity of communication when I work as a facilitator and a dramaturg.

Facilitation and Dramaturgy

I use the term facilitation to describe situations in which I provide artists with experiences that can nourish their future work in ways of their own choosing.

While I do teach martial arts jībĕngōng, tàolù, and partner games in this context, I do so in the hope that some element of what I share will be of use to them later, rather than in a performance I'm directing or choreographing myself. The outcomes of facilitation can range from a modest introduction, to new somatic experiences, to subtle choreographic choices in later works that are known only to the artists themselves, to the artists' direct use of some of the procedures I've introduced.

I use the term dramaturgy in the sense established by Guy Cools, who describes his work as a dance dramaturg in terms of the three roles of witness, dialogue partner, and editor (2019: 47–50). My silent presence as witness in the rehearsal studio supports the artists' work, offering them the discreet, tacit support of my somatic responses to their proposals. Outside of the rehearsals proper, my conversations with the artists not only offer them my reflections on what is being created, but also support the establishment, maintenance, and development of the conditions they need to keep working. In the final stages of the process, my familiarity with the work allows me to assist in the editing together of the various fragments that have been created, suggesting the order in which they are presented and how transitions between them might be achieved.

To explain the role of the pulse and the maelstrom in these two activities, I offer the following examples. In 2018 I introduced students and recent graduates of the contemporary dance program at Fontys University of the Arts in Tilburg, the Netherlands to the partner games and exercises of the Chinese martial arts. In 2021 I helped facilitate the meeting of Naishi Wang and Jean Abreu, two choreographer-dancers who were working together for the first time developing *Deciphers*, a contemporary dance piece, at the National Arts Centre of Canada in Ottawa. *Deciphers* premiered in January 2024 at the PuSh Festival in Vancouver, Canada. Beginning in the fall of 2022, I served as a dramaturg for choreographer-dancer Katherine Ng as she created a solo for the CanAsian Dance Festival. *Calm and Dormant with Strength and Power; Sinuous and Flowing* premiered in Montréal, Canada in May of 2023.

Martial Movement at Fontys University of the Arts

In November and December of 2018, I facilitated approximately 40 hours of studio work for the contemporary dance program at Fontys University of the Arts in Tilburg, the Netherlands at the invitation of teachers Ulrika Kinn Svensson and Dirk Dumon, whom I had met through Guy Cools. The participants included 10 recent graduates of the dance program and three students from the choreography stream.[143] The alumni group met for three hours a night, four

---

[143] The participants in the alumni group were Steffi de Leeuw, Sergio Debevère, Laila el Bazi, Martina Gunkel, Dylan Holly, Tommy Pham, Kevin Ruijters, Suzan Stouthart, Kelly Vanneste,

nights a week over three weeks. I met with the choreography students separately for approximately nine hours and attended the performances of the first performances they had created for the program, contextualizing our time in the studio in terms of what I had seen in their dance pieces.

During these sessions I shared the first section of the first tàolù of Chén Tàijí Quán and a series of partnering games based on avoidance and entanglement like the suite shared in chapter 2. I took the participants through the process of setting duets and turning them into solos, and used a simple writing exercise to generate texts for them to speak during extended improvisations that incorporated all the elements we'd worked on.

The Fontys group were enthusiastic, highly trained, and used to intense physical work. They learned everything I shared quickly and precisely. In an early session, while most of the participants continued to improvise, I quietly took two of them aside to coach a nuance of manipulating a partner's arm using the huà jìn 化勁, or transformational movement skill, of Tàijí Quán. When one partner resists the other's attempted rotation, the partner initiating the movement can increase the force of their turn by adding a slight extension along the line of their arm to overcome that resistance. I only explained this detail to two of the participants, but over the next few minutes I watched this new skill spread through the room as though by induction as the two dancers I had coached used it with their colleagues, who tacitly adopted it without a word being spoken.[144]

The avoidance and entanglements games we played lent themselves a little more easily to the creation of maelstroms, dependent as many of them were on sectional movement patterns. In this video example, dancers Martina Gunkel, Kevin Ruijters, and Julia van Rooijen improvise with avoidance and entanglement. The long-armed winding movements Kevin and Julia use at 0:35–37 demonstrate their growing comfort with the shapes and dynamics used to create maelstroms:[145]

https://vimeo.com/915667547?share=copy

---

and Julia van Rooijen. The choreography students were Leo Rathmann, Laura Schönlau, and Celina Schröter.

[144] While the element of huà jìn I describe here sounds like a simple movement, the kind of angular momentum or torque it creates is very surprising when felt for the first time. One of the participants, dancer Kevin Ruijters, had a black belt rank in Jūdō and extensive competition experience. During our work we found that we had a great number of throws in common, but that he knew quite I few I'd never seen. He was also flummoxed by huà jìn. He laughingly explained that he believed that he could throw me most of the time, which he really could have, "but then you do that *thing*. I never felt anything like that before!"

[145] Thanks to dancer and impromptu videographer Dylan Holly, who arrived at the studio while this improvisation was already underway and who took the camera from me, taking over the shooting so I could make notes.

I hoped to share how the suspended moment created at the conclusion of a maelstrom or a pulse could enable a shift where new and unusual elements could be introduced. One novel element we worked with was having the dancers switch from moving to speaking. I asked the dancers to write short individual texts to have words to speak during our improvisations. I asked the dancers to each write and memorize five questions they might pose if they met themselves 10 years in the future, as well as five statements using the very open-ended template of "this is…," "it feels like…," "she is…," "they are…," "and … is all around us."

In this longer excerpt from our work, the dancers began with simple combinations of speaking, moving, and watching, and gradually incorporated fragments of the solo choreographies we had created using our martial games. While the dancers were free to speak in their mother tongues for ease of recall, everyone in this example elected to speak in English:

https://vimeo.com/915681934?share=copy

After two and a half weeks of practice, the dancers demonstrated the beginnings of both júbù lì and zhěng hé lì. The large winding motions they accomplished with their arms were increasingly driven by the sectional coordination of their legs, waists, and torsos. Their clear moments of suspension, the tight stops that punctuated their phrases, began to have the quality of pulses, projecting the reaction force generated by their downward momentum through their entire bodies. Their daily improvisations further led to the discovery of a correlate suspension at the end of a spoken question or statement where the dancers could elect to return to movement, speak again, or direct their attention to one of their fellow performers.

I learned a lot from this experience. It was fascinating to watch the dancers absorb the martial games and through them express the beginnings of júbù lì and zhěng hé lì. I do not know how this intensive workshop influenced their subsequent work, yet their generous participation allowed me to better understand the movement structures that inform my aesthetic perceptions and preferences, and to more clearly articulate how I understand the role of maelstrom and the pulse onstage.

Deciphers

In the November and December of 2021, at the invitation of Sionêd Watkins, I helped to facilitate the first meeting of Naishi Wang and Jean Abreu, two choreographer-dancers in residence at the National Arts Centre of Canada.[146]

---

[146] In his professional work, Wáng Nǎishí 王乃石 uses the Pīnyīn Romanization of his name without the tonal markings and the Euro-American convention of listing the family name last.

Jean and Naishi had been planning to create a duet performance together, inspired by their different experiences of emigration as younger dancers. Jean had moved from Brazil to the UK to dance, and Naishi had moved from China to Canada for the same reason. The COVID-19 pandemic that broke out in the late winter of 2020 postponed their meeting. When they arrived in Ottawa to begin to work on *Deciphers* in the fall of 2021, they had written many letters to one another and communicated online, but had yet to work in person. My role was to offer Jean and Naishi new ways to explore moving together.[147] We met twice for two-hour sessions, during which I led them through the games of avoidance and entanglement as well as the sticking sword fencing game, all presented in chapter 2. After our work in Ottawa at the end of November, we decided to meet for three more two-hour sessions at the Harbourfront Centre in Toronto in early December.

Jean and Naishi were already very experienced creators when I met them. As our work sessions were short, I kept my intervention very focussed and active, spending as much of our time as possible on movement. Jean and Naishi's maturity and good humour helped our process enormously. Both dancers had the ability to switch instantly from smiling, informal conversation to concentrated and intense work, which made the time we spent together very productive indeed.

When I introduced the sticking sword exercises, I discovered that Naishi was already familiar with solo manipulation of the jiàn. In his teens he had been a full-time student at a state wǔshù school in Tianjin, where he had specialized in the performance of Bāguà Zhǎng tàolù.

At the end of our time at the National Arts Centre, Sionêd Watkins helped us make a video of all the elements we had covered for the dancers to refer to in their future work. As the martial games initially limited momentum and maintained a slow and even speed, they more easily lent themselves to the development of the sectional movement of júbù lì than they did to the short, sharp pulses of zhěng hé lì, as can be seen in our archive:

https://vimeo.com/916784046?share=copy

A few weeks later, in December of 2021, Naishi and Jean asked me to join them again, this time at the Harbourfront Centre in Toronto, to help with a puzzle that had emerged in their work. The dancers were curious about the effect of different breathing patterns on the shape of the body. If the body were struck, would it freeze, inhale or exhale? How would these different responses change the shape of the body? How could a soloist move convincingly using the same reactions he would have if he were struck? To help answer these questions,

---

[147] *Jīngjù* artist William Lau, dancer and somatics expert Sionêd Watkins, and the late choreographer, dancer, and teacher Tedd Robinson (1952–2022) also worked as facilitators for this project, for which Guy Cools served as dramaturg.

I taught Naishi and Jean how to punch me in the abdomen. I had them use a predictable rhythm to target spots just above or just below my navel where I could easily absorb their shots.

As I coached them to improve the quality of their punches, I also demonstrated different ways in which I could receive their hits. Depending on the angle and power of Jean or Naishi's punches, I could keep my abdominal muscles firm, allow them to soften away from the blow, or expand them to try to interrupt the incoming fist. As we played, their punches became stronger, and I had to control my abdomen more precisely to absorb them. I used a method of breathing and moving called *hēng-hā*, which is found in some versions of Tàijí Quán and other northern Chinese martial arts.

Hēng-hā breathing is named after a pair of Chinese deities, the Hēng-Hā Generals or Hēng-Hā Èr Jiàng. These two martial deities appear in *The Canonization of the Gods* or *Fēng Shén Yǎnyì* 封神演义, an anonymous Ming dynasty compendium of fantastical tales written in vernacular Chinese that appeared in the early 1600s. Set in the late Shang and early Zhou dynasties, *The Canonization of the Gods* tells the stories of successful Léi Fǎ, or Thunder Rituals (see chapter 3), through which troublesome local spirits were transformed into benevolent deities honoured by the larger ritual networks of China due to the ritual actions of intrepid Daoist sorcerers and heroes. This unusual piece of writing can be described as a blurred genre, as it overlapped with theatre, where these stories were acted out as apotropaic entertainments, and with the actual martial rituals that enfeoffed irksome spirits or renewed the ties of canonized deities with their human congregants. As Mark Meulenbeld explains:

> What ultimately defines these three genres of novel, ritual, and theatre as the intertwined elements of a single cultural complex is that each in its own way articulates the "work of the gods" …—their miracles and meritorious deeds—as they can be reconstituted by mortals in the form of ritual and theatrical performance and, derived from these, in the form of novels. The re-enactment of the work of the gods in each of these three genres naturally implies the reconstitution of the gods themselves in that they are embodied by religious professionals in ritual, played by actors on stage, and brought to life by texts that incorporate them within larger theoretical frameworks. What these genres elucidate is the merit of particular gods and the specific ways these gods have attained their merits. By re-enacting the work of the gods it is ultimately possible to re-create their efficacy. (2015: 3)

In *The Canonization of the Gods*, the Hēng-Hā Èr Jiàng were powerful Zhou dynasty warriors, posthumously transformed into virtuous spiritual guardians. Zhèng Lún 鄭倫 became known as General Hēng and Chén Qí 陳奇 as General Hā. The two warriors had both studied with a Daoist adept named Dù È 度厄 in the Kunlun mountains, and they had learned special powers they employed on the battlefield. Zhèng Lún could exhale a white cloud from his nostrils which was accompanied by a powerful ringing sound. This would annihilate his enemies physically and spiritually, destroying their bodies and preventing them from reaching the afterlife. Chén Qí cultivated a lethal yellow gas in his belly which he would blow out of his mouth, killing his opponents en masse. Both perished in the magical battles that took place in the transition from the Shang to the Zhou dynasties. In the afterlife, the sage Jiāng Ziyá 姜子牙 (c. 1156–1017 BCE) commanded them to guard temple gates, and their statues became fixtures of Chinese shrines. As door guardians, they also overlapped with the double manifestation of the Indian and Himalayan Buddhist protector deity or Dharmapāla Vajrapāṇi, or Zhíjīngāng Shén 執金剛神 in Chinese.[148] They can still be seen today, General Hā mouth open and General Hēng mouth closed.

In addition to being a part of temple iconography and appearing in the *Canonization of the Gods*, Chén Qí & Zhèng Lún also appeared on stage. In *Jīngjù* theatre or Beijing Opera the two characters figure in the drama *Qīnglóng Guān* 青龙关 or *Blue-Green Dragon Pass* which recounts their story. In the role types of Chinese theatre, they are martial heroes or *jing* 淨 characterized by their colourfully painted faces or *huāliǎn* 花臉.

In the oral tradition explained to me by Ismet Himmet, Daoist initiates would slowly chant *hēng* or *hā* while visualizing white clouds or yellow fog during exorcisms and non-ordinary combat with spirits or other sorcerers (Himmet, personal communication). Hēng-Hā breathing can thus be seen to have functioned ritually, theatrically, and tactically. Incanted slowly in martial ritual, these sounds were apparently used to prepare for spiritual battle and exorcism. In theatre, they became the characteristic sounds of iconic stage characters. Sounded quickly and powerfully, hēng and hā are tactically valuable physical techniques of duelling and skirmishing.

The vocalized syllable hā is used to support a strike with a small surface area, such as a punch or a blow with the elbow. The vocalization hēng braces the body for impact and can be used defensively against a strike or offensively when performing a body-slam.[149] In hā breathing, the player makes a whispered, rasping

---

[148] Vajrapāṇi's dual manifestation included Nārāyaṇa or Nàluó Yán Jīngāng 那羅延金剛, General Hēng and Guhyapāda or Mì Jī Lìshì Jīngāng 密跡力士金剛, General Hā.

[149] The use of sounds varies widely among different styles of Tàijí Quán. There are no audible exhalations in the Dōng Píng Tàijí Quán I learned from Sui Meing and Sui Vuey Wong. Chén Zhōnghuá frequently uses the hā sound, but I've never heard him make the hēng sound. The *Wǔdāng Dān Pài Xuán Mén Tàijí Quán* 武当丹派玄門太極拳 馬杰, which I saw demonstrated by the late Mǎ Jié 馬杰 (d. 2013) and that I later studied with Zhāng Wùnà and Lǚ Měihuì, emphasizes the hēng sound.

   While I didn't study Tàijí Quán with him, Ismet Himmet clearly demonstrated the uses of both sounds to me during the private instruction he gave me in his approach to the jiàn of the Wǔdāng Xuánwǔ Pài in 2018. Ismet learned *hēng-hā* breathing from his red sand palm *Zhūshā Zhǎng* 朱砂掌 teacher Long Jin Ju. Long had apparently been Máo Zédōng's bodyguard for about 18 months in the 1960s. Long was allegedly champion of a martial arts competition

vocalization in two parts, that sounds like *ho-waht*: the *ho* is less emphasized and the *waht* is louder—*ho-WAHt*! In hēng breathing, the sound is made with the mouth held closed and resembles clearing one's throat using the sound *mmm*. It too is done in two parts with the second sound emphasized: *mmm-MMH*. Chén Zhōnghuá made the hā sound throughout his demonstration of the Chén Tàijí Quán Pào Chuí in the video above. Ismet Himmet demonstrated his expression of both the hēng and the hā in a short video shot at his training centre on Hainan Island in the early 2000s:

https://vimeo.com/919640546?share=copy

The hēng and hā sounds themselves are secondary to the global effect they produce in the body. When the adepts I've met use hēng or hā, their abdomens draw in on the inhale and expand on the exhale.[150] We automatically breathe like this when weeping, or lifting a very heavy weight, reversing the more commonly sought relaxed deep breathing in which the abdomen expands on inhalation and retracts on exhalation. In my experience, hā creates an outward pulse in the abdomen to which hēng adds a marked expansion through the ribs. The two expressions are quite similar, but hā makes it easier to reach out with the arms, while hēng firmly stabilizes the torso.

The sudden expansion of the abdomen on exhalation is also an important element of zhěng hé lì. During our time in the studio, when I used hēng-hā breathing to absorb Jean and Naishi's punches, I explained how they could also use these methods as part of striking. When we began our experiments, the dancers were generating the power with which they hit me by swivelling their waists to turn their torsos to drive their punches. Over our three sessions they experimented with dropping one hip and extending a fist while mimicking my hā sound, experiencing the rudiments of creating a pulse within their own bodies. We spent our last session together joyfully roughhousing, incorporating both hitting and absorption into our games of entanglement and avoidance.

---

organized by Máo in the mid-60s, employing a method known as *Fēng Zhǎng* 風掌, or *wind palm*, to drop his fellow contestants with seemingly light touches. He changed his name after he left Máo's service, hoping to maintain a low profile. I do not have the characters for Long's name.

[150] 20th-century texts on Tàijí Quán refer to the contraction of the abdomen on the inhale as *nì shì hūxī* 逆式呼吸, or reversed abdominal breathing. Much as he often uses the hā sound to support his movements, Chén Zhōnghuá does not approve of this general contemporary description: "Reversed breathing has been promoted by Tang Hao and Gu Liuxin (1963, Chen Style Taijiquan). As no one can say what this means and how to do it, it became popular" (Chen 2012: 41). I interpret his ironic tone here to mean that breathing patterns should emerge downstream of the parameters governing the entire body, as the use of hēng or hā creates a more complex movement pattern in the torso than is produced by voluntarily contracting the belly on the inhale and expanding it on the exhale.

Figures 24 & 25: A maelstrom and a pulse in *Deciphers*, created and performed by Jean Abreu and Naishi Wang, photo by Maya Yoncali.

Jean and Naishi's performance underwent a long gestation from our work in the fall of 2021 to its premiere in January of 2024. Over this time, *Deciphers* developed into a passionate yet introspective meditation on their experiences of emigration, expressed on stage in terms of language, translation, movement, and solitude. Clear traces of our time together appeared in the final choreography. Our work with maelstroms appeared in an extended sequence of grappling between the dancers, while our explorations of pulses created moments of suspension that punctuated the piece, seen in Figures 24 and 25 above. Martial movement training was also decisive in Katherine Ng's 2022 solo performance. Unlike in *Deciphers*, where it appeared briefly as a part of the actual choreography, in Katherine's performance our martial work was more like an underground river whose invisible trajectory and influence was known only to the choreographer-dancer.

Calm and Dormant with Strength and Power; Sinuous and Flowing

In 2021 Gitanjali Kolanad became interim artistic director of the CanAsian Dance Festival. Gita, a *Kalarippayattu* martial artist, *Bharatanatyam* dancer, contemporary choreographer, and author whom I had previously met through both martial arts and theatre colleagues, invited me to be the dramaturg for Ottawa-based dancer Katherine Ng's first solo choreography.[151] Katherine's was among the four proposals by emerging artists from across Canada selected by the festival in May of 2023.

Katherine was a very skilled young dancer whose experience ranged from contemporary dance explorations with Montréal-based companies to

---

[151] Katherine Ng uses her English name professionally. Her name in Chinese is 伍宇晴, Ńgh Yúh Chìhng in Cantonese or Wǔ Yǔqíng in Mandarin.

commercial work for MGM Macao directed by the late pop star Michael Jackson's choreographer Travis Payne. When we first met to discuss her project in August of 2022, Katherine was training intensively with Cirque du Soleil contortion coach Alixa Slobodyan, adding inverted equilibrium and virtuosic spinal flexibility to her already considerable skills. During our first conversation, Katherine explained that she had already created a short preliminary sketch of her solo that she would be presenting informally in September, and that she would like to start building on this material. She further asked me if I'd be willing to teach her some wǔshù. While Katherine's family hails from South China, she had never played any Chinese martial arts before. Our work together thus included both facilitation and dramaturgy. We decided that we would meet for weekly 90-minute sessions of wǔshù training for 12 weeks, and that I would accompany her for 30 hours as dramaturg, adding 20 hours to the 10 subsidized by the festival, to better understand and support her work.

Wǔdāng Wǔshù

From late August until mid-December I taught Katherine the *Wǔdāng Tàihé Quán* 武当太和拳, a short and simple tàolù whose name means "grand harmony fist," which I had learned from Simon Cox. Katherine absorbed the form quickly and precisely. It offered her a good introduction to the movement patterns of júbù lì and zhěng hé lì, as well as to Daoist cosmological ideas. In this video from 2013, Simon Cox demonstrates the Wǔdāng Tàihé Quán, which was his *dānxiàng bǐsài* 單項 比賽, or individual competition specialization—the set that he would perform at wǔshù tàolù events in China:

https://vimeo.com/912349852?share=copy[152]

The Tàihé Quán is mainly characterized by júbù lì. The chain of force running from the ground, up the extended leg of the long, lunging archers' stances or *gōng jiàn bù* 弓箭步, is clearly visible in Simon's execution. The sectional, winding use of the body is very clear in the movement phrases named *zuǒ kāi xuán mén* 左開玄門 and *yòu kāi xuán mé* 右開玄門, or "opening the mysterious gate to the left and the right" (1:07–1:16). Similarly, the movement phrase "swan spreads its wings," or *tiān'é zhǎn chì* 天鹅展翅, shows a clear pulse of zhěng hé lì (1:44–1:45).

Each of the 25 short movement phrases in the quán pǔ, or "form score," of the Tàihé Quán has a poetic description with multiple Daoist meanings. As Simon Cox notes, the Tàihé Quán is

---

[152] Simon Cox's teacher Yuán Xiūgāng demonstrating the Wǔdāng Tàihé Quán: https://vimeo.com/922496800?share=copy.

full of esoteric and alchemical symbolism, through which one re-enacts the Daoist creation of the universe, from primordial chaos of *wuji* to the implicit duality of *taiji* to the explicit duality of *liangyi*, the creation of heaven and earth, and the skillful transformations of Yin and Yang, from which all things spring. The form ends as you pace the eight-trigram circle, returning to the origin, the unlimited primordial state (*wuji*) from which it began. (Cox 2022b: 4)

I also introduced Katherine to a tuī shǒu tàolù or push-hands pattern, so she could begin to practice applying the martial movements of the Tàihé Quán on me. We concentrated on the two movement phrases mentioned above. We used kāi xuán mén to practice a progressive tangle and knock-down using júbù lì, and tiǎn'é zhǎn chì to work on body-slamming skill or *kào jìn* 靠勁 using zhěng hé lì. As Katherine was much smaller and lighter than I, it was rewarding for both of us when she eventually managed to crisply break my balance and stagger me. During these months, Katherine was also working very intensively on her contortion training, which took up to four hours daily. We made sure not to overload her already fatigued shoulders, forearms, and wrists with hard impact or sudden twists. In tandem with this careful work on the Tàihé Quán, we also started to develop her performance.

A Work-in-Progress

In September of 2022 Katherine shared a work-in-progress version of her solo at an evening presented by the Ottawa-based Dark Horse Dance Projects. This sketch introduced most of the elements that would eventually determine the form of her finished piece. The space was defined by a large red rectangle of fabric on the ground, and by smaller pieces of red fabric scattered on and about it. Katherine wore a long red skirt. The dancing took her first around the edge of the rectangle, and then across it lengthwise. Katherine danced slowly and at walking speed, alternating between standing, kneeling, and lying positions. Her initial peregrination around the edge of the space gave her dancing a timeless feel. Her subsequent crossing and return along the length of the red rectangle, punctuated by significant gestures and sharp silhouettes, created a sense of beginning, middle, and end. The performance took place along a wide hallway in Ottawa's School of Dance which had bright acoustics due to its high ceiling, hard plaster walls, and granite-tiled floor. Katherine was accompanied by a sparse, occasional soundtrack of percussive sounds sampled from recordings of Southern Chinese drumming that she had created for herself. Muffled sounds and music from other performances also drifted into the hall from various rooms. A video archive of this version of the solo can be seen here:

https://vimeo.com/922880624?share=copy

Dramaturgy

This work-in-progress performance provided me with an enormous amount of information. I parsed it in terms of the dancing, the space, the sounds, and the costume. I further divided my reception of the dancing into elements I could describe concretely and structurally, and the more subjective phenomenology of how those elements affected me personally. While I was, of course, curious about Katherine's motivations and the meanings she ascribed to her choices, I kept most of my questions about them to myself, as I didn't want her to feel compelled to rationalize her intuitive decisions. I conceived of Katherine's job as a choreographer as having to figure out how to create a bridge between the movements and images that inspired her and her eventual audiences. How could the movements she'd chosen to dance and the environment she'd created to dance them in best conjure meaning in audiences' imaginations? And how could I assist her? To keep our work practical, I framed my questions in terms of *how* an element of the performance was working or might be changed, rather than asking *why* an element had been included. I consciously avoided abstract questions that could have made Katherine feel that she had to justify her interests to me, unhelpfully shifting her mindset from a creative to a self-critical one. My role as dramaturg was to assist her in making her choices potentially meaningful to viewers rather than to elucidate, cohere, or correct the possible discursive meanings of her dance.

To begin, I asked Katherine how she saw the different sections of the performance and where she thought the transitions between them occurred. I described to her the sections I had seen, and where I believed the transitions took place. Based on this conversation, we co-created a structural map of the performance to which we could both refer. I then asked Katherine where she thought she'd like to add material, and what sort of movement she imagined it would be. This seemingly simple conversation gave us a shared idea of what had been created, and a list of elements to make in future rehearsals. Katherine explained to me that she planned to replace the potentially slippery red cloth on the ground with a piece of red Marley dance flooring, a heavy plastic matting that would offer much better traction and permit faster movements. She also was going to work with a composer to elaborate the simple musical accompaniment she'd created for her first version. Having made an outline and a plan, I began to visit Katherine regularly in the studio, sometimes to watch her at work, and sometimes to see a run-through of all the material she had made to date.

While the roles I played were encompassed by Guy Cools' description of the dramaturg as a witness, a partner in dialogue, and an editorial assistant, in our process I performed them in an idiosyncratic fashion. As one of the first things I did was to watch the sketch Katherine had made before I joined the process, our discussions about structure and editing became our first point of collaboration rather than a later phase of work. While we had many spoken conversations about the performance, our physical and tactile dialogue developed first, as we practiced the Tàihé Quán and played tuī shǒu together. I watched a lot of work in the studio, but I shared the role of daily witness with dancer Jocelyn Todd, who assisted Katherine as rehearsal director, and whose presence and insights were also decisive in the process. While all the decisions in the process were Katherine's, we had important conversations about the dancing, costumes, music, and text, which I will discuss in turn. Here is an archival video of the completed performance of *Calm and Dormant with Strength and Power; Sinuous and Flowing*, shot in Toronto on May 13, 2023:

https://vimeo.com/922925006?share=copy

Dancing

In keeping with the title of the piece, Katherine's preferred movement quality was sinuous and flowing, and she tended to move at a contemplative walking pace. My goal was to help her create contrasts in her slow and smooth actions without departing from her desired aesthetic. We tried to find subtle ways of varying the undulating, uninterrupted character of her dancing and the main trajectory used in the piece, where Katherine danced from upstage to downstage along the red floor. We created two kinds of contrasts: differences within the domain of movement, and differences between the domains of movement and sound. For example, working with composer Jonathan Bendavid, Katherine added rapid percussive music to slow and calm movement. These cross-domain choices were later supported by Jareth Li's lighting design, which arrived in the last weeks of rehearsals. The location, intensity, and quality of the light allowed Katherine to create even further variations.

While such large contrasts as sudden running and frozen suspensions were very clear to the viewer, Katherine also made small changes in the sequencing of her movements that created new syncopations in how she expressed the general pattern of circumnavigating the red rectangle and progressing along its length. For example, having established a slide on the ground where her hips moved forward at the same time as her legs, seen at 5:27, 5:35, and 5:43, she created a more articulated change of hip and leg position which can be seen at 6:43. While this might have appeared to be a completely new movement, we developed it as a variation of previously established material. Creating such nuances was an important part of our work together. They preserved the overall atmosphere Katherine wanted to create while also producing a subtle sense of progress and development within the repetitions the piece seemed to require.

Costumes

The red skirt and top that Katherine had made for her work-in-progress presentation were evocative, but they obscured her movements when she danced on the ground, as the skirt tangled around her legs and hid her waist. At the same time, we didn't want to lose the mysterious figure she presented at the beginning of the solo who, thanks to the volume and length of the skirt, seemed to float timelessly about the space. My suggestion to Katherine was to introduce the skirted figure and then change her costume to reappear wearing a 1970s-style dark-red Adidas tracksuit, a more gender-neutral choice than the long, feminine skirt. This would let her move freely and visibly while also evoking very different associations in the audience. For me, born in 1971, her new costume evoked childhood. It also reminded me of the outfits worn by Chinese wǔshù competitors in the 1970s and early 1980s. By 2018, this dated look had once again become a contemporary dance fashion choice—the Fontys dancers I worked with in the Netherlands all wore Adidas pants! The changes from the drapery of the floating skirt to the slimmer lines of the tracksuit, and from the loose red floor fabric to the hard edges of the red Marley floor brought me from a timeless ritual world to the 20th- and 21st-century rituals of athleticism. The progression from what I thought of as the private ritual world to the more public, athletic world was made more meaningful to me by the transport Katherine danced to the music of Teresa Teng.

Music

During Katherine's initial work in progress presentation, I had mistaken the music drifting into the hallway from other performances going on in the building to be a part of her piece. The effect struck me as a fortuitous combination of the mysterious and the nostalgic. It reminded me of an instructional video by American expert martial artist Tak Wah Eng 伍德华 (*Jyutping* Ng5 Dak1 Waa4, *Pīnyīn* Wǔ Déhuá) in which he played a sword tàolù named *Pán Lóng Jiàn* 蟠龙剑, or Coiling Dragon Sword, in the Bo Law 寶羅 (*Jyutping* Bou2 Lo4, *Pīnyīn* Bǎo Luó) martial arts studio in Lower Manhattan, New York. The video preserved the ambient sounds of the other studios in the building and of the streets outside. During Eng's performance, Chén Fēnlán's 陳芬蘭 1973 Mandarin pop song *Yuèliàng Dàibiǎo Wǒ de Xīn* 月亮代表我的心, or "The Moon Represents My Heart," drifted into the studio from somewhere else in the building. The version playing in the background is probably the one made famous in 1977 by Taiwanese singer Teresa Teng 鄧麗君. When I shared Tak Wah Eng's video with Katherine, she was enthusiastic about both the atmosphere and the song, which she said was a favourite of her mother's. She decided to incorporate it into the soundscape of her dance. In Jonathan Bendavid's eventual score, the warm, melodic character of *Yuèliàng Dàibiǎo Wǒ de Xīn* emerged from a thicket of more percussive effects (13:16).

This fragment of the dance made me feel that Katherine had discovered something familiar in the unknown environment of her dream-like journey. Her position on the floor, which hitherto had evoked discovery, exploration, and confusion, was transformed into a space of recognition. After this episode, I felt that the pattern of repeatedly descending the red rectangle could be resolved. The feeling of homecoming created by the song and its Mandarin lyrics led Katherine to the text she used as her conclusion.

Text

"I've added a poem," Katherine told me before a run-through in mid-April. At the very end of the performance, she spoke the following lines as she was leaving the stage:

> You bend your neck towards the sky and sing.
> Your white feathers float on the emerald water,
> Your red feet push the clear waves.

Her English text was most of *Yǒng É* 咏鹅, a poem by celebrated Tang dynasty author Luò Bīnwáng 駱賓王 (619–684 CE), allegedly written when he was only seven years old. It is regularly taught to very young Chinese children as part of their language and cultural education. The poem's title can be translated as "Calling Goose." While the pronunciation has likely changed since the seventh century, the Chinese word for goose—*é*—is pleasingly onomatopoeic, and sounds very much like the honking cry of the water bird. The entire poem reads:

> 鹅、鹅、鹅，曲项向天歌。
> 白毛浮绿水，红掌拨清波。

> *É, é, é, qū xiàng xiàng tiān gē.*
> *Bái máo fú lǜ shuǐ, hóng zhǎng bō qīng bō.*

> Goose, goose, goose, you bend your neck toward the sky and sing.
> Your white feathers float on the emerald water, your red feet push
> the clear waves.

This concluding text offered a light and humorous counterpoint to the seriousness and mystery of the dancing that had preceded it. While it didn't erase or resolve that mystery, its declarative tone suggested that the figure Katherine had danced might have known what was going on all along, rather than being an innocent on a voyage of discovery. The text also gently provided some retroactive guidelines by which the audience could interpret dramatic but very open moments in the dance, such as the one at 9:59 when, among other possibilities, Katherine's vertical arm and flexing hand suggested the neck and head of a goose. While Katherine kept her original title *Calm and Dormant with Strength and Power; Sinuous and Flowing* for the festival performances, between us we decided that the real name of the dance was *Goose, Goose, Goose*. For me, the ritualistic opening, the athletic yet mysterious middle, and the childlike, matter-of-fact spoken conclusion represented a life cycle in reverse, an ingenious conceptual complement to the technically accomplished cyclical form of the dance.

Conclusion

The influence of the Chinese martial arts on Katherine's dance can be divided into explicit and implicit strands. In our practice of the Tàihé Quán, Katherine and I tried to move within specific martial parameters. We discussed the Daoist cosmology revealed by the names of the movements in the form, and we spoke about the Chinese martial concepts that structured the fighting techniques we applied on one another. In making her dance, however, we didn't expressly try to create martially derived maelstroms and pulses. These ideas tacitly informed my comments where I saw suggestions of similar coils and suspensions in Katherine's movements, but they were not elements we intentionally attempted to build. We concentrated on creating a dance that would ignite our audiences' imaginations, and while we spoke about the piece all the time, we were parsimonious with any abstract or conceptual discussions and remained focussed on talking about *how* the dance was done.

At the end of chapter 2 I described how the Chinese martial arts are principally transmitted nonverbally, an approach to teaching called bù yán zhī jiào. I believe that a similar tacit and immersive quality characterized all the collaborations I've described in this chapter, even though the facilitator and dramaturg occupy more modest and less directive positions than the teacher. Guy Cools described this unspoken quality as somatic, and brought it to the foreground (2019: 47):

> [D]ramaturgy has been mainly associated with the theoretical, rational component of knowledge: the "outside eye" which from a distance keeps an overview and gives meaning and coherence to the embodied practice of the makers and doers, the artists.

> Contemporary dramaturgical practices, however, blur this dichotomy. The creative "friendship" between dramaturg and choreographer presumes as much proximity and intimacy as distance. (2019: 50)

The work at Fontys, on *Deciphers*, and on *Calm and Dormant with Strength and Power; Sinuous and Flowing* depended on close physical and personal contact between the artists and me. Orthodox tuī shǒu tàolù practice and the original martial games I developed cultivated tactile responses through collaborative play. While offering the dancers an interactive physical vocabulary and novel principles they could use to structure their movement, these games also set up resonances between us as we experienced the spacetime of the studio through the medium of each other's motion. Using touch, we gained a direct insight into one another's physical experience and decision-making process, combing the extended physiological proprioception mentioned in chapter 2 with the enjoyment and mutual appreciation implicit in collaborative martial play, a nonverbal and somatic experience.

These examples of facilitation and dramaturgy were enabled by the experiential understanding of spacetime cultivated by the practice of the Chinese martial arts. Much as it took me many years of practice to develop it, I believe that this understanding can be shared to some degree through concrete, physical work in the studio, and subsequently described conceptually, as I have done here.

Conclusions

Each chapter of this book has considered a patch of the sky of the Chinese martial arts as seen from the bottom of a different well. I suggest we use the tolerance of seeming contradictions provided by the idiom "ruò wáng ruò cún" as we review some of the details of the general perspectives we have considered: wǔshù as a method of combat, wǔshù as religious expression, and wǔshù as theatre and dance.

Combat

Wǔshù curricula all appear to have contained methods of teaching and learning to fight, but the instruction they offered in self-defence, duelling, and skirmishing was, historically, far from uniform. Wǔshù's relationship to military training, to civil defense, to personal defense, and to sporting combat has varied widely, determined by contextual and contingent factors.

Contemporary wǔshù curricula such as the Chói Lěih Fáht Kyùhn, Chén Tàijí Quán or Wǔdāng Jiàn we examined in chapters 1 and 2 appear to offer educational pathways that develop the novice's capacities for personal combat. As we can see from the genesis of Tàijí Quán in late Qing- and Republic-era Beijing discussed in chapter 3, wǔshù in the late 19th and early 20th centuries was also a virtuosic serious leisure activity created by and for people already skilled in fighting. Early 20th-century wǔshù adepts combined their experience of combat and the sophistication of their martial serious leisure to create simplified battlefield methods for enlisted men and civilian militias. Participation in wǔshù also prevented people in precarious circumstances from becoming involved in anti-social violence in the first place. The Fujian Shàolín White Crane methods associated with the Tiāndìhuì societies in the 1760s seen in chapter 4, and the later dissemination of Chói Lěih Fáht Kyùhn by the Hùhng

How to cite this book chapter:
Mroz, D. 2025. *Resonant Space: Religion, Theatre, and the Chinese Martial Arts.* Pp. 177–180. Cardiff: Cardiff University Press. DOI: https://doi.org/10.18573 /book11.j. Licence: CC-BY-NC-ND

Sing Association in the mid-19th century discussed in chapter 1, are examples of martial training that kept initiates busy with demanding physical conditioning, while also offering them kinship ties, responsibilities, and in-group privileges.[153]

While written references to wǔshù abound in Chinese history, documents we would understand today as technical or instructional are rarer and much more recent. As seen in chapter 5, wǔshù heroes, theory, and ethics are found in the *Zhuāngzǐ* and in the histories of Sīmǎ Qiān 司馬遷. Manuals attempting to teach armed and unarmed combat only appeared much later, in the Ming dynasty and after.[154]

We can learn much about the historical contexts in which different social groups practiced wǔshù, and in which the texts we can still examine today were written, but due to its embodied, ephemeral nature, the broader structures and phenomenology of historical wǔshù must be triangulated using a wide range of subjects and sources. Key among these are what contemporary Euro-American scholarship and common knowledge refer to as religion and theatre.

Religion

Wǔshù can be understood as a part of the Huárén Jiào—Jordan Paper's neologism for the ensemble of Chinese religions. Martial arts had an important relationship with jīndān or nèidān, the golden, inner elixir practices that developed within different Chinese traditions from 200 CE on. The vocabulary and imagery of jīndān and nèidān were adopted by martial artists as a developmental framework, and wǔshù itself has been seen as a way of practicing internal alchemy. As we discussed in chapters 1 and 2, reversals of perspective, or fǎn, which were decisive in the conceptual ontologies of jīndān, offer an excellent description of the changing phenomenology of perception experienced by martial artists in training. In the early 20th century, Republic-era martial artists equated the phenomenology of mature wǔshù practice with the fruition of nèidān, as seen in chapter 5.

Tàolù, contemporary solo choreographies of mimed martial movement, seem to find precedent in the rituals of state war magic and the popular practices

---

[153]   The distinction between demimonde organizations and mutual aid societies is a blurry one in Chinese history. In addition to providing group bonding and hierarchy within a subculture, wǔshù training clearly offered tactical skills to enforcers or defenders associated with such groups.

[154]   For example, the *Jiàn Jīng* 劍經, or "Sword Treatise," is a short manual actually about staff combat appearing in the *Zhèngqì Táng Jí* 正氣堂集, the *Compilation from the Hall of Orthodox Qì*, a 1550 military encyclopedia authored by General Yú Dàyóu 俞大猷 (1503–1579). The *Jìxiào xīnshū* 紀效新書 of 1560 by General Qī Jìguāng (1528–1588) briefly discusses which folk, civilian martial art practices are suitable as adjunct training for soldiers. In 1676 Huáng Bǎijiā 黃百家 (1643–1709), the son of the Ming loyalist scholar Huáng Zōngxī, published a terse and gnomic pamphlet on the *Internal Boxing of Wáng Zhēngnán* or the *Nèi Jiā Quán* 內家拳.

descended from them. As we saw in chapter 5, martial movement was a part of the magical rituals of Song armies. In chapter 3 we explored the contexts in which Ming Daoist ritual specialists might have created martial movements as a part of their state-appointed roles as performers of Léi Fǎ, or Thunder Rituals. Such rites also appeared at local levels of administration and seem to have included vernacular martial arts practiced alongside militia training for civil defence. As we saw in chapter 7 with the Hēng-Hā breathing and its associated deities and spiritual powers, contemporary wǔshù styles contain lore and practices that can be correlated with much older religious texts, such as the Ming dynasty Fēng Shén Yǎnyì, The Canonization of the Gods. The apotropaic action of martial movement was a root that nourished not only the actions of religious professionals in ritual but also the portrayal of gods on stage by actors.

Dance and Theatre

As Jo Riley described in chapter 1, even in the late 20th century village temples were the sites where ritual, wǔshù training, and theatrical performance took place, braided together through the practice of martial movement. The vocabulary of wǔshù was central to Chinese theatres, which historically combined religious action with staged entertainment. As we saw in chapter 4, apotropaic and martial lion and qílín spirit-puppets played a vital role in the calendar of the religious year, bringing theatrical, supernatural figures to the streets and courtyards of daily life.

This heritage offers us two perspectives on the relationship between wǔshù and contemporary theatre and dance in the 20th century, discussed in chapter 4. One is an explicit and interdisciplinary view, in which wǔshù is a secondary artistic discipline placed at the service of dance or theatre, which remain primary, as with White Crane Silat and the actor training developed by W. S. Rendra. The other is an implicit, genealogical view in which Chinese martial ritual and contemporary theatre are not two distinct kinds of performance, but rather linked communal and transformational expressions, as I suggest occurred in Móu Sēn his and collaborators' production Bǐ'àn Hé Guānyú Bǐ'àn De Hànyǔ Yǔfǎ Tǎolùn.

These explicit and implicit strands have also informed my own work as an artist, teacher, facilitator, and dramaturg. In chapter 2 I proposed the idea of spatial projection, a skill equally grounded in wǔshù's combative, religious, and theatrical qualities, and described how it manifested in my production of Ismene. In chapter 6 Colin Lalonde elaborated on how choreographic elements made using martial movement contributed to novel experiences of agency for performers and audiences, using examples drawn from our creation and presentation of And Treat the Distant Peoples with Kindness. In chapter 7 I described the very different ways in which wǔshù was used to facilitate the process of choreographers and performers Jean Abreu, Naishi Wang, and Katherine Ng. In all these artistic processes, martial movement offered fruitful working methods while decisively informing the way my collaborators and I experienced space and time in the studio, and on stage.

Onward

The idea of explicit and implicit strands might also be useful in determining trajectories of future research. We might use the explicit structural categories we can find in the Chinese martial arts to organize our investigations. By doing so, we conceive of wǔshù as interdisciplinary. We could examine how different styles of wǔshù in various periods developed combat skill. We might investigate their methods of religious enaction and their relationships with local jiào. How did and do different Chinese martial arts manifest as participatory recreation, competitive athleticism, and performed entertainment? The parsing of wǔshù into these different elements would allow us precision and focus.

We could also look at wǔshù's implicit phenomenological strand. The Chinese martial arts enable unusual personal experiences. They facilitate somatic mutability, recreating adepts' bodies, imaginations, and relationships. The varieties of somatic pluralism they produce resist categorical parsing. Rather than seeing inter-disciplines combining discrete structural elements, we might instead see wǔshù as a poly-ontological meta-discipline, as an ensemble of practices best understood by the ways in which they develop our senses of space and time.[155] What dynamics are at play in the interaction and interpenetration of wǔshù's conceptual and pragmatic ontologies? What bodies do they conjure, and what worlds do they allow us to tune into as they initiate us into new ways of experiencing space and time? I have only begun to examine these possibilities, and such questions offer much to future researchers. I hope that this book will be of some assistance to them.

---

[155] Thanks to my collaborator Damon Honeycutt, who has used the term "meta-discipline" to explain how he viewed his practice of the martial arts in relationship to his work as a dancer, choreographer, composer, and visual artist.

Postface by Guy Cools, PhD

...worth of a sword

The book that you have just finished reading is an excellent example of how artistic research weaves together different disciplines, cultures, and past and present—traditional Chinese martial arts and contemporary performing arts practices. I am a complete neophyte in the first, and the little I know, I know through my exchanges with Daniel in and out of the studio, and from sleeping in his library, which is probably one of the largest private collections on the subject. But it is easily to recognize in these pages the master swords-and-pen man, who combines rigor of thought with fluidity of articulation. To paraphrase Seamus Heaney, Daniel's pen is not snug as a gun, but has the worth of a sword.

I do know the other field, contemporary performing arts, dance in particular, which has been my own professional biotope and field of study for almost 40 years. I feel honored that Daniel cites and reflects further on my own writings on the dramaturg as witness, dialogue partner, and editor, and uses it to situate himself. I was also lucky to have been a privileged witness of several of the projects he describes in this book, such as his staging of *Ismene* (chapter 2) or the project *Deciphers* by the choreographers Jean Abreu and Naishi Wang (chapter 7), which we both accompanied at different stages.

The closest I got to gaining an insight into this unique bridge Daniel creates between Chinese martial arts and performing practices was in 2017, when we spent a couple of days in the studio together with Siôned Watkins and Lin

Snelling exchanging our respective practices: the grid and the practice of pre-arranged movement patterns (tàolu) of Chinese martial arts he discusses in chapter 2, and our *Rewriting Distance* performance practice (see also www .rewritingdistance.com). Coming from opposite ends—an extremely free improvisation score versus a highly codified language—we met halfway to find joy and laughter in playing together.

Being invited to be one of the first readers of this book, I felt like I was on a treasure hunt, (re)discovering some of the gems of insights Daniel offers us through his practice and his reflections, such as:

- the importance of the use of negative space when we create for the stage;
- how the secular and the sacred are not a binary, but different perspectives on our experiences, both grounded in the body;
- how specific the Chinese and Indian body maps are;
- how my awareness of space and time is guided by differentiation and alternation, which both result from changes in the body and its relationship to the environment, due to movement.

In the end. the main conviction I share with Daniel is that the moments we are looking for, witnessing other people's creative processes, are moments of transformation. Any form of knowledge, mastery, or creative practice is only relevant insofar as it supports individual transformation, and the sharing of these experiences can also initiate collective transformation.

As you discovered with me, reading his book, Daniel as a practitioner and a scholar, as a mentor and a pedagogue, is a masterfully talented shapeshifter moving among these different fields he has made his own. He is also very gifted, as he has shared his talents with all of us in this book.

Guy Cools is a dance dramaturg and professor in the Département de danse de l'Université du Québec à Montréal. He completed his PhD at Ghent University in 2014. Cools is a much sought-after choreographic and dramaturgical mentor, and has worked as a production dramaturg with, among others, Jean Abreu (UK), Koen Augustijnen (Belgium), Sidi Larbi Cherkaoui (Belgium), Danièle Desnoyers (Canada), Alexander Gottfarb (Austria), Lia Haraki (Cyprus), Christopher House (Canada), Akram Khan (UK), Joshua Monten (Switzerland), Arno Schuitemaker (Netherlands) and Stephanie Thiersch (Germany).

His most recent publications include The Ethics of Art: Ecological Turns in the Performing Arts, *co-edited with Pascal Gielen (2014)*; In-Between Dance Cultures: On the Migratory Artistic Identity of Sidi Larbi Cherkaoui and Akram Khan *(2015)*; Imaginative Bodies: Dialogues in Performance Practices *(2016)*; The Choreopolitics of Alain Platel's Les Ballets C de la B, *co-edited with Christel Stalpaert and Hildegard De Vuyst (2019); and* Performing Mourning: Laments in Contemporary Art *(2021).*

Excerpt from *Ismene* by Michael Geither

Scene 10 – Ismene and Creon

(...Ismene is telling Creon stories about Antigone—in particular, that she built cairns).

Creon: What are cairns?

Ismene: They're stacked-up rocks.

Creon: Cairns?

Ismene: It's hard to pronounce. So she takes us into the cave and there are about thirty cairns, substantial ones—about five feet tall. It looked like a museum. I said, "What are they for?" She said, "I make one every time I come here. I'll go now." I said, okay, and me and my boyfriend watched her get in a rowboat and start back to Thebes.

Creon: Your mother said she raised herself.

Ismene: She did. And she disappeared. She'd leave for a night or two at a time.

Creon: Where?

Ismene: After a while we didn't get worried because she always came back. It was like she understood that she had a calling and she was going to follow it.

Creon: Making cairns.

Ismene:	Or whatever. I always felt like I was seeing a rock on the ground when I saw her, a rock that was really the top of a mountain growing miles down.
Creon:	She was a mystery.
Ismene:	But she always stayed close. The week before I was told I couldn't stay at school, one of the worst weeks in my life—
Creon:	I remember.
Ismene:	The week before she made me a dress, bought me two books, slept in my room, made me a doll, took me to the movies. It was like she knew something was coming.
Creon:	How could she have? Why are you telling me this?
Ismene:	Drink some more wine.
	He does.
Creon:	You see that I'm still alive?
Ismene:	Sometimes it's hard to tell with you.
Creon:	Only my niece could say that and live.
Ismene:	What family do you have left?
Creon:	You. I have you.
Ismene:	Until tomorrow.
Creon:	And if I don't banish you?
Ismene:	I'll go anyway.
	Creon drinks.
Creon:	Go ahead.
Ismene:	So, the crazy part. Antigone filled seventeen composition notebooks when she was twelve. I used to read them.
Creon:	She let you?
Ismene:	It started in secret, but one day she walked in when I was reading one and she looked at me and lay down for a nap. I was still reading when she got up and left.
Creon:	What were they?
Ismene:	The first one was sort of a long prayer to a "Mister Glass." It asked him questions and told him what was going on in her life, what she thought about people and things. I remember one sentence from it because it was so weird:
All:	"I am a bird screaming glass."
	Creon feels strange.
Ismene:	You feel that feeling you have right now?
Creon:	Yes.
Ismene:	That's Antigone.
Creon:	Okay.
Ismene:	That's her.
Creon:	Okay.
Ismene:	That's all?

Creon:	I think I'm not surprised.
Ismene:	I told you it was poisoned.
Creon:	It's not.
Ismene:	*I* poisoned it.
Creon:	Funny.
Ismene:	On our way back from Thebes, Antigone and I paid visit to Tiresias.
Creon:	Who could have stopped everything if he had come earlier.
Ismene:	Antigone asked him what lay ahead for us with our parents dead and our brothers dead. And, at first, he wouldn't speak. But Antigone wore him down. She told him jokes. No pleading. She made him laugh. And finally he said:
All:	"You've already died. Both of you died with your mother. You know you've died. And you'll die again with one another." *Ismene photographs Creon, who has died.*
Ismene:	Here I am still breathing.

Excerpts from *And Treat the Distant Peoples with Kindness* by Michael Geither

Overture

Gabrielle: La beauté de ton sourire ton sourire en cristaux les cristaux de velours le velours de ta voix ta voix et ton silence ton silence absorbant

David: When de Gama reached Calicut, he ordered his men to parade Indian prisoners and hack off their hands, ears and noses. The amputated pieces were piled in a small boat.

Katelin: What is he saying? That love was never meant to crack between man and woman?

David: When all the Indians were thus dismembered, he ordered their feet to be tied together,

Katelin: and so he loves and he loves his sons and loves as he pleases.

David: So as the Indians should not untie their feet with their teeth, he ordered his men to strike upon the prisoners' teeth with staves, knocking teeth down their throats

Katelin: But there is a great law over him which—is as it is.

Gabrielle: Absorbant comme la neige

Katelin: The wind blowing,

Gabrielle: La neige chaude et lente

Katelin:	the mud spots on the polished surface.
Gabrielle:	Lente est ta démarche
Katelin:	the face reflected in the glass
Gabrielle:	Ta démarche diagonale, diagonale
Katelin:	which as you advance the features disappear
David:	Then a Brahmin was sent to Calicut to plead for peace, but the brave de Gama had his nose and ears cut off and the ears of a dog sewn on instead.
Gabrielle:	Soif, soir, soie
Katelin:	leaving only the hat
Gabrielle:	Et flottante, flottante comme les plaintes
David:	When de Gama reached Calicut, he ordered his men to parade Indian prisoners
Katelin:	and as you draw back the features return
David:	then hack of their hands
Katelin:	the tip of the nose
David:	ears
Katelin:	the projection over the eyebrows,
David:	and noses.
Katelin:	the cheekbones, the bulge of the lips, the chin last.
Gabrielle:	Les plantes sont dans ta peau ta peau les décoiffe elles décoiffent ton parfum ton parfum est dans ma bouche ta bouche est une cuisse une cuisse qui s'envole elle s'envole vers mes dents mes dents te dévorent je dévore ton absence,
Katelin:	I remember, she said, we had little silver plaques with a chain on it to hang over the necks of the bottles, whiskey, brandy, or whatever it was. And a box of some kind of wood, not for the kitchen but a pretty box. Inside it was lined with something like yes, pewter, all inside and there was a cover of metal too with a little knob on it, all inside the wooden box.
Gabrielle:	Ton absence est une cuisse / Cuisse ou soulier / Soulier que j'embrasse / J'embrasse ce soulier / Je l'embrasse sur ta bouche / Car ta bouche est une bouche, elle n'est pas un soulier / Miroir que j'embrasse
Sean:	Le choléra est une infection de l'intestin causée par la bactérie Vibrio cholerae.
Gabrielle:	De même que tes jambes, de même que tes jambes, de même que tes jambes, de même que tes jambes, tes jambes
Sean:	Les symptômes comprennent la diarrhée sévère, une bouche sèche, peau sèche, les yeux enfoncés et vitreux,
Gabrielle:	Jambes du soupir / Soupir du vertige / Vertige de ton visage /
Sean:	la léthargie, un pouls rapide, soif inextinguible, et de violents vomissements.
Gabrielle:	J'enjambe ton image comme on enjambe une fenêtre

Sean:	Al Qahira, «la victorieuse»—la plus grande ville en Afrique
Gabrielle:	Fenêtre de ton être et de tes mirages / Ton image /
Sean:	—fondée en 969—
Gabrielle:	Son corps et son âme / Ton âme et ton nez
Sean:	troisième plus ancienne université au monde—la plus grande bibliothèque de l'Ouest.
Gabrielle:	Étonné, je suis étonné.
Sean:	La transmission du choléra se produit principalement en raison de la consommation d'eau ou d'aliments qui ont été contaminés par les selles d'un individu infecté.
Gabrielle:	Nez de tes cheveux.
Katelin:	You would open the outer cover.
Gabrielle:	Ta chevelure en flamme.
Katelin:	and inside was the lid.
Gabrielle:	Ton âme en flammes et en larmes
Katelin:	When you would take that off
Gabrielle:	Comme les doigts de tes pieds
Katelin:	you would see the tea
Sean:	Rebaptisé Caire en 1250,
Gabrielle:	Tes pieds sur ma poitrine
Katelin:	with a silver spoon for taking it out.
Sean:	il a été un carrefour sur la route des épices entre l'Europe et l'Asie
Gabrielle:	Ma poitrine dans tes yeux tes yeux dans la forêt
Sean:	et a prospéré comme centre d'érudition islamique.
Gabrielle:	la forêt liquide et en os
Sean:	En 1340, il était la plus grande ville à l'ouest de la Chine.
Gabrielle:	les os de mes cris
Sean:	Le choléra est une maladie très virulente qui touche les enfants et les adultes.
Gabrielle:	J'écris et je crie de ma langue déchirante / Je déchire tes bras, tes bas
Sean:	elle peut tuer un adulte en bonne santé en un jour
Katelin:	But now, here are the roses—three opening. Out of love. For she loves them and so they are there. They are not a picture. Holbein never saw pink thorns in such a light.
Sean:	et un enfant en quelques heures.
Katelin:	Nor did Masaccio...

Torture

de Conti:	The world is a sphere.
	In the North, the oceans freeze and ships cannot pass.

At the center, the water is interrupted by land.

Far to the South there is a ring of uninterrupted water between the lands and the southern ice.

These are cold seas where storms and squalls form easily and violently, throwing up vast waves between which lurk giant pieces of floating ice.

To reach these desolate oceans, ships must follow the west coast of Africa to its southern tip. They must round the cape of that vast continent, where raging storms and massive gates of ice will welcome them.

Once there, they must be sure to voyage only from West to East or the wrath of the oceans will smash them asunder, shattering them like beetles.

de Conti: Bracciolini?

Bracciolini: What?

de Conti: In the harbor, the *Fiore Rosso*. In my quarters—the maps—inside a vase—in my bed.

Bracciolini: ...

de Conti: Eight maps and as many journals. Within the last journal is an explanation of the calculation of latitude at sea.

               Pause.

Bracciolini: I'll seek your pardon.

de Conti: If you please.

Les Ateliers du corps 2009–2012

Activities

In fall and winter, we met for three-hour sessions, three times a week, for 12 weeks. In the spring periods we worked full-time, eight hours a day, five days a week, for four weeks. Exceptionally, in 2011 we worked full-time for six weeks. Guest teachers taught additional introductory sessions lasting three hours, although Natasha Nikeprelevic and Gey Pin Ang taught 30 hours for a week each, and Chen Zhonghua usually taught eight hours a day for two days. The entire project involved approximately 1,150 hours of practical work in the studio.

Full-time periods in the spring concluded with public performances. *Circe/Landfall* was presented at the 2010 Canada Dance Festival (June 10, 11, 12; 120 spectators). *Shah Mat* was presented at the Ottawa Dance Directive in 2011 (July 7, 8, 9; 120 spectators). *And Treat the Distant Peoples with Kindness* was presented in 2012 at the Academic Hall Theatre of the Department of Theatre, University of Ottawa (August 9, 10, 11; 181 spectators).

Guest artist Natasha Nikeprelevic presented *Vicinity: music theatre for a singing actress* at the Ottawa Dance Directive, June 4, 2011, and offered *Sinfonia: music for an improvised choir*, a public class at the Ottawa Dance Directive, June 5, 2011.

Guest artist Gey Pin Ang presented a combined lecture and performance, *A Creative Stream*, which included parts of her performance *Feast of Yóu Shén* at the Ottawa Dance Directive on June 18, 2011.

Collaborators Fall 2009

Participants
  Amelia Schembri
  Brandon Groves
  Colin Lalonde
  Emmanuelle Lussier Martinez
  Emmanuelle Pépin
  Gabrielle Lalonde
  Stuart Lee
  Katelin Richards
  Mary Catherine Jack
  Tracey Guptill
  Jennifer Venning

Collaborators Winter 2010

Participants
  Amelia Schembri
  Brandon Groves
  Colin Lalonde
  Emmanuelle Lussier Martinez
  Gabrielle Lalonde
  Katelin Richards
  Mary Catherine Jack
  Tracey Guptill

Invited Teachers
  Sui Meing Wong (Chói Lĕih Fáht Kyùhn)
  Chén Zhōnghuá, MA (Chén Tàijí Quán)
  William Lau, MA (Introduction to Jīngjù)
  Rainer Weins (Introduction to complex rhythms)
  Michael Saso, PhD (Introduction to Zhèng Yī Daoist ritual and medita-
  tive practices)

Collaborators Spring 2010

Performers (in *Circe/Landfall*)
  Amelia Schembri
  Brandon Groves
  Colin Lalonde
  Emmanuelle Lussier Martinez
  Gabrielle Lalonde

Katelin Richards
Mary Catherine Jack
Tracey Guptill

Apprentice Director
Fanny Gilbert-Collet

Assistant Apprentice Director
Ekaterina Shestakova

Invited Artists
Paul Auclair (lighting design)
Marie-Louise Gariépy (video artist)
Michael Geither, MFA (playwright)
Sean Green (technical director)
Dominique Lafon, PhD (literary dramaturg, translator)
Tedd Robinson (dance dramaturg)

Collaborators Fall 2010

Participants
Amelia Schembri
Artem Barry
Brandon Groves
Colin Lalonde
Gabrielle Lalonde
Katelin Richards
Tracey Guptill

Collaborators Winter 2011

Participants
Amelia Schembri
Artem Barry
Brandon Groves
Colin Lalonde
Gabrielle Lalonde
Katelin Richards
Tracey Guptill

Collaborators Summer 2011

Performers (in *Shah Mat*)

Amelia Schembri
Artem Barry
Brandon Groves
Colin Lalonde
Gabrielle Lalonde
Katelin Richards
Tracey Guptill

Guest Performers Spring 2011
Emmanuelle Lussier Martinez
Marc Tellez, MSc

Apprentice Director Spring 2011
Fanny Gilbert-Collet

Invited Teachers
Natascha Nikeprelevic (*Receiving the Spirit of the Very Moment*)
Gey Pin Ang (*Sourcing Within*)
Rainer Wiens (complex rhythms)

Invited Artists
Paul Auclair (lighting design)
Jean-François Dubé (video artist)
Michael Geither, MFA (playwright)

Collaborators Fall 2011

Participants
David Benedict Brown
Gabrielle Lalonde
Andrea Pelegri
Katelin Richards
Sean Sonier

Invited Teacher
Lola Ryan (contemporary dance)

Collaborators Winter 2012

Participants
David Benedict Brown
Gabrielle Lalonde

Katelin Richards
Sean Sonier

Invited Teacher
Chén Zhōnghuá, MA (Chén Tàijí Quán)

Collaborators Summer 2012

Performers (in *And Treat the Distant Peoples with Kindness*)
David Benedict Brown
Gabrielle Lalonde
Katelin Richards
Sean Sonier

Apprentice Director
Colin Lalonde

Invited Artists
Paul Auclair (lighting design)
Michael Geither, MFA (playwright)
Gabrielle Lalonde (translation)
Jean-Michel Ouimet (video artist)
Rainer Wiens (composer, complex rhythms in performance)
Sionêd Watkins (somatics)

APPENDIX D

Videos

Videos in the Body of the Text:

Chapter 1: Martial & Theatrical Movement: https://vimeo
.com/901925713?share=copy

Chapter 2: Video 1—*Jībĕngōng*: https://vimeo.com/935113528?share=copy

Chapter 2: Video 2—*Tàolù*: https://vimeo.com/935118737?share=copy

Chapter 2: Video 3—*Tuī shŏu*: https://vimeo.com/935146975?share=copy

Chapter 2: Video 4—*Nián Jiàn*: https://vimeo.com/935149191?share=copy

Chapter 2: Video 5—Avoidance game, no contact: https://vimeo.com
/935155592?share=copy

Chapter 2: Video 6—Avoidance game with contact: https://vimeo.com
/935158724?share=copy

Chapter 2: Video 7—Entanglement game in turns: https://vimeo.com
/935166015?share=copy

Chapter 2: Video 8—Proactive entanglement: https://vimeo.com
/935172945?share=copy

Chapter 2: Video 9—Duet by Emma Hickey & Stephanie Velichkin: https://
vimeo.com/935176102?share=copy

Chapter 2: Video 10—Solo by Emma Hickey: https://vimeo.com
/935186049?share=copy

Chapter 2: Video 11—Solo by Jasmine Massé: https://vimeo.com
/935194326?share=copy

Chapter 2: Video 12—Ensemble duets: https://vimeo.com
/935197527?share=copy

Chapter 2: Video 13—Scene from *Ismene*: https://vimeo.com
/935202723?share=copy

Chapter 6: The Overture of *And Treat the Distant Peoples with Kindness*:
https://vimeo.com/908004606?share=copy

Chapter 6: The Conclusion of *And Treat the Distant Peoples with Kindness*:
https://vimeo.com/908005491?share=copy

Chapter 6: The Torture Scene of *And Treat the Distant Peoples with Kindness*:
https://vimeo.com/908005760?share=copy

Chapter 7: Chén Zhōnghuá performing *Chén Tàijí Quán Pào Chuí*: https://
vimeo.com/912349999?share=copy

Chapter 7: Chiu Kwok Cheung performing *Chói Lěih Fáht Daaih Sahp Jih
Kyùhn*: https://vimeo.com/914012873?share=copy

Chapter 7: Fontys Alumni Group Dancers Playing Martial Games: https://
vimeo.com/915667547?share=copy

Chapter 7: Fontys Alumni Group Dancers Improvise with Text and Martial
Movement: https://vimeo.com/915681934?share=copy

Chapter 7: Jean Abreu and Naishi Wang Playing Martial Games:
https://vimeo.com/916784046?share=copy

Chapter 7: Ismet Himmet demonstrates *Hēng-Hā* breathing: https://vimeo
.com/919640546?share=copy

Chapter 7: Simon Cox performs the *Wŭdāng Tàihé Quán*: https://vimeo
.com/912349852?share=copy

Chapter 7: Katherine Ng First Draft:
https://vimeo.com/922880624?share=copy

Chapter 7: Katherine Ng Final Performance:
https://vimeo.com/922925006?share=copy

Daniel Mroz, Performance Videos:

2010   *Circe/Landfall* https://vimeo.com/15460624?share=copy

2011   *Shah Mat* https://vimeo.com/36102375?share=copy

2011   *Liberté [in Motion]*, a Documentary about *Les Ateliers'* Summer Intensive 2011 https://vimeo.com/34557158?share=copy

2013   *And Treat the Distant Peoples with Kindness* https://vimeo.com/5569
4239?share=copy

2017   *Ismene https://vimeo.com/250012072?share=copy* & https://vimeo.com
/250012072?share=copy

Videos Linked in Footnotes:

Chapter 1, Note 5: David Palmer with Martin Tse, *The Civil-Martial structure in Chinese Communal Religion: A Buddho-Daoist Jiao ritual in northern Guangdong*: https://www.youtube.com/watch?v=RAkjt2I9mlI   (archived here: https://vimeo.com/891091968?share=copy)

Chapter 1, Note 6: Plum Blossom International Federation, *Spear vs Double Broadsword Two-person Weapon Set* https://www.youtube.com/watch?v =5tXl6xv8Sks (archived in the video example in the body of the text)

Chapter 5, Note 114: The Workcenter of Jerzy Grotowski and Thomas Richards' *The Living Room*: https://www.youtube.com/watch?v=abvov7z5W6c (archived here: https://vimeo.com/806112082/b6edc5cadb)

Chapter 7, Note 144: Yuán Xiūgāng demonstrating the *Wǔdāng Tàihé Quán*: https://vimeo.com/922496800?share=copy

References

Adda, M. (2022). Martial art-acting in dictatorial Indonesia: *Antigone* (1974) and *Lysistrata* (1975) directed by W. S. Rendra. *Theatre, Dance and Performance Training, 13*(3), 397–415. DOI: https://doi.org/10.1080/19443927.2022.2046631

Adda, M. (2019). Rendra 2.0: Cross-cultural theatre, the actor's work and politics in dictatorial Indonesia. In P. B. Zarrilli, T. Sasitharan, & A. Kapur (Eds.), *Intercultural acting and performance training* (pp. 217–245). Routledge.

Akiyama, N., & Drachman, J. (2008). *Karate and ki* (K. Ushiro, Trans.). Aiki News.

Alay, A. & Hun, J. G. (2017). *La danza del leon c hino en Cuba.* Ediciones Extramuros.

Amdur, E. (2023). *Little bird & the tiger.* Edgework Books.

Amos, D. (2021). *Hong Kong martial artists: sociocultural change from World War II to 2020.* Rowman & Littlefield. DOI: https://doi.org/10.5040/9798881810641

Amos, D. (1997). A Hong Kong southern praying mantis cult. *Journal of Asian Martial Arts, 6*(4), 31–61.

Ang, G. P., & Tay, K.X.R. (2022). Cultivating vessel and voice: embodiment as a way of being in performer training. *Theatre, Dance and Performance Training, 13*(2), 214–221. DOI: https://doi.org/10.1080/19443927.2022.2066337

Archimbaud, Michel. (1992). *Francis Bacon in conversation with Michel Archimbaud.* Phaidon.

Aristotle. (1987). *De anima (On the soul)* (H. Lawson-Tancred, Trans.). Penguin.

Armstrong, H. B. (1988). Pre-arranged movement patterns. *Hoplos: The Journal of the International Hoplology Society, VI* (1 & 2). 18–20.

Avalon, A. (John George Woodroffe & A. B. Ghose). (1919). *The serpent power.* Luzac & Co.

Bagchi, P. C. (1930). Compte-rendu de Benoytosh Bhattacharyya, edition de la Sādhanamālā. *Indian Historical Quarterly, 6,* 584–587.

Baier, K. (2012). Mesmeric yoga and the development of meditation within the Theosophical Society. *Theosophical History, 16*(3–4), 151–161.

Baker, I. (2019). *Tibetan yoga.* Thames & Hudson.

Baker, I. (2012a). Embodying enlightenment: physical culture in Dzogchen as revealed in Tibet's Lukhang murals. *Asian Medicine, 7*(1), 225–264. DOI: https://doi.org/10.1163/15734218-12341249

Baker, I. (2012b). Tibetan yoga: somatic practice in Vajrayana Buddhism and Dzogchen. In K. Baier, P. A. Maas, & K. Preisendanz (Eds.), *Yoga in Transformation* (pp. 335–384). Vienna University Press. DOI: https://doi.org/10.14220/9783737008624.335

Bandem, I. M., & DeBoer, F. E. (1981). *Kaja and Kelod Balinese dance in transition.* Oxford University Press.

Barba, E. (2010). *On directing and dramaturgy: burning the house.* Routledge.

Barba, E. (1995). *The paper canoe.* Routledge.

Belyea, C., & Tainer, S. (1991). *Dragon's play.* Great Circle Lifeworks.

Biagini, M. (2022). Changes: from the Workcenter to the academy of the unfulfilled. *TDR: The Drama Review, 66*(3), 184–193. DOI: https://doi.org/10.1017/S1054204322000466

Blavatsky, H. P. (1877). *Isis unveiled: a master-key to the mysteries of ancient and modern science and theology.* Bouton.

Bogart, A., & Landau, T. (2005). *The viewpoints book.* Theater Communications Group.

Boretz, A. (2011). *Gods, ghosts and gangsters.* University of Hawai'i. DOI: https://doi.org/10.21313/hawaii/9780824833770.001.0001

Bowman, P. (2019). *Deconstructing martial arts.* Cardiff University Press. DOIs: https://doi.org/10.2307/j.ctvv41849 and https://doi.org/10.18573/book1

Bowman, P. (Ed.) (2018). *The martial arts studies reader.* Rowman & Littlefield.

Brask, P. (1992). The anthropology of performance: an Interview with Richard Fowler. *Canadian Theatre Review, 71,* 81–88. DOI: https://doi.org/10.3138/ctr.71.011

Brunton, P. (1935). *A search in secret India* (R. Hurst, Trans.). New York: Dutton.

Burt, R. (2006). *Judson Dance Theatre – performative traces.* Routledge. DOI: https://doi.org/10.4324/9780203969663

Butler, M. (2007). *Reflections of a military medium: ritual and magic in eleventh and twelfth century Chinese military manuals.* [Doctoral dissertation, Cornell University].

Carmona, J. (1997). *Sur les traces du Baguazhang.* Guy Trédaniel.

Carmona, J. (2007). *La transmission du taijiquan.* Vega.

Chan, M. (2016). Tangki war magic: Spirit warfare in Singapore. In D. S. Farrer (Ed.), *War magic* (pp. 25–46). Berghahn. DOI: https://doi.org/10.2307/jj.6879783.5

Chao, S. Y. (2011). *Daoist ritual, state religion, and popular practices: Zhenwu worship from Song to Ming (960–1644)*. Taylor & Francis Group.

Chen, F. (1924/2023). *Quányì Shùzhēn 拳意述真 (Boxing Concepts Explained)* (L. Sun, Trans.). Amazon, Kindle Edition.

Chen, Z. (2012). *Chen taijiquan practical method introduction*. Hunyuan Taiji Academy.

Chenagtsang, N. (2020). *Nejang, Tibetan self-healing yoga*. Sky Press.

Cheng, C.-Y. (1990). Chinese metaphysics as non-metaphysics: Confucian and Taoist insights into the nature of reality. In R. Allinson (Ed.), *Understanding the Chinese mind: The philosophical roots* (pp. 167–208). Oxford University Press.

Chierchini, S., & Amdur, E. (2021). *The phenomenologist: interview with Ellis Amdur*. Ran Network.

Childs, C. (2020). *Choy Lay Fut Kung Fu*. Amazon.

Chin, C., Chen, C., & Tsai, L. (2010). The evolution of song-jiang battle array and the relationship between song-jiang battle array and the rural society of southern Taiwan. *Asian Culture and History*, 2(2), 120–132. DOI: https://doi.org/10.5539/ach.v2n2p120

Cleary, T. (Trans.) (1991). *The secret of the golden flower*. Harper Collins.

Co, A. (1997). *Five ancestor fist kung fu*. Tuttle.

Cohen, K. (1997). *The way of qigong*. Ballantine.

Cools, G. (2019). On dance dramaturgy. *Revista Cena*, 29, 42–52. DOI: https://doi.org/10.22456/2236-3254.97633

Coons, R. J. (2015). *Internal elixir cultivation*. Tambuli.

Copenhaver, B. P. (Trans.). (1995). *Hermetica: the Greek* Corpus Hermeticum *and the Latin Asclepius*. Cambridge.

Corbin, N. (1977). *Spiritual body and celestial Earth* (N. Pearson, Trans.). Princeton University Press.

Cox, S. (2024). *Subtle Energy: A Few Trajectories*. Text of a conference presentation at *Mapping Subtle Bodies and Esoteric Anatomies 2*, December 8–13, 2024, Esalen Institute, Big Sur, California, USA.

Cox, S. (2022a). *Zòu Chuán Hùn Liàn Fàshì 奏傳混煉法式*. "Model rites for submission, dispatch, fusing, and refinement." Unpublished translation.

Cox, S. (2022b). *太和拳谱 Tàihé Quán Pǔ*. "Grand harmony fist manual." Unpublished translation.

Cox, S. (2021). *The subtle body: a genealogy*. Oxford University Press. DOI: https://doi.org/10.1093/oso/9780197581032.001.0001

Cox, S. (2019). *The subtle body, a genealogy*. [Doctoral dissertation, Rice University.]

Crossley, P. (1990). *Orphan warriors*. Princeton University Press. DOI: https://doi.org/10.1515/9780691224985

Dean, K. (1998). *Lord of the three in one*. Princeton University Press. DOI: https://doi.org/10.1515/9780691261218

de Bono. E. (1993). *Water logic*. Penguin.

Debreczeny, K. (Ed.). (2019). *Faith and empire: art and politics in Tibetan Buddhism*. Rubin Museum of Art.

De Marinis, M. (2017). Maud Robart, student/teacher. *TDR: The Drama Review, 61*(1), 114–123. DOI: https://doi.org/10.1162/DRAM_a_00626

De Michelis, M. (2004). *A history of modern yoga: Patanjali and western esotericism*. Continuum.

Doherty, D. (2009). *Tai chi chuan: decoding the classics for the modern martial artist*. Crowood.

Dong, P., & Raffill, T. (1996). *Empty force*. Element.

Efurd, Y. K. (2012). *Baiyunguan: The development and evolution of a Daoist temple*. [Doctoral dissertation, University of Kansas].

Eliade, M. (1958). *Yoga: Immortality and Freedom*. Bollingen.

Elias, L., & Saucier, D. (2006). *Neuropsychology: clinical and experimental foundations*. Pearson Education.

Eno, B., & Schmidt, P. (1975/2001). *Oblique strategies: over one hundred worthwhile dilemmas*. Opal.

Estrella Sanchez, J. (2011). *One man one destiny*. Thesis submitted for as a requirement for the grade of 6th duan, Hong Kong: Hong Kong Wushu Association.

Evans-Wentz, W. Y. (1954/2000). *The Tibetan book of the great liberation*. Oxford University Press.

Falk, A. (Trans. & Ed.). (2022). *Zhang Wenguang's chaquan and tantui spring kick drills*. TGL Books.

Falk, A. (2019). *Falk's dictionary of Chinese martial arts: Chinese to English*. TGL Books.

Farrer, D. S. (2018). Captivation, false connection and secret societies in Singapore. *Martial Arts Studies, 5*, 36–51. DOI: https://doi.org/10.18573/mas.48

Farrer, D. S. (Ed.). (2016). *War magic*. Berghahn.

Farrer, D. S. (2011). Coffee shop gods: Chinese martial arts of the Singapore diaspora. In D. S. Farrer & J. Whalen-Bridge (Eds.), *Martial arts as embodied knowledge* (pp. 203–237). SUNY.

Farrer, D. S., & Whalen-Bridge, J. (Ed.). (2011). *Martial arts as embodied knowledge*. SUNY.

Feuerstein, G. (Ed.). (2011). *The encyclopedia of yoga and tantra*. Shambhala.

Filliozat, J. (1969). Taoisme et yoga. *Journal Asiatique, 257*(1969), 41–87. DOI: https://doi.org/10.2307/20634306

Frantzis, B. K. (1993). *Opening the energy gates of your body*. North Atlantic.

Friday, K. (2005). Off the warpath: military science & budō in the evolution of ryūha bugei. In A. Bennett (Ed.), *Budō perspectives* (pp. 249–265). Kendo World Publications.

Gao, X. (2012). *Aesthetics and creation* (M. Lee, Trans). Cambria Press.

Gao, X. (1998). The other shore (Jo Riley, Trans). In M. Cheung and J. Lai (Eds.), *An Oxford anthology of contemporary Chinese drama* (pp. 149–183). Oxford University Press.

Geertz, C. (1980). *Blurred Genres: The Refiguration of Social Thought* in *The American Scholar*, Spring 1980, Vol. 49, No. 2, pp. 165–179. Cambridge: Phi Beta Kappa Society.

Geither, M. (2017). *Ismene.* Unpublished manuscript.

Geither, M. (2012). *And treat the distant peoples with kindness.* Unpublished manuscript.

George, D. (1991). *Balinese ritual theatre.* Chadwick-Healey France.

Green, N. (2008). Breathing in India. *Modern Asian Studies, 42*(2–3): Islam in South Asia, 283–315. DOI: https://doi.org/10.1017/S0026749X07003125

Green, T. A., & Svinth, J. R. (2010). *Martial arts of the world: An encyclopedia of history and innovation* (2 Vols.). ABC-CLIO. DOI: https://doi.org/10.5040/9798400683169

Grotowski, J. (1995). From the theatre company to art as vehicle. In T. Richards (Ed.), *At work with Grotowski on physical action* (pp. 133–135). Routledge.

Grotowski, J. (1989). «Tu es le fils de quelqu'un.» *Europe, 726* (Octobre 1989), 13–25.

Hamilton, G. (1998). An interview with Master Zhu. *Tai Chi Chuan Magazine, 10* (Autumn/Winter 1998), n.p.

Hammer, O. (2004). *Claiming knowledge: strategies of epistemology from Theosophy to the New Age.* Brill. DOI: https://doi.org/10.1163/9789047403371

Hanegraaf, W. (2013). *Esotericism: a guide for the perplexed.* Bloomsbury.

Hanegraaf, W. (Ed.). (2006). *Dictionary of gnosis and western esotericism.* Brill.

He, S. (2006). Foreword. In Hong Junsheng, *Chen style practical method, volume one: theory* (Z. Chen, Trans.) (xxiv–xxix). Hunyuan Taiji Press.

Henning, S. (1999). Academia encounters the Chinese martial arts. *China Review International, 6*(2), 319–332. University of Hawaii Press. DOI: https://doi.org/10.1353/cri.1999.0020

Henning, S. (1981). The Chinese martial arts in historical perspective. *Military Affairs, 45*(4), 173–179. DOI: https://doi.org/10.2307/1987462

Herrigel, E. (1948). *Zen in the Art of Archery.* Routledge.

Hinton, D. (2008). *Classical Chinese poetry.* Farrar, Strauss and Giroux.

Holmberg, A. (1996). *The theatre of Robert Wilson.* Cambridge University Press.

Horowitz, R. S. (2002). Beyond the marble boat: the transformation of the Chinese military, 1850–1911. In D. A. Graff & R. Higham (Eds.), *A military history of China* (pp. 153–174). Westview Press.

Hu, W. C. (1995). *Chinese lion dance explained.* Ars Ceramica & Chinese Performing Arts Foundation.

Huang, A. (1973). *Embrace tiger, return to mountain: the essence of tai ji.* Celestial Arts.

Huang, F., & Hong, F. (Eds.). (2018). *A History of Chinese martial arts.* Routledge. DOI: https://doi.org/10.4324/9781315628073

Huang, Y. (Ed.). (2016). *The big red book of modern Chinese literature: writings from the mainland in the long twentieth century.* Norton.

Huber, J., & Chuan, Z. (2013). *The Body at stake: experiments in Chinese contemporary art.* Transcript Verlag. DOIs: https://doi.org/10.1515/transcript.9783839423097 and https://doi.org/10.14361/transcript.9783839423097

Huxley, A. (1946). *The perennial philosophy.* Chatto and Windus.

Jacobs, B. (2023). *Dragon body, tiger spirit.* Mushin.

Josephson-Storm, J. (2017). *The myth of disenchantment.* UCP. DOI: https://doi.org/10.7208/chicago/9780226403533.001.0001

Judkins, B., with Neilson, J. (2015). *The creation of wing chun.* SUNY.

Jung, C. (1999/1937). *The psychology of kundalini yoga.* Princeton University Press.

Jung, C. (1977/1956). *Mysterium coniunctionis.* Princeton University Press.

Kang, G. (1995). *The spring and autumn of Chinese martial arts.* Plum Publications.

Katchmer, G. (1993). *The Tao of bioenergetics.* YMAA Publishing.

Kennedy, B., & Guo, E. (2010). *Jingwu: the school that transformed kung fu.* Blue Snake Press.

Kjellberg, P. (Trans.). (2001). "Zhuangzi." In P. J. Ivanhoe and B. W. Van Norden (Eds.), *Readings in Classical Chinese Philosophy* (pp. 207–254), 2nd edition. Hackett Publishing Company.

Kozma, A. (2011). *Warrior guards the mountain.* Line of Intent.

Lagerwey, J. (2010). *China: a religious state.* Hong Kong University Press. DOI: https://doi.org/10.1515/9789882205512

Lalonde, C. (2012). *And treat the participants with kindness: the search for emancipatory performance creation practices.* [Master's thesis, University of Warwick].

Lee, J. C., & Bernard, L. (2021). *Authentic white crane kung fu.* Kontact Sports.

Leadbeater, C. (1927). *The chakras.* Theosophical Publishing House.

Leadbeater, C. (1919). *The inner life.* Theosophical Publishing House.

Leland, K. (2016). *Rainbow body.* Nicolas-Hays, Inc.

Lei, D. (2006). *Operatic China.* Palgrave. DOI: https://doi.org/10.1007/978-1-137-06163-8

Lévi, E. (A. L. Constant). (1856/2008). *Dogme et rituel de la haute magie.* Arbre d'Or.

Lo, V., & Stanley-Baker, M. (Eds.), with Yang, D. (2022). *The Routledge handbook of Chinese medicine.* Routledge. DOI: https://doi.org/10.4324/9780203740262

Lorge, P. (2012). *Chinese martial arts: from antiquity to the 21st century.* Cambridge University Press. DOI: https://doi.org/10.1017/CBO9781139029865

Lowell Lewis, J. (1992). *Ring of liberation.* University of Chicago Press.

Luca, G. (1953). *Héros-limite.* Soleil Noir.

Lu, K. Y. (1970). *Taoist yoga: alchemy and immortality.* Weiser.

Lu, Z. (2019). *A history of Shaolin: Buddhism, kung fu and identity.* Routledge.

Lu, Z. (2018). *Politics and identity in Chinese martial arts.* Routledge.

Mallinson, J. (2016). The Amṛtasiddhi: haṭhayoga's tantric Buddhist source text. In D. Goodall, S. Hatley, H. Isaacson, and S. Raman (Eds.), *Śaivism*

and the tantric traditions (pp. 409–425). Brill. DOI: https://doi.org/10.1163
/9789004432802_019

Masich, Sam. (2020). *Taijiquan lun* 太極拳論. Unpublished manuscript.

McGuire, C. (2016). [Review of the book *The fighting art of pencak silat and its music: from Southeast Asian village to global movement*, by Uwe U. Paetzold and Paul H. Mason]. *Martial Arts Studies, 2*, 105–108. DOI: https://doi.org/10.18573/j.2017.10100

McGuire, C. (2010). Rhythm skills development in Chinese martial arts. *The International Journal of Sport and Society, 1*(3), 209–218. DOI: https://doi.org/10.18848/2152-7857/CGP/v01i03/54024

McMahan, David L. (2008). *The Making of Buddhist Modernism*, Oxford University Press. DOI: https://doi.org/10.1093/acprof:oso/9780195183276.001.0001

Mei, X. (1993). *Fukien ground boxing* (C. Cai, Trans). Sugawara.

Ménard, D. (Trans.). (2003). *Le voyage aux Indes de Nicola de Conti (1414–1439)*. Chandeigne.

Menzies, G. (2002). *1421: The year China discovered the world*. Bantam.

Mershon, K. E. (1971). *Seven plus seven: mysterious life rituals in Bali*. Vantage.

Mesmer, F. (1779). *Mémoire sur la découverte du magnétisme animal*. Didot.

Meulenbeld, M. (2015). *Demonic warfare: Daoism, territorial networks, and the history of a Ming novel*. University of Hawaii Press. DOI: https://doi.org/10.21313/hawaii/9780824838447.001.0001

Míng, L. (2007). *Sleep, dream, and the Dao of night*. Da Yuan Circle.

Misner, C. W., Thorne, K. S., & Wheeler, J. A. (1973). *Gravitation*. W.H. Freeman.

Morris, A. (2004). *Marrow of the nation: A history of sport and physical culture in republican China*. University of California Press. DOI: https://doi.org/10.1525/9780520354982

Morris, G. (1993). *Path notes of an American ninja master*. North Atlantic.

Mroz, D. (2022). Spatial projection. *Theatre, Dance and Performance Training, 13*(3), pp. 443–462. DOI: https://doi.org/10.1080/19443927.2022.2032300

Mroz, D. (2020). *Tàolù*: the mastery of space. *Martial Arts Studies, 10*, 9–22. DOI: https://doi.org/10.18573/mas.111

Mroz, D. (2017). *Tàolù*: credibility and decipherability. *Martial Arts Studies, 3*, 38–50. DOI: https://doi.org/10.18573/j.2017.10094

Mroz, D. (2011). *The dancing word: an embodied approach to the preparation of performers and the composition of performances*. Rodopi. DOI: https://doi.org/10.1163/9789401200264

Murray, D., and Qin, B. (1996). *The origins of the Tiandihui*. Stanford University Press.

Nair, S. (2007). *The restoration of breath*. Rodopi. DOI: https://doi.org/10.1163/9789401205177

Naquin, S. (1976). *Millenarian rebellion in China: the eight trigrams uprising of 1813*. Yale University Press.

Needham, J. (1956). *Science and civilisation in China* (Vol. 2). Cambridge University Press.

Needham, J. (1954). *Science and civilisation in China* (Vol. 1). Cambridge University Press.

Needleman, J. (Ed.). (1996). *Gurdjieff: essays and reflections on the man and his teachings*. Bloomsbury.

Palmer, D. (2021). Isomorphism, syncretism, and poly-ontological dynamics. In C. Seiple & D. R. Hoover (Eds.), *The Routledge handbook of religious literacy, pluralism, and global engagement* (pp. 120–135). Routledge. DOI: https://doi.org/10.4324/9781003036555-11

Paper, J. (2019). *Chinese Religion and Familism*. Bloomsbury. DOI: https://doi.org/10.5040/9781350103641

Paper, J. (1992). *The Spirits Are Drunk*. SUNY.

Pavis, P. (Ed.). (1996). *The intercultural performance reader*. Routledge.

Pegg, R. (2015). Chinese sword and brush masters of the Tang dynasty. In M DeMarco (Ed.), *Chinese swords: an ancient tradition and modern training*. Via Media Publishing. Kindle Edition.

Perry, E. (1980). *From rebels to revolutionaries: peasant violence in Huai-Pei 1845–1945*. [Doctoral dissertation, University of Michigan.]

Phillips, S. P. (2019a). *Tai chi, baguazhang and the golden elixir*. Angry Baby Books.

Phillips, S. P. (2019b). Zhang San Feng conundrum. *Journal of Daoist Studies*, *12*, 96–122. DOI: https://doi.org/10.1353/dao.2019.0004

Phillips, S. P., & Mroz, D. (2016). Daoyin reimagined. *Journal of Daoist Studies*, *9*, 139–158. DOI: https://doi.org/10.1353/dao.2016.0006

Phillips, S. P. (2008). Portrait of an American Daoist: Charles Belyea / Liu Ming. *Journal of Daoist Studies*, *1*, 161–176. DOI: https://doi.org/10.1353/dao.2008.0006

Pregadio, F. (2019). *The way of the golden elixir*. Golden Elixir Press.

Raiport, G. (1998). *Red gold*. Tarcher.

Reiter, F. (2007). *Basic conditions of Taoist thunder magic*. Otto Harrassowitz Verlag.

Reynolds, J. M. (Trans.). (1989). *Self-liberation through seeing with naked awareness*. Station Hill.

Riley, J. (1997). *Chinese theatre and the actor in performance*. Cambridge University Press.

Rousselle, E. (1960). Spiritual Guidance in Contemporary Taoism. In J. Campbell (Ed.), Papers from the Eranos Yearbooks, Eranos 4: Spiritual Disciplines (pp. 59–101). Princeton University Press. DOI: https://doi.org/10.1515/9781400885787-007

Samuel, G. (2013). Subtle-body processes: towards a non-reductionist understanding. In G. Samuel & J. Johnston (Eds.), *Religion and the subtle body in Asia and the west: between mind and body* (pp. 249–266). Routledge. DOI: https://doi.org/10.4324/9780203558249

Samuel, G. (2008). *Origins of yoga and tantra: Indic religions to the thirteenth century*. Cambridge University Press. DOI: https://doi.org/10.1017/CBO9780511818820

Salter, D, Móu, S., & Wú, W. (1996). China's theatre of dissent. *Asian Theatre Journal*, *13*(2), 218–228. DOI: https://doi.org/10.2307/1124526

Saso, M. (2012). *The teachings of Daoist Master Zhuang.* Oracle Bones.

Saso, M. (1990). *Taoism and the rite of cosmic renewal.* Washington State University.

Saso, M. (1991). *Blue dragon, white tiger.* University of Hawaii Press.

Sawyer, R. (1993). *The seven military classics of ancient China.* Westview Press.

Schechner, R., & Wolford, L. (Eds.). (1997). *The Grotowski sourcebook.* Routledge.

Schinz, A. (1996). *The magic square: cities in ancient China.* Axel Menges.

Schmidt, R. A. (2008). *Motor learning and performance: a situation-based learning approach* (4th ed.). Human Kinetics.

The Secret of the Golden Flower (R. Wilhelm, Trans.). (1931). Harcourt, Brace, Jovanovich.

Selby, S. (2000). *Chinese archery.* Hong Kong University Press. DOI: https://doi.org/10.1515/9789882200661

Shahar, M. (2019). The Chinese cult of the horse king, divine protector of equines. In R. Kowner, G. Bar-Oz, M. Biran, M. Shahar, & G. Shelach-Lavi (Eds.), *Animals and human society in Asia* (pp. 355–390). The Palgrave Macmillan Animal Ethics Series. Palgrave Macmillan. DOI: https://doi.org/10.1007/978-3-030-24363-0_12

Shahar, M. (2008). *The Shaolin monastery: history, religion, and the Chinese martial arts.* University of Hawaii Press. DOI: https://doi.org/10.21313/hawaii/9780824831103.001.0001

Shank, T. (1996). Mou Sen on *File Zero. Theatre Forum, 8,* 7–11.

Shi, X. (2015). The influence of Buddhist Sanskrit on Chinese. In W. Wang & C. Sun (Eds.), *The Oxford Handbook of Chinese Linguistics* (pp. 236–247). Oxford: UK.

Siff, M. (2016/1995). *Facts and fallacies of fitness.* Westside.

Simpson, D. C. (1974). The choice of control system for the multimovement prosthesis: extended physiological proprioception (EPP). In P. Herberts (Ed.), *The control of upper-extremity prostheses and orthoses* (pp. 146–150). Charles Thomas.

Spatz, B. (2020). *Making a laboratory.* Punctum Books. DOI: https://doi.org/10.21983/P3.0295.1.00

Spatz, B. (2015). *What a body can do.* Routledge. DOI: https://doi.org/10.4324/9781315722344

Spineto, N. (2001). Mircea Eliade and traditionalist thought. *Aries, 1*(1), 62–63. DOI: https://doi.org/10.1163/157005901X00048

Stanley-Baker, M. (2022). *Qi* 氣 a means for cohering natural knowledge. In V. Lo & M. Stanley-Baker (Eds.), with D. Yang, *The Routledge handbook of Chinese medicine.* Routledge. DOI: https://doi.org/10.4324/9780203740262-4

Stebbins, R. A. (1992). *Amateurs, professionals and serious leisure.* McGill-Queen's University Press. DOI: https://doi.org/10.1515/9780773563346

Sutton, D. (2003). *Steps of perfection: exorcistic performers and Chinese religion in twentieth-century Taiwan.* Harvard University Asia Center. DOIs: https://doi.org/10.1163/9781684173785 and https://doi.org/10.2307/j.ctt1tg5nf9

Swetz, F. (2008). *Legacy of the Luoshu: the 4,000-year search for the meaning of the magic square of Order Three*. A.K. Peters. DOI: https://doi.org/10.1201/b10589

Szymanski, J. (2023). Xingyiquan, a sort of history. in B. Jacobs (Ed.), *Dragon body, tiger spirit*. (pp. xxiii–xxxiii). Mushin.

Tan, M. G. (2005). Ethnic Chinese in Indonesia. In M. Ember, C. Ember, & I. Skoggard (Eds.), *Encyclopedia of diasporas: immigrant and refugee cultures around the world* (pp. 795–808). Springer. DOI: https://doi.org/10.1007/978-0-387-29904-4_82

Tanaka, M. (2001). *Karate-Dô perfecting kumite* (Schlatt, Trans.). Götzelmann.

Taylor, K. (2001). *Sir John Woodroffe, tantra and Bengal*. Routledge.

Teo, S. (2009). *Chinese martial arts cinema*. Edinburgh University Press. DOI: https://doi.org/10.3366/edinburgh/9780748632855.001.0001

Tu, W. M. (1997). Chinese philosophy: a synopsis. In E. Deutsch & R. Bontekoe (Eds.), *A Companion to World Philosophies* (pp. 3–22). Blackwell.

Tyrey, B., & Brinkman, M. (1996). The Luoshu as taiji boxing's secret inner-sanctum training method. *Journal of Asian Martial Arts*, 5(2), 74–79.

Valusi, E. (2022). Daoist sexual practices for health and immortality for women. In V. Lo & M. Stanley-Baker (Eds.), with D. Yang, *The Routledge handbook of Chinese medicine*. Routledge. DOI: https://doi.org/10.4324/9780203740262-35

Van Kerkhoven, M. (1997). Le processus dramaturgique. *Nouvelles de Danse, Dossier Danse et Dramaturgie*, 31, 18–25.

Velan, A. S. (1963). *Siddhar's science of longevity and kalpa medicine of India*. Sakthi Nilayam.

Ward, B. (1979). Not merely players: drama, art and ritual in traditional China. *Man*, 14(1), 18–39. DOI: https://doi.org/10.2307/2801638

Warrington, P. (2009). *Alchemists of the stage* (M. Schino, Trans.). Icarus.

Wells, M. (2005). *Scholar boxer*. North Atlantic.

Wetzler, S. (2018). Martial arts as a coping strategy for violence. In P. Bowman (Ed.), *The martial arts studies reader* (pp. 123–136). Rowman & Littlefield International.

White, D. G. (2014). *The yoga sutra of Patanjali: a biography*. Princeton. DOI: https://doi.org/10.1515/9781400850051

White, D. G. (1996). *Alchemical body*. University of Chicago Press. DOI: https://doi.org/10.7208/chicago/9780226149349.001.0001

Wile, D. (2016). Fighting words: four new document finds reignite old debates in taijiquan historiography. *Martial Arts Studies*, 4, 17–35. DOI: https://doi.org/10.18573/j.2017.10184

Wile, D. (1999). *T'ai chi's ancestors*. Sweet Ch'i Press.

Wile, D. (1996). *Lost t'ai-chi classics from the late Ch'ing dynasty*. SUNY Press. DOIs: https://doi.org/10.1515/9781438424064 and https://doi.org/10.2307/jj.18255579

Williams, W. C. (1970). *Imaginations*. New Directions.

Wolford-Wylam, L. (2008). Living tradition: continuity of research at the Work-center of Jerzy Grotowski and Thomas Richards. *TDR/The Drama Review*, 52(2), 126–149. DOI: https://doi.org/10.1162/dram.2008.52.2.126

Wong, K. K. (1993). *The art of Chi Kung*. Element.

Wong, K. K. (1976). *Introduction to Shaolin kung fu*. Paul Crompton.

Wong, Y. M. (2010). Taijiquan: Heavenly Pattern Boxing. *Journal of Chinese Martial Arts*, 1(2), 28–37.

Yamada, S. (2001). The Myth of zen in the art of archery. *Japanese Journal of Religious Studies*. 28/1–2. DOI: https://doi.org/10.18874/jjrs.28.1-2.2001.1-30

Yang, J. M. (2006). *Qigong meditation—small circulation*. YMAA.

Yang, J. M. (1994). *Shaolin white crane*. YMAA.

Yates, F. (1964/2001). *Giordano Bruno and the hermetic tradition*. Routledge.

Yuasa, Y. (1993). *The Body, Self-Cultivation & Ki-Energy*. SUNY Press.

Yung, S. (2005). Moving body: the interactions between Chinese opera and action cinema. In M. Morris, S. Li, & S. Chan (Eds.), *Hong Kong connections: transnational imagination in action cinema* (pp. 21–34). Hong Kong University Press. DOI: https://doi.org/10.1515/9789882201583-004

Zarrilli, P. (2020). *(Toward) a phenomenology of acting*. Routledge. DOI: https://doi.org/10.4324/9780429322525

Zarrilli, P. (2009). *Psychophysical acting*. Routledge.

Zarrilli, P. (1998). *When the body becomes all eyes*. Oxford University Press.

Zhang, Y. (2016). *The taijiquan classics*. Ying Chen Gong Fa.

Zhouxiang, L. (2019). *Politics and identity in Chinese martial arts*. Routledge. DOI: https://doi.org/10.4324/9781315108438

Zhouxiang, L. (2020). *A history of Shaolin: Buddhism, kung fu and identity*. Routledge. DOI: https://doi.org/10.4324/9780429261626

Ziporyn, B. (Trans.) (2020). *Zhuangzi: the complete works*. Hackett. DOI: https://doi.org/10.1002/9781119009924.eopr0446

References in Chinese

陳攖寧、《中華仙學》

Chén, Y. (1962). *A Study of the Chinese Immortals*. Taibei: Zhenshanmei Publishing House.

吕锁森、《中国戏曲武打概論》

Lü, S. (2009). *An Introduction to Martial Arts in Chinese Opera*. Beijing: National Academy of Chinese Theatre Arts.

马贤达、《中国短兵教学训练竞技》

Mǎ, Xiándá. (2003). *Chinese Short Weapon Fencing*. Xi'an: San Qin.

唐豪、《少林武當考》

Táng H. (1968/1930) *Shaolin Wudang Research*. Hong Kong: Unicorn Press.

唐豪、顧留馨、《太極拳研究》

Táng H. & Gù L. (1964/2004) *Taijiquan Research*, Taipei: Dah-jaan Publishing House.

湯, 汝昆、《意拳淺釋》

Tāng R. (n.d.) *A Brief Explanation of Yì Quán*. Publication information unavailable.

严雙军、《太极拳》，浙江人民出版社.

Yan, S. (2007). *Taijiquan*. Zhejiang People's Publishing House.

余水清、《中国武术史概要》，湖北科学技术出版社.

Yú, S. (2006). *Essentials of Chinese Martial Arts History*, Hubei Science and Technology Publishing House.

钟云龙、《武当太极拳》

Zhōng, Y. (2014). *Wǔdāng Tàijí Quán*. Beijing: CIP.

Online Sources

Anon—*Collège de France*. https://www.college-de-france.fr/fr/chaire/jerzy-gro towski-anthropologie-theatrale-chaire-statutaire/biography (01/12/2023)

Anon, trans. P. Brennan, circa 1875. *Explaining Taiji Principles, attributed to Yang Banhou*. https://brennantranslation.wordpress.com/2013/09/14/explaining -taiji-principles-taiji-fa-shuo/ (18/07/2022)

Atmadja, D. PGB *Teropong Newsletter* (*Telescope Newsletter*) trans. anon. https://web.archive.org/web/20170622142811/https://silat.de/flashback_of _pgb_en.html (16/10/2023)

Bates, C. 2012. *Hiyaa Martial Arts Podcast—Interview with Chris Bates*. https:// archive.org/details/podcast_hiyaa-martial-arts-podcast_bonus-episode -1-interview-wi_1000448481908 (7/12/2023)

Cox, S. (1) *History of Wudang Sanfeng Pai Taijiquan*: https://www.okanaganval leywudang.com/wudang-taijiquan (1/5/2022)

Cox, S. (2) *On the Historical Mystery of Zhang Sanfeng*: https://www.okanagan valleywudang.com/on-the-historical-mystery-of-zhang-sanfeng (1/5/2022)

Cox, S. (3) 2023. *Subtle Bodies and Occult Energies*. Catherine Kerr Vital Energy in Health and Healing Lecture Series. Brown University Contemplative Studies Initiative and the Carney Institute for Brain Science. Online lecture, 7:00pm EST. https://www.youtube.com/watch?v=rd1UWdncxWM (and archived here: https://vimeo.com/907927630?share=copy) (10/11/2023)

Cox, S. (4) trans. Shuì Xiǎojié 稅曉潔 Searching for Daoist Master Guo Gao Yi: on living in a cave and cultivating the Dao 寻郭高一道长：老道洞潜心修行. https://www.okanaganvalleywudang.com/searching-for-guo-gaoyi (1/5/2022)

Debrezceny, K. *War Magic: The Wizarding World of Tibetan Sorcery*. https:// rubinmuseum.org/spiral/war-magic-the-wizarding-world-of-tibetan-sorcery/ (18/07/2022)

Friday, K. *Interview with Historian, Professor Karl Friday*. http://www.thesho gunshouse.com/2009/08/interview-with-historianprofessor-karl.html (18/07/2022)

Gu, R. trans. Brennan, P. 1936. *Taiji Boxing*. https://brennantranslation.word press.com/2013/08/20/the-taiji-manual-of-gu-ruzhang/ (18/01/2024)

Judkins, B. *Tang Hao: The First Historian of the Chinese Martial Arts*. https:// chinesemartialstudies.com/2014/03/14/lives-of-chinese-martial-artists -12-tang-hao-the-first-historian-of-the-chinese-martial-arts/ (18/07/2022)

Kavanagh, C. *Religion Without Belief* in *Aeon* 2016. https://aeon.co/essays/can
-religion-be-based-on-ritual-practice-without-belief (18/97/2022)

McCarthy, Patrick. 2005. *Sometimes you don't know how to fit in until you break
out.* Self-published, Koryu-Uchinadi Website. http://www.koryu-uchinadi
.org/KU_HAPV.pdf (09/08/2020)

Redana, B. *Rendra and Martial Arts.* https://www.insideindonesia.org/editions
/edition-1016/rendra-and-martial-arts (19/09/2023)

Roth-Lindberg, D. 2020. *Musings on "Silk Reeling" and Buddhism in Chen style
Tai Chi Chuan.* https://taichithoughts.wordpress.com/2020/09/13/musings
-on-silk-reeling-and-buddhism-in-chen-style-tai-chi-chuan/ (18/07/2022)

Stebbins, R. *The Serious Leisure Perspective.* https://www.seriousleisure.net
/concepts.html (18/07/2022)

Sun, L. 1924. trans. Meredith, S. 2011. *Quányì Shùzhēn* 拳意述真 (*Boxing Concepts
Explained*), Chapter 8: http://www.stickgrappler.net/2014/12/sun-lu-tang-my
-personal-experience.html (6/7/2022)

Sun, L. 1924 trans. Brennan, P. 2013. *Quányì Shùzhēn* 拳意述真 (*Boxing
Concepts Explained*), Chapter 8: https://brennantranslation.wordpress
.com/2013/04/29/the-voices-of-sun-lutangs-teachers/ (6/7/2022)

Zhōu, B. http://www.kungfuloung.com.tw/engbooka0201.htm (22/3/2010)

Online Sources in Chinese

Hè, Y. 贺奕, *Móu Sēn Shíyàn Xìjù "Bǐàn"* 牟森实验戏剧《彼岸》 (*Móu Sēn's
Experimental Drama "The Other Shore"*). https://movie.douban.com/review
/12622620/ (18/09/2023)

Huáng, S. 黄颂茹, *Wénhuì Yuèdú Shēntǐ Lìshǐ Chuàngzào Wǔdǎo Wèilái* 文
慧 阅读身体历史 创造舞蹈未来 (*Wen Hui Read the History of the Body
to Create the Future of Dance*). https://par.npac-ntch.org/cn/article/doc
/ES9IGBXE0T# (13/10/2023)

Lǐ, Y. 李晏, *Xiāoshī Zài 20 Shìjì De Zhōngguó Xìjù* 消失在 20 世纪的中国戏剧
(*The Disappearing Chinese Theatre of the 20th Century*). http://renshengda
butong.com/Article/Content/index/content_id/943%20 (18/09/2023)

Yáng. H. 楊海, 《丹道非发现也，乃发明也。》 *The Elixir practice was not
Fa Xian (discovered) but Fa Ming (Created).* https://www.youtube.com
/@HaiYangChannel/community (16/12/2023)

Yáng, S. 杨舒帆, *Móu Sēn: Cóng Xiānfēng Zǒuxiàng Zhèngdiǎn* 牟森：从先锋
走向正典 (*Móu Sēn: From Pioneer to Canon*). http://www.chinawriter.com
.cn/n1/2018/0424/c404005-29944984.html (18/09/2023)

Yú, J. 于坚, *Yú jiān: Guānyú `Bǐànde Yī huí Hànyǔ Cíxìng Tǎolùn* 于坚：关于
「彼岸」的一回汉语词性讨论 (*Yú Jiān: A Discussion of the Other Shore and
its Philology*). https://www.zgnfys.com/m/a/nfwx-58842.shtml (18/09/2023)

Personal & Public Communications

Adda, M. 5/9/2023, 10/12/2018, & 8/8/2014.

Albastaki, F. "The Search for the Tiger: Silat Harimau in an Austrian Transnational Context." Martial Arts Studies Conference, Sheffield, UK, 21/7/2023.

Bailey, R. 06/5/2024

Barlow, G. 05/7/2020

Cartmell, T. 11/8/2023

Cox, S. 6-17/7/2022

Eisner, C. 21/2/2019

Hé, Y. 11/10/2024

Himmet, I. 9/15/2018 & 8/3/2024

Mǎ, Y. 马越. 23/2/2019

Liu, M. (Belyea, C.) 15/5/2008

Riley, J. 10/6/2020

Wells, M. 15/8/2022

Wetzler, S. 8/7/2023

Ziółkowski, G. 17/3/2024

Index

Italicized page numbers indicate figures, illustrations, and photographs.

About the Author

Figure 26: The author performing *Tiān'é Wò Xuě* 天鵝臥雪 or *Swan Lying in the Snow* (photo by Laura Astwood, July 2010).

Daniel Mroz, PhD is Associate Professor in the Department of Theatre of the University of Ottawa in Ottawa, Canada where he teaches acting, directing, history and theory to graduate and undergraduate students. He has directed original theatre in Canada and the United States and worked as a dramaturg and facilitator for contemporary dancers in Canada and Europe. He has taught professional actors, directors, dancers, and choreographers in North America, Great Britain, Europe, and Asia. He has practiced Chinese martial arts since 1993 and his research focusses on the use of *wǔshù* in contemporary theatre and dance. He contributes regularly to Martial Arts Studies, a research area that he has helped to establish in collaboration with colleagues from around the world.

www.ingramcontent.com/pod-product-compliance
Lightning Source LLC
La Vergne TN
LVHW052019080426
835513LV00018B/2080